The Long Road to *Blessed*

The Long Road to *Blessed*

Keep Putting One Foot in Front of the Other

MICHAEL WILLIAMS

Archway Publishing books may be ordered through booksellers or by contacting:

Archway Publishing
1663 Liberty Drive
Bloomington, IN 47403
www.archwaypublishing.com
1 (888) 242-5904

ISBN: 978-1-4808-6695-9 (sc)
ISBN: 978-1-4808-6696-6 (hc)
ISBN: 978-1-4808-6694-2 (e)

Library of Congress Control Number: 2018914121

Print information available on the last page.

Archway Publishing rev. date: 11/28/2018

DEDICATION

To my children, I hope this is something you can appreciate. I want you to understand where your family came from and the changes I have tried to make on your behalf. I want you to know but not to repeat the mistakes of the past. Learn from them and grow. I have loved you with all the power I possess. I have tried to shield you from evil while showing you that it exists. I want you to take what I have taught you and run with it to greater things that than I ever thought possible. And to my amazing wife who changed my life. Without you none of this would be possible.

CONTENTS

How It Began 1
My Early Years. 9
Becoming A Teenager. 21
Troubled Teen 33
Back To Misery 43
To Go Or Not To Go 53
Limbo 67
The Avalanche 79
A New Beginning 91
The Inevitable End. 103
What To Do Now?. 115
First Impressions 125
Could This Be Real? 131
The Horror 143
Trying To Find "Normal" 153
Roll With The Punches 167
Ups, Downs And New Experiences. 181
The Smell. 197

God's Plan Is Revealed. 203
Not Out Of The Woods Yet 213
Tragedy Strikes 221
New Challenges 233
Moving Forward 245
Pure Determination 253
Trying To Find Normal 263
God Is Still Working. 275
Past Present And Future. 287
Looking For The End 295
A Pain Worse Than My Own 305
What's The Point? 309

CHAPTER ONE

How It Began

I was born November 4, 1977. My mother was 16 years old at the time. She said she named me after some guy she dated. My middle name comes from her brother. My middle name is the same as his. My last name is her maiden name from her father. To tell my story I think it would be best to know a little background that led to some of the situations I'm about to describe.

My family tree has been traced back as far as the 1700's in North Carolina. The farthest I was able to trace it myself was an Irishman who moved from North Carolina to Knoxville Tennessee where his wife gave birth to a son. That son moved to Kentucky and started his own branch of the family tree. Generations later, a coal miner and his wife had 13 kids. One of these was my grandfather. Judging from the research I've done myself and the stories told to me, the occupations of my ancestors were varied. I have heard and read about farmers, moonshiners, coal miners, electricians and many were in the United States Military. I have no idea what the original immigrants' status was, but from what I can tell, as far back as Knoxville Tennessee we've been poor Irishmen.

My grandfather was in the army around the time the Vietnam conflict was beginning. He was stationed in Germany where he spent most of his time drinking with the locals. When he came home he decided to travel the U.S. He went from state to state doing different jobs. He made his way around the country drinking, fighting and sleeping with as many women as possible. After a while he found himself in Chicago Illinois, where he met the granddaughter of some Irish immigrants (my grandmother). Her father passed away very young and she was raised by her mother. When they met, my grandmother already had 6 kids that she had either given up for adoption or lived with other relatives. She had her first when she was 14 years old. When he showed up to pick her up for their first date, my great grandmother was not happy that a man was there to see her daughter. My great grandmother was barely five foot tall and my grandfather was around six foot. When she answered the door and he asked for her daughter she punched him in the face so hard it knocked him backward off the porch. It's safe to say they never liked each other but this didn't prevent my grandmother from dating him. They eventually married and had five kids. The first was given up for adoption because there was some question about who the father was. In 1961 my mother was born, then her brother and two more sisters all in Chicago. This brought my grandmothers' total number of children up to eleven.

While in Chicago, my grandfather worked in factories and spent his evenings in the local bars. Three of his brothers had moved to Chicago to find work with him. I was told a story about him and two of his brothers. The story went like this. The three of them were in a bar drinking and the two elder of them decided to have some fun at their little brothers' expense. When the youngest and shortest of the three went to the bathroom, the other two went to each guy in the bar and told them that he was planning to start a fight with them. They went outside and watched through the big window in the front of the bar. When he came out the guys in the bar started a fight with him. He cleared the entire bar and when the last man fell to the floor he looked around to figure out what had happened. He saw his two brothers outside the window laughing. He pointed at them and said "you're next." It was also in one of these bars that my grandfather tried to stop an armed robbery. Two men came into the bar waiving a pistol around demanding all the money. He stood up and confronted the men. He forced them out into the street where he ended up on the ground with one of them. While they were struggling the gun went off and my grandfather was shot. The two men ran away and he was left with a bullet in his body that couldn't be removed. It was quite a heroic act but my grandmother was not impressed. He had not proven to be the best of husbands. She eventually decided to start seeing someone else and kicked him out. This someone else just happened to be his brother. This led to some confusion about which brother was actually the father of the youngest daughter. My grandfather moved back to Eastern Kentucky. My grandmothers' new relationship didn't last long and eventually all the brothers moved back to Kentucky.

At this point the timeline gets a little confusing but somewhere along the line, my grandfather and his brother spent some time in prison. They liked fast cars and they loved to drink and fight. Three of them were out together one night and one of them was messing around with a married woman. They dropped the woman off at her house and her husband happened to be home. He came out and shot at the car as they drove away. A mile or two down the road they realized that the brother who was in the back seat had been shot in the back of the head. They rushed him to the hospital and then formed a plan to kill the guy who shot their brother. They went back to his house but he wasn't there. They took his wife and daughter instead, thinking that when he showed up to get them back they would kill him. The plan didn't work out anything like they thought. They waited all night but the guy never showed up. The next morning they heard someone on a loud speaker telling them to come out with their hands up. They thought it was the local police. They wanted to look good in the picture they put in the paper so when they walked out onto the porch each of them had a shotgun in one hand and a bottle of whiskey in the other. To their surprise it wasn't the local police. The entire front yard was full of FBI. You see, they lived in an area where in those days you had to cross a winding mountain pass to get from where they lived to the next town where they had taken the women from, crossing two state lines in the process. This made it a federal offense. Their brother survived being shot, but of course they served time in prison for their actions. While in prison, they decided to use their time wisely and learn a trade. They made an agreement that they would each learn a trade that worked with the others and they would go into business together when they got out. I don't know the details but they didn't go into business together. They were never able to get along very well, so I'm sure that had everything to do with it.

My grandmother decided to raise her last four kids. She and her mother moved to Missouri to work in a shoe factory that had recently opened. As my mother and her siblings came into their teens they started to make friends and party. They drank a lot and tried a few drugs. Each of them had their preferences whether it was marijuana, pills or alcohol. I don't know how much of this happened before I was born but I know there was a lot of it after.

My mother was waiting for the school bus when my father first saw her. She was 15 and my father would have been around 22. He was from Western Tennessee and he had a wife and daughter. He and his wife were separated at the time and he was in town visiting relatives. He was born with juvenile diabetes and had been in poor health his entire life. It didn't help that he drank and didn't take care of himself very well. His father was a farmer and he had four sisters and no brothers. I've seen several of his family grave markers. There were some of his uncles who served in the military during wartime. That is about as much information as I was able to find on my fathers' family tree.

He and my mother dated over a short period of time. After he moved back my mother found out she was pregnant. She was pregnant at 15 by a man who was married to another woman and living in another state. My grandmother advised her to abort the baby and never tell him she was even pregnant. My mother refused and decided to have the baby. She didn't tell my father until after I was born. I was told he came to visit me a couple times but he was sent to prison for burglary before I was old enough to remember seeing him. While he was in prison he wrote letters to my mom. She told me he talked about wanting to see me someday but never actually said he was in prison. She said one day she would let me read his letters but they were lost in one of our many moves.

It would have been around this time I started bonding with my moms' brother Ted. I always felt close to Ted. I was too young to remember but my mom told me that he took me with him places and spent time with me. He even got me drunk for the first time when I was two years old. He told me years later that he regretted doing that but he said at the time it was funny. After being in Missouri for a couple years, my grandmother decided to move to southern Illinois and Ted didn't want to go. He was 16 so he and a friend of his who had a car decided they would move to Florida on their own. They had a car but no money, so they just stole what they needed along the way. I know, great planning right? They made it all the way to Georgia before they were caught and arrested. Ted was sentenced to a few months in a juvenile detention center. When it came close to time for him to be released, my grandmother had no way to get to Georgia to pick him up. She called my grandfather in Kentucky. He agreed to drive to Illinois, pick her up, drive to Georgia to pick up their son, drive them both back to Illinois and pay for the trip. When he got to Illinois, he went to the bar where she was working. He asked her if they could go somewhere and talk. Now my great grandmother was running the bar and she didn't like him at all. She sees what is happening and said "don't have sex with him unless he pays for it." You see they were running prostitution out of this bar and my grandmother was one of the prostitutes. He told me this story in front of my grandmother and she didn't deny a single word of it. She looked horribly embarrassed but never denied it. He even admitted that even though this was his son too, he expected something in return and when they said he had to pay for it, he became angry and left. He ended up getting pulled over and arrested for drinking and driving later that night. I'm not sure what else happened that night but he never got his driver license back from the state of Illinois and wasn't able to get one in any other state. It's my understanding that he still provided the money to go and get Ted. Sometime shortly after this my grandmother moved back to Missouri with her kids.

CHAPTER TWO

My Early Years

After moving back to Missouri, my mom and her siblings continued to party. Her sister Tina got pregnant and had a baby boy. She named him James. He was almost three years younger than me. My very first memory is playing with him when he was a baby. My aunt babysat me sometimes and my cousin and I became close. We were like brothers from the start. My other aunt, Tracey had a daughter and moved to another town. I don't remember seeing her very often but when I got a little older we would go visit from time to time.

My mom started dating a new guy and she got pregnant a second time. He told her if they got married he would raise me as his own son. They married and when I was four years old my sister Anna was born. My second memory was being at the hospital when she was born. Tracey was there with me in the waiting room. My mom would have been 20 years old at this time. After we got my sister home, I remember looking into her basinet. I loved that little baby and wanted to protect her. Protect her from what you might ask? Any number of things really. We didn't start off with the easiest of lifestyles. Not that anyone truly has it easy. Life is hard. It's meant to be that way. But, by this time our mother was a heavy drinker and there were always parties and strange people in our house. My mom and her new husband didn't always get along and they were both violent. I remember there was always tension. I could tell he didn't really like me. I knew he wasn't my father but I was forced to call him dad and if I slipped up and called him by his name he got very angry. There was one day my mom was at work and I was in front of our house playing with the neighbor kid. We were riding tricycles. The other boy picked up a cigarette butt off the sidewalk and pretended to smoke it, so I did too. I didn't think there was anything wrong with it because I saw people smoking every day and no one had ever told me not to. As soon as my lips touched it, my step-dad burst out the front door and jerked me up. As he carried me by one arm I could feel his huge hand pounding onto my back and butt all the way up the sidewalk, through the house and to the bedroom where he threw me onto the bed and I cried myself to sleep. It was no different for my mom. They argued constantly and I can remember waking up nights to find them yelling and hitting each other. Sometimes the neighbors would call the cops and they would both get arrested. My sister and I would have to stay with someone else until our mom could get out of jail and come get us. They eventually divorced. I'm not sure how long they were married but it couldn't have been very long because Anna was still very young. We left and for at least one night we hid at a friends' house.

Mom remarried soon after divorcing my sisters' father. Her next husband was much nicer to us but it didn't last long. This marriage was so short in fact that I don't even remember the guys' name. The only thing I remember about this one was that I liked when he would take me with him to ride the three-wheeler and that his family really disliked my mom. Some of his relatives would make fun of me because we were poor and my mom got my clothes at the Salvation Army. As far as I was concerned my mom was doing the best she could at the time and I refused to listen to anyone bad mouth her.

After they split up we moved in with my grandma and I started kindergarten. Sometime during that year my mom got a letter from my father that said he was out of prison and wanted to see us. I was so excited when my mom asked me if I wanted to see him that I jumped up and down and yelled "YES!" I knew I had seen him before but I was too young to remember, so as far as I was concerned, I was going to meet my dad. My Aunt Tina wanted to come along for the trip and brought Jimmy with us. We loaded up and headed out. It wasn't what I expected at all. There was no cheerful reunion or playing catch in the yard. My father had lost his sight by this time and really wasn't able to do much of anything because of his health. He was nice to me but didn't pay a lot of attention to me. He and my mom did a lot of talking but I was never allowed to hear the conversations or if I did I was too young to understand what was being said. She told me years later that he offered for us to move there with him. I asked why she wouldn't have moved and let me be around my dad. She said there was a catch. He lived with his dad and step mother and said he couldn't handle little kids around because of his health. He said my mom could live with him if she would let his ex-wife raise me and my sister with her kids. She had three kids, one of which was his. My mom said no. I have to give her credit for one thing; she refused to give us up to anyone. She did her best to keep us together. That was the last time I saw my father. It was the only time I actually remember seeing him.

We moved to Eastern Tennessee next. Me, my sister and our mom moved in with my grandfather and his new wife. They had a nice home and she had three kids, a son in his twenties, a nineteen year old son and a daughter in high school. I started first grade while we lived with them. It was hard trying to make friends but that became a lifelong struggle. I was awkward and extremely shy. That Christmas, Papaw (that's what I called my grandfather) bought me my first bicycle. It was awesome! It was the first time I remember getting something I really wanted. I loved having something of my very own. Just as I was starting to get comfortable there, mom started wanting to go out to bars and meet men. Papaws wife was very much against this. She thought my mom should be staying home taking care of her kids. I woke up in the middle of the night to screaming and fighting and my mom being arrested again. My mom was a confrontational person and very irrational when she was drinking. When she got out of jail we moved to a rundown trailer park that was barely fit for human habitation. It was always so cold in that place, with holes in the floors and paper thin walls. There was a place at the end of the gravel road where people threw their trash. It was a tiny makeshift landfill that wasn't regulated or checked, maybe fifty yards from our trailer. Some of the kids in the trailer park would go there and find things people had thrown out to play with. I went once and my mom yelled at me for it.

My Aunt Tina had moved close to the same area. When we would go to her house and visit, I would get to play with Jimmy. We would catch lightening bugs and play in the rain, anything you could find to do in the country when you're a kid we did it. We loved each other like brothers and as we got older we competed like brothers as well. Games, sports, girls, everything was a contest. One of our favorite games was to see who would chicken out first. Whether it was jumping off the highest point in a tree or off a roof or any other ridiculous dare we could come up with. If one did it, the other had to or you were the chicken. There was never a winner because neither of us would allow our self to be called chicken.

That winter my mom received a letter that said my dad had passed away. I remember there being people at our trailer so my mom took me into the bedroom and sat me down on the bed and told me the news. I cried hard but in my head I wondered, "Why? I never really knew him anyway." Then I stopped crying and tried to look big for the people in the other room. I was seven years old. I spent my entire childhood looking for a father figure. My Uncle Ted and I were close but he had gotten married and moved away. I could tell my Papaw felt bad about the way things ended at his place. He would come around from time to time to visit us but I didn't see him as often as I would have liked to.

We moved from that trailer park to another one. This time the owner gave my mom a deal on the rent or deposit or both I guess. The deal was that we had to clean up after the last tenants. The utter filth that I saw that day almost made me vomit. There was trash piled up all over the floor in every inch of that place. There were dirty diapers and a ton of garbage everywhere. It was my mom and me, at all of seven years old, cleaning this disgusting place up so we could move in. You couldn't see the floor there was so much trash. I don't know a single person today who would have lived in that place but we made it work for a while. Mom made some friends and went back to throwing parties at home with us kids there. There was one night a guy that lived next door was at our kitchen table by himself so I went to see what he was doing. He had a large bag of marijuana and was putting rolling papers together to make one giant joint for everyone to share. When he finished, my mom told me to go to bed. I was curious so I snuck back into the living room and stood by the door. They passed the joint around until the guy standing next to me tried to pass it to me. I stood there and looked at it not knowing what I should do. Then my mom saw me from across the room and ran over to send me back to my room and yelled at the guy who just passed a joint to her kid. Of course my mom was still frequenting the local bars and I woke up one morning to find her beat up. She had a black eye, marks on her neck and she was visibly upset. Not long after this we moved back to Missouri. I found out years later that Papaw moved out and divorced his wife so that he could have a place of his own anytime his kids needed a place to stay. He and my mom never got along so there is no way they would ever live under the same roof again. Ted stayed with him years later after his divorce and Tina may have at some point as well.

This brings us to another rundown trailer park in Missouri. Mom woke me up one night and told me to hurry up and put my shoes on, we had to leave. The trailer next door was engulfed in flames. We were told by one of the firemen to get out of our trailer because the flames were blowing our direction. We waited in a neighbors' trailer until the fire was out. When we were allowed to go back home, mom turned to me and yelled "cover your eyes!" The firemen were bringing out a body from the ruble. We found out that the man who lived there had been tied to a kitchen chair. Whatever happened there was enough to scare my mom into moving. She found another small trailer court that was cheap enough for her to rent something. When she went to sign me up for school, I was sent to the elementary school across town. We were told the one closest to us was full. This meant I had to attend a different school than all the other kids in my neighborhood. If you can remember being this age, being the kid that's different usually doesn't bode too well. I finished the last part of first grade and the rest of elementary school there. Mom still went out to bars pretty much every weekend and this time she brought a guy home named Dean and he moved in with us. Mom swears that we met him a few times before he moved in but all I can remember is him being there one day and from that day forward he lived with us. There hadn't been a man living with us for a long time and I had not had good experiences with it. I did not like the idea of a strange man moving in but mom didn't seem to care much about my opinion.

Dean had a history of his own. He had served in the Army and he had other kids with his ex-wives that he didn't see very often. He had been to prison and he had been involved with some pretty hard drugs. He had left the hard drugs in his past but he still smoked pot and was a heavy cigarette smoker. He didn't use marijuana in front of us but I knew he did because I saw it all the time. I hated the cigarette smoke. This was one of the things we argued about the most because he would get mad when I would say anything about it. I finally got told by my mom if I didn't like it to go in another room while he was smoking. I was terrified of him because he was a mean looking guy and would get mad at me and yell if I did anything wrong. His voice would cut through me like a knife. They would throw wild parties in the living room and tell me to go to the bedroom and go to sleep. I didn't like it but I would get yelled at if I didn't do as I was told. Over time I learned that my mom had a guilty conscience and would be nicer than usual to me when she was drinking. She was falling deeper and deeper into alcoholism and it bothered me. She would get drunk and want to fight with whoever was around. Luckily Dean didn't believe in hitting women so he would watch her get stupid and swing at him or kick at him and he would just move out of the way and let her hit inanimate objects and laugh at her. This only made her angrier but he thought it was hilarious. Once she broke her toe kicking the refrigerator.

My grandmother came to pick me up and take me on a trip to visit family over the summer. She did this a few times over the next several years. She would pick me up and we would take a greyhound bus to wherever she planned to go that summer. We visited my Uncle in New Orleans before he got divorced and moved to Tennessee. We also visited cousins in Chicago and in North Carolina. I knew when she showed up we were going somewhere but I never knew where or why. I always had fun but I wondered why my mom let me go away so often and for such long trips. Did she not want me around? When I came home after this trip, I had a surprise waiting for me. I had a new baby sister! My sister Lucy was born while I was away.

One day a man and his wife knocked on our door and said they were from a local church. They wanted to know if we would come to their church if they picked us up in the church van. We didn't have a car. We had not ever had a car that wasn't borrowed. Anna and I got very excited and begged our mom to let us go. She agreed but very rarely would go with us. We loved going to church. It was fun and the people were nice to us. I know now that I'm older they probably pitied the little poor kids that came without parents but at the time I felt like I belonged there. It was a huge building filled with what I considered at the time to be rich people. They were local business owners and people who were just not on the same economic playing field as us. While we were at church, they seemed to really care about us and I felt comfortable there. I didn't have anything in common with the other kids that went there but at least most of them weren't mean to me like a lot of kids at school were. They picked us up on the van every Sunday and every Wednesday. On Wednesdays I participated in the Royal Ranger program and Anna was part of the Missionettes. Royal Rangers went on camping trips and learned first aid and knot tying along with learning bible verses. I loved it and I was learning a lot. This was a great part of my childhood. Dean even came on a father son camping trip with me once.

One day during service the pastor gave an alter call and I felt God calling to me. I knew I needed to get down to the front and talk to God. It felt as if he had his hand on my heart and was pulling me towards the front of the church. I went up there knelt down and prayed a sincere prayer. I felt God enter my heart that day and he has not left me since. I made a decision to try to be good, to do the right things and to live how God would want me to. As you will read, I have not always kept my end of the bargain but God has always taken care of me in every situation. I may not always understand things but I know God is with me.

Now that there were three kids, mom and Dean decided to move two trailers down the gravel road to a larger trailer. They didn't always get along and lived together off and on for years. One of the times Dean moved out, my grandma came to stay with us. She would babysit us while my mom would go out on the weekends. I got tired of it and I asked her to stay home. I begged her not to go to the bar one Saturday night. She explained to me that she would go talk to men and if she was nice to them they give her money to help pay the bills. Can you imagine explaining this to your nine year old? Yes, my mom was a prostitute, at least for a period of time anyway. She had a job but she was a single mother of three kids and had only made it through the tenth grade. She wasn't able to make enough to actually support us on her own. We were always very poor and there were strange men around from time to time. I know that she cared for us and I believe she really tried for a long time but she didn't have an example in her life of what a good parent was. This was the lifestyle she was taught and what she thought to be normal. I also think she was a little selfish at times by putting her emotions above what was best for her kids. We had family in Tennessee that would have helped us and I loved it there but mom couldn't get along with anyone for very long so living close to family was out of the question. Living in Missouri we didn't have family anywhere close enough to be a problem for her so she was more comfortable there, even considering the lifestyle we had to live.

I made good grades all through school but I had a real hard time making friends or even just getting along with other kids. I wanted to fit in and have nice things like the other kids and I began to resent the kids that were better off than we were. They made fun of me for not having cool clothes or the expensive shoes they were wearing. I always felt like the outsider. There were other kids in the trailer park to play with. We would play baseball on the gravel road in front of the homes, climb trees, ride bicycles and build forts. It never failed though, by the end of the day we would be fighting. Maybe it was because I had sisters instead of brothers. I was always being told not to play too rough because they were girls. I didn't know how to play with boys my own age. Maybe it was because I didn't have a dad to teach me how to play sports or how to act around other guys. When Dean was around he didn't pay much attention to me. We couldn't afford for me to play organized sports and be on a real team. Half the time it felt like a special occasion if I was able to get a haircut. I didn't mind that so much because I liked my hair long anyway. I was usually picked on by the bigger kids and ignored by everyone else. Like the time in elementary school when a kid wanted to fit in with some older guys so they put him up to picking a fight with someone. They looked around the playground and I guess they decided to pick on the little poor kid. He walks up to me and starts shoving me around. I tried to avoid a fight because I didn't want to get in trouble, plus the guy was bigger than me. He wouldn't quit so I punched him. He stumbled back but kept coming so I punched him again. By this time a teacher saw us and we were both sent to the principal.

I wasn't always safe from being picked on at church either. There was a youth lock-in on New Year's Eve and they had ordered pizza for everyone. There were several boys gathered around the pizza and there seemed to be plenty so I waited for them to finish eating before I sat down. As they were getting up I picked up a slice and one of the boys saw that I was the last one to eat so he tried to eat as much pizza as he could to keep me from getting any. When he couldn't eat any more he licked every piece except the one already in my hand. Then he ran over and told all the other kids I was eating a piece of pizza he licked because I got one piece before he could get to it. It was like this all through my childhood. Girls were even more difficult to talk to. The first time I worked up the courage to ask a girl to a movie she said "with you?", then she laughed at me and walked away. I never even knew what I did wrong but it seemed as if I couldn't find a place to fit in.

CHAPTER THREE

Becoming A Teenager

Mom and Dean worked things out and got back together. We moved in with him this time. He had rented a mobile home outside of town and it was the nicest place we had lived yet. This was the most stable period of my childhood. They were both working at this time and the partying was much less but they had not completely quit drinking. My sisters and I would get off the school bus at a day care until they got off work. There was one Friday that no one showed up to get us. We were left there all weekend. The lady who ran it kept asking me over and over "Are you sure you don't know where your parents are?" Luckily, the lady ran the daycare out of her home and she was very nice to us but that doesn't excuse leaving us there. Another weekend the same lady came to our house and watched us but again I have no idea why. Mom would just disappear sometimes and show back up with no explanation like it never happened and everything was normal. To this day I can't tell you where they went or why.

Over the previous couple of years, Dean and I grew to tolerate each other but we weren't exactly close. He watched football on TV every Sunday, which I thought was boring so I would aggravate him by asking questions while he was trying to watch the game. To my own surprise, I started to learn a little about how it is played. And then it happened... ..... Watching a Chicago Bears game, they gave the ball to a guy wearing #34, Walter Payton. This running back did things that made the defense look like they were standing still. It was the most exciting thing I had ever seen! I fell in love instantly and started enjoying the games. The next year I would have been old enough to play football for the first time but we missed the deadline for sign-ups. Dean talked my mom into letting me play football the following season. I finally got to join a real team! This was very important to me and I even got to be a running back like Walter Payton! I was a fullback not a halfback but at that age it didn't really matter and I got to run the ball occasionally. I wasn't going to be the star of the team or anything but I wasn't half bad and this started a lifelong love for the game.

That spring, Dean had told me he would pay me to clean up the yard. The trailer we lived in was much nicer than what we had been living in before, no holes in the floors or walls, no cockroaches and we had central heat and air for the first time ever. The one problem was a barn had been torn down in the back yard and the wood was still lying all over the place. My job was to pull out all the nails and sort the wood by size. I did the entire job by myself and had it done by the time the football season started. When I asked to be paid for it, he said I had already been paid because he paid the fee for me to play football and bought me a pair of cleats. In that moment what I thought was progress between him and I went down the drain. I thought we had started to develop a relationship and to me this felt like a betrayal. I didn't say a word. I just let it go. I did get to play football after all and I felt I had found something better to concentrate on. I couldn't wait for football season to come around every year. It got more and more exciting the more I played and the more I learned about it. It was the release I needed. I got to let out all the frustration in my life and have fun doing it.

Things went ok at home for a while but there was still tension. Some of it was my fault. We would occasionally have a family game night and play a board game or something and I was a terrible loser. If I lost I would throw a fit like a little child and ruin the night for everyone. It frustrated Dean to no end that I acted this way. He would tell my mom she was too easy on me. Dean wasn't a horrible person. He worked hard every day and provided for us. He made sure we ate healthy even if all we could afford at times was pinto beans. I learned a lot by being around him, like some carpentry, how to care for a garden and that it's wrong to hit women. He wanted to be the father figure in my life but I never felt like he really cared for me all that much. He was a hard man who had lived a hard life. Looking back I would be willing to say that he cared but had no idea how to show it. He offered to adopt me and my sister and have the three of us take his last name. When we didn't want to give up our family names he was hurt. I still didn't think of him as my father even though he was the closest thing I had to it my entire life. We went fishing a few times and he would take us to the local racetrack once in a while but I don't remember us playing catch or doing father son activities on a regular basis like I desperately wanted someone to. It seemed like he was always angry at me for something and I never felt wanted at home. I remember praying and asking God for help dealing with my emotions and wondering if he really heard me.

Jimmy came to visit for a couple weeks the next summer. We rode bicycles all over the area and we ran into a guy I had gone to elementary school with but had moved away. His name was Devin and he lived just a mile or two down the road from me. We hit it off right away and became friends. After Jimmy went back home, Devin and I hung out quite a bit. I think we got along so well because we were both outcasts. He was my only friend for a very long time. One day he and his parents came over and asked if I could go with them to Six Flags. I had never done anything this cool before. We couldn't afford to go to places like Six Flags. Those types of things were way beyond anything we ever dreamed of doing. I couldn't believe mom and Dean said yes. The main reason I got to go was because Devin's parents offered to pay for everything. His parents weren't rich either but there was no possible way my family could afford something like Six Flags. We had to ride in the bed of his mom's Ford Ranger all the way there because it only had two seats. It was a chilly morning and after the cold wind blowing across us for over two hours it took our legs about an hour to thaw after we got there. We didn't care because we were having so much fun. It was one of the best days of my childhood, not only because we had fun all day but mainly because someone picked me to hang out with. Someone picked me to do something that cool with. Devin told me on the way home that I wasn't his first choice or even his second but the kids he asked before me couldn't go. That hurt and it took a little bit away from the memory but it was still a great day.

In middle school I came up with a plan to get noticed. We were learning wrestling in PE so I figured I would challenge the toughest kid in school to a wrestling match. I was tiny and if I could just hold my own I'd get noticed. He easily won the match but it worked. Everyone was asking me about what happened. Later that day, two other kids got into a real fight and I was forgotten again. The next year when a kid in shop class twice my size tripped me, I decided that I wasn't being the punching bag any longer so I told him to meet me after school. He showed up right on time. He towered over me but I ran up to him and hit him right between the eyes as hard as I could. It barely slowed him down and he took me to the ground and pummeled me. I may have lost the fight but I proved to myself that I didn't have to allow anyone to pick on me ever again. In junior high I tried to make friends with the guys in my gym class. One kid told me to leave him alone. I thought he was kidding around. After class, I was walking out of the locker room and a kid jumps out from behind some lockers and grabs me from behind. He held my arms behind my back while the kid I was trying to make friends with punched me over and over in the gut. When he was finished he ran out of the locker room and I followed him. I caught up with him and told him to come outside for a fair fight. When we got outside he punched me in the nose and I bled everywhere. I didn't even throw a punch. The fight was over before it started and it was seen by several kids who told everyone how I got my butt kicked. It was at the end of the school day and I usually rode the bus but for some reason my mom was there to pick me up. When she saw the bloody nose, she made a huge scene and took me in to see the principal. I was the one who got beaten up but just for participating in a fight I got the same punishment as the other kid. I decided that day, I wasn't losing another fight. I was going to get in trouble whether I won or lost and I didn't feel like I could avoid fights because I got forced into them whether I wanted to or not. I started overcompensating by being very cocky.

It seemed like almost every summer we were going to Kentucky to visit or stay for a while. I would stay at my Aunt Tina's so Jimmy and I were able to hang out every day. When we were there, I would go to church with Tina in a small country church and I loved it. I started to learn more about God and I got to go to church camp two summers in a row. I spent one summer working for Tina's husband mowing grass. His lawn service was how he was earning a living. I was only 13 and was glad to get a chance to make some money. He said he would pay me by the hour but when I had to go home he paid me $30 total for weeks of mowing. I didn't mind too much because they were as poor as we were. When my mom was ready to go back, I begged her to let me stay so Jimmy and I could go to the same school but she wouldn't.

I loved traveling and spending time with relatives. I always wanted to stay in Tennessee or Kentucky to be closer to family. My grandma and great grandma had moved to Tennessee, where my Uncle Ted was now living. I talked mom into letting me move to Tennessee and live with my grandma towards the end of my eighth grade year. School had not let out for summer yet so I got signed up and started school there. To my surprise, being the new kid in school wasn't all bad. Everyone wanted to meet me, I made friends quickly and every girl in the school wanted to date me. It was great! School let out and Ted said he could get me a job working for a local tobacco farmer to make my own money so I wouldn't be a burden to my grandmother. So at fourteen, I started working on a tobacco farm. We would start at sunrise and didn't quit until sundown. It was rough filthy work for little pay but it was nice to make my own money.

I told my mom I loved it there and I wanted to stay. She agreed and I started my freshman year of high school. I signed up for football and started lifting weights with the team. I had already been lifting a little and I started filling out. At my old school there were a lot more kids competing for starting spots and playing time so I had learned to work hard to get noticed. The school I was at now was much smaller and the coach was impressed with how hard I was working. I ended up playing in some varsity games as a freshman and I really enjoyed my time there. Ted took me deer hunting with him once that fall, it was the first time I had ever been. We saw a few doe and a really nice buck but I missed the shot. He and I started to bond again like we had when I was small. Papaw came over and picked me up a few times to hang out with him as well. Eventually my mom showed up. She and Dean had another fight and she was moving to Tn. While she was there, Tina brought Jimmy for a visit. We had rented a video game system and Jimmy was beating me at a game. He had a way of pushing my buttons and I snapped on him. When my mom walked in to break us up, I had him pinned down choking him. My mom had no idea what to do and decided to sign me into the mental ward of a hospital to have me evaluated by a psychiatrist. I told the therapist I had been living the past few weeks with my great grandmother, grandmother, mother and two sisters in a two bedroom house. You could say it was a little stressful. They kept me in the hospital for two weeks. I was fourteen and in a facility with drug addicts and legitimate crazy people. Some would talk to themselves or walk the hall looking like zombies. It wasn't exactly a vacation on the beach but honestly, it was quiet and more peaceful than living with my mother. I kind of enjoyed it. They evaluated me and said I was fine. When they let me out my mom had made up with Dean and forced me to move back to Missouri with her. I found somewhere I thought I could be happy and she showed up and ruined it.

Mom and Dean tried one last time to work it out. He started taking me places with him. We went fishing and he took me with him to the races. I thought he was finally making a real effort to connect with me. This last effort that he and my mom were trying fell apart and I realized the only reason he was taking me places was because mom forced him to. She thought he was fooling around and if I was with him he couldn't cheat on her. She had not been faithful to him but she became uncontrollable when she found out he had seen someone else. It seemed like every time I got close or even thought I was getting close to someone it fell apart. I started to feel like I was destined to be alone.

We started going to a new church mom had found. She went with us this time. I met a girl there and we started talking. Her name was Emma and she was very shy and quiet. Emma was beautiful. She was by far the most attractive girl who had given me the time of day and she seemed genuinely interested in me. Her family liked me and we got along well. After mom and Dean started fighting again, the people of this small church helped mom get on her feet. When she decided to leave Dean for the final time, they gave us a place to stay and even though I was only fifteen, one of the members offered me a job to help us earn some money. It was only part time through the Christmas rush but it helped.

We bounced around a little bit for a few months but the next spring mom found an actual house to rent. The rent came out of the small amount of money my mom was receiving from social security on my behalf after my father passed away. She had waited a few years after his death to even apply for it because she didn't understand how it worked. The house had two and a half bedrooms. It was very small but it was in good shape. The first night after renting it, we stayed there because we didn't have anywhere else to stay. We hadn't moved any of our stuff in yet but mom and I slept on the floor. Mom had found someone to keep Anna and Lucy while she and I got the house ready. That first night was awful. We were sleeping on the living room floor which was a thin carpet over a concrete slab. We didn't even have blankets. The house was so completely infested with cockroaches that they were falling off the ceiling and hitting us like rain drops. I was so disgusted that I went out to the car mom had gotten from my papaw and tried to sleep there. As soon as I lay down, I started hearing gun shots. They were close and they went on for what seemed like hours. I found out there had been a gun battle between two rival gangs a couple blocks away. The police had gotten in the middle of it and at least one officer was shot. He lived thankfully, but this was the introduction to our new neighborhood. There was an area in the town we lived that was a heavily black neighborhood and if you were a white teenager you just knew you didn't go there. The house mom had rented was a few blocks away from the highway that separated our neighborhoods.

We moved in and I got the half bedroom. I call it a half bedroom but in reality I don't think it was intended to be a bedroom at all. It was a small room with a window but no closet. It was probably intended to be for storage. I made due and I was ok with it. There was just enough room for a twin size bed and a stereo. At least my sisters had a room and we were together. Mom worked as a waitress but continued to drink and stay out late on the weekends. It wasn't often that she got really drunk through the week but I do remember waking up for school one morning and she was hung over too bad to get out of bed. I made sure my sisters got ready for school and Anna got on the bus. For some reason Lucy needed a ride to school. I woke mom up and asked her if she was going to take her. She wasn't very cooperative. Lucy was still very young and I didn't want to leave her there alone with my mom in that shape. I asked mom if I should take her. I was only 15 but she said yes and let me have the keys. I took Lucy to school and everything went fine on the way there. Getting home was a different situation. As I pulled up to the line of cars waiting at the stop sign, the brakes gave out. I didn't want to hit the vehicle in front of me so I swerved to the right. I hoped the grass would help me slow to a stop but it was no use, I was headed right for the stop sign. I plowed through the sign and it snapped off at the ground and flew over the top of the car just like you see in the movies. As I uncontrollably rolled out onto the highway, I frantically looked to see if I could make it without hitting an oncoming car. I had enough room to make a right turn, luckily that's the way I needed to go. Now I had to make a quick decision. I was 15, I had no driver license, my grandfather had given my mom this car so the car was not in my moms' name, it had out of state plates and there was no insurance. I could let the car coast to the shoulder and take whatever punishment was coming or I could keep going and hope nobody followed me. I had about five miles of straight flat road in front of me without a single car ahead of me. I floored it! I kept it to the floor long enough to get away but let off with enough room to gradually slow down to my turn. Now when I say the brakes went out, I mean I had zero braking ability. I drove that car all the way home and made every turn. I did use one more street sign to help slow me down to avoid some kids waiting at a bus stop though. I got it all the way to our driveway and threw that piece of junk in park so hard I was hoping it would trash the transmission. I went inside and told my mom not to drive the car because the brakes were out. She didn't even remember telling me I could take Lucy to school. After all that, I still made it to my bus stop in time to catch my bus.

CHAPTER FOUR

Troubled Teen

It was around this time I started to change. Everything we had been through so far really hadn't changed who I was. I tried very hard to be a good person. I looked out for my sisters. I went to church as often as I could. I was very respectful and polite and I always did my best at everything I tried. This was a point in my life that something was different. A feeling started to come over me that I had never felt before. I sat my mom down and tried to talk to her about it. I told her that for some reason I couldn't explain, I felt the urge to get into trouble. I knew people who had this problem, like my cousin Jimmy. He almost seemed to enjoy doing things that he knew was going to get him into trouble. My mom used to say that he was going to end up in prison. I had never had this feeling before and it scared me a little. I wanted to do something with my life and this didn't feel like the way to get there. My mom didn't have any helpful advice. She simply said "Oh no, that's your grandpa coming out in you. Just don't get in too much trouble." That was the end of the conversation. No advice, no help, nothing. I realized that day that there was a good chance I could end up in some pretty bad situations.

The next date I had with Emma was our last. We had dinner at her house and watched a movie in the living room with her parents. She fell asleep on my shoulder and it was really nice. Her parents even commented about how cute we were. Her dad gave me a ride home that night and I explained to him how I felt. I knew my life was about take on a different look. I told him I like to party and drink. Not a conversation you would like to have with your girlfriends' father when you're15 right? I respected her and her family and I didn't want to be a bad influence on her. Whatever path her life was going to take, I didn't want it on my conscience that I led her down the wrong path. I had been hoping to find someone I could connect with and here I was throwing it away. It didn't make sense but it was for the best. I knew it then and I still know it now. I had a whole lot of trouble headed my way and I probably would have dragged her into it. I heard that she got kind of wild herself for a while but at least it wasn't because of me. I looked her up years later and found out she now has a great career and she even did some modeling. My only regret in that situation was that I didn't break it off with her in person. I should have but I just couldn't.

Mom got me a job working with her at a restaurant. I started as a dishwasher but legally I could only work so many hours at my age. Outside of work I started hanging out with people who did nothing but party. I was still only 15 so it was somewhat limited what I was able to do but I really didn't have a lot of restrictions.

My mom didn't give me a curfew or a lot of rules to follow. I would catch a ride with someone who had a car or I would walk wherever I wanted to go. I would try to find people to hang out or drink with and I started smoking pot.

Jimmy came for another visit. When I spent summers in Kentucky with him, we were left home alone during the day and would do whatever we wanted. We always had fun but we had different views on a lot of things. The biggest thing was that I liked going to church and he didn't. Probably because he was forced to go by his mom and I went because I wanted to. We did go to church camp together one summer and had a blast. It always seemed like when we were together we ended up in some kind of trouble though. This visit was a little different. I hadn't been going to church and had gotten a little wilder. We were bored and looking for something to do so I asked him if he had ever smoked pot before. He told me yes but he hadn't. We went for a walk and I gave him his first hit off a joint. This meant that I was the first person to give him drugs. It seemed cool at the time. I found out later it wasn't so cool. He ended up doing some much harder drugs when he got older.

It seemed like I was always getting into fights. I had been picked on for so long that I stopped caring about getting hurt and just started fighting anyone who posed the slightest threat. I fought at school, in our neighborhood or even just walking down the street. I can't count how many times I was jumped, followed or told not to come around anymore. There was one time in particular that mom asked me to walk to the store to get her a case of soda. I was on my way back and it was getting dark. A group of girls saw me and started making fun of the white boy. I kept walking without saying a word. A few blocks later a really tall guy saw me and went into a house. He came back out with two other guys. All three of them were bigger and older than I was. They followed me for two blocks and I knew what they were after. I thought about running but I was determined to stand my ground even if it cost me my life. They came up to me, one on each side and one behind me. The biggest one came up on my right and punched me in the jaw. I was tired of being pushed around. I made a promise to myself a couple years earlier that I wasn't going to lose a fight because I didn't fight back. If they were going to beat me, they were going to have to earn it. I turned to face him and he said "give me the soda." I threw the soda on the ground and put my fists up and said "Come get it." The package busted and the sodas rolled out down the street. Instead of coming at me like I expected, they each grabbed a soda and ran away. I couldn't believe that didn't turn into a beating. I stood my ground and was ready to fight all three of them and they just ran off. I picked up the rest of the soda and took it home. I told my mom what happened and she just looked disgusted and walked away. I heard her tell someone later that she didn't believe me and thought I gave the soda to my friends.

Mom hadn't changed a bit. She was waitressing through the week and had different guys at the house on the weekends. I told her one night not to take a guy to her room because my sisters were home and she was setting a bad example. She wasn't happy about it but she made the guy leave. Not long after this I woke up early one morning to hear some arguing coming from my moms' room. I walked in the door and asked if everything was ok. Mom had been out drinking and was lying on her bed drunk. There was a guy I had never seen before standing at my moms' bedroom window asking to come in. She had been saying no but he wouldn't shut up and leave. It was summer and we didn't have an air conditioner so we had the windows open to stay cool. The only thing keeping him out was a screen we had stapled to the window sill. I went back to my room and got a .22 rifle I had gotten for Christmas from Dean a few years earlier. I loaded it and went into mom's room. He must have heard me because when I entered the room he was running back to his car. Mom looked very surprised but didn't say a word.

I came home from school one day and there was a note on the table. It said "be back in a week." There was a $20 bill on the letter to last me a week. I had no idea where my sisters were or where my mom had gone. I called Dean and he came over to explain. Mom had met some truck driver and left Anna and Lucy with Dean so she could ride in this guys' truck for a week. I was furious! She forced me to come home from Tn. where I was happy, to pull some irresponsible stuff like this. I had enough. I went to stay with Dean for the week with my sisters. When mom got back we convinced her to go to rehab. Dean kept us while she completed a 30 day rehab and then we went back to living with mom. She kept dating the trucker. He would basically live with us while he was in town but he actually lived in another state. He didn't seem like a bad guy but it was obvious we weren't going to like each other. Mom drastically reduced her drinking after that last stint in rehab but she was still the same person. She wasn't going to change.

Dean offered to give me a driving lesson and a friend of his let me borrow a car to take my driver test. After I got my license, my mom would have me take my sisters to the skating rink on the weekends and keep an eye on them. I would hang out with my friends and win money playing pool while my sisters skated. Anna started wanting to date so I volunteered to chaperone her first couple of dates because I didn't trust my mothers' judgment. It was pretty innocent and I was sort of ok with that, I guess.

The following summer we got a surprise visit from my Aunt Tracey and her husband. They wanted to know if I wanted to come live with them in Kentucky for a while and work with him in construction. I begged my mom to let me go. She agreed. I threw some clothes together and left that night. The construction company I was working for was owned by a relative through marriage and my direct boss was my aunts' husband. I was pretty much a gopher but I was making decent money for a 16 year old and the job was easy. I started going to church again with Tracey and my cousins. I was enjoying myself but it didn't last long.

We had to go out of town to finish a job one weekend. The company had rented an apartment for the employees. My uncle dropped me off with the other workers and left. I stayed up all night hanging out with the construction guys who were all at least ten years older than me. I ended up losing my virginity that night to some random chic that was at the party. She was 29 and I didn't have a condom but at the time I didn't care. I wasn't going to pass up a chance to be with a woman. After the job was finished I got really nervous that I might have gotten some kind of disease from this older woman who was willing to sleep with a construction worker she didn't know. I was too embarrassed to tell any of the guys so I asked Tracey to take me to a clinic to get checked out. (I was clean) She started asking a lot of questions that I didn't know how to answer. I thought I was covering for her husband by saying he wasn't there and he didn't know what I had done. I thought she was mad because he let me do something I shouldn't. She was actually mad because he was cheating on her and using me as an alibi. He had told her that he was with me the whole time. They sent me to live with my Aunt Tina after this. I lost my job and Tracey got divorced. I felt terrible for a long time but she ended up much better off once she got herself together.

I stayed with Tina for a week or two until Papaw showed up to pick me up. I decided to stay with him and spent the rest of the summer working on tobacco farms in Tennessee again. It was still sunup to sundown but I was a little older now so the work got harder as I was expected to do more. To start the season, tobacco had to be "set," which basically meant planting the small plants into the field. This wasn't difficult but very time consuming. Eventually the plants would develop flowers at the top which had to be cut off so the plants would grow taller. This was called "topping." When the plants were full grown they had to be cut. When we cut "'baccer" as they called it, we would use a small hatchet to cut the 6 foot plants and spear them onto a wooden pole, called a stick. You needed six full plants to make one "stick." We spent long days in the hot summer sun getting paid 25 cents per stick. We would cut an entire field and while the sticks full of tobacco would sit out in the sun to dry, we would go to the next field and start cutting it. Once every field was cut we went back to the first field to load all the sticks and take them to a tall barn, where we climbed up into the rafters and hung them to finish drying. There would be one guy on the trailer handing up the sticks and 4-5 guys up in the barn. Each man was a level higher than the last, standing with each foot on skinny poles made to hold the tobacco sticks. It required a decent amount of balance and core strength to reach down to the guy below you, grab a 30-40lb stick and hand it to a guy standing above you in a barn, while balancing on thin poles with your feet wider than your shoulders. By the time the barn was half full, the tobacco blocked any air movement and it became a sauna in the top of the barn. Then you would pray you didn't disturb any wasp nests because you had nowhere to go to get away but straight down. You would continue this until you had and an entire barn, five layers high, filled with tobacco to finish curing. Then we moved on to the next barn. Once the tobacco was cured, it had to be taken back down in the same manner and the leaves were picked, graded and baled to get it ready to sell. Working on a tobacco farm was not a job for someone who was out of shape. I've seen more than one person nearly pass out or start vomiting while working. It was grueling work and every part of it was done by hand. I surprised more than one farmer who thought I wouldn't last a day. I hung in there with guys who had grown up doing this and even out worked a couple guys who were a few years older than me. I made enough money to carry my own weight and gave some money to my grandfather to help pay bills.

School was about to start and I asked my mom to let me stay and live with papaw. I had proven I wasn't going to be a burden and I loved it there. She agreed and we got a temporary custody approved to sign me up for school and I started my junior year. I told Papaw I wanted to play football and he told me he wasn't coming to watch me play and I had to find my own transportation. I played football for myself, not to have people watch me, so I agreed. I spent my time playing football and did my own thing. He had a girlfriend that he spent his time with but there were times we would hang out together. There was one day we went to visit with his brother at the house their parents had owned before they passed. This was the same house they had been arrested at when they were sent to prison. We played horseshoes all day and drank. I had my first transaction with a bootlegger because it was illegal to buy whiskey in that county. When it got too dark for horseshoes we went inside and played poker. We were all drunk and playing for money. There was a couple hundred dollars on the table and I caught a guy dealing off the bottom of the deck. This led to a fight between Papaw and his brother. They started tearing the kitchen up and beating on each other. I went to jump on the other guy in the room who had been cheating and he put his hands up and said "I just got out of prison. I don't want any trouble, just let them fight it out," so I left him alone. I wasn't going to beat on a guy that wasn't going to fight back. I watched my grandpa and his brother fight until they both called it quits. The fight was pretty even but Papaw didn't see it that way. On our way back home it was completely quiet until Papaw broke the silence and said "I guess I'm going to have to learn karate and kick his butt real good one time… … ….na, that'll take too long… … … I'm just gonna get a gun and shoot him." Knowing my grandfather the way I do I found this hilarious, but at the same time I know he was dead serious.

Papaw and I got along great. I took care of myself and we spent time together on the weekends. We would play cards and fish or sometimes he would have me be his designated driver so he could try to pick up women in bars. It may not have been the ideal situation for a 16 year old but I loved my Papaw and in my eyes there wasn't much he could have done that would make me think poorly of him. He had taken me in, cared about me and spent time with me. That's all I ever wanted. I didn't realize until years later that he wasn't really as great of a guy as I thought he was. I was very naïve. It didn't occur to me how dangerous his severe alcoholism was because I had been around alcoholics my entire life. He drank from the time he woke up till he went to bed at night. This was his daily routine. There was not a single day he didn't do this. He was never mean to me in any way but I've seen him get violent with people when he was drunk. He was a good looking man for his age and tried to stay in shape into his sixties. He considered himself to be a ladies' man and he didn't quite understand why he wasn't able to bed as many women as he did in his younger days. He wasn't exactly the best role model to say the least. Especially considering how much I looked up to him.

CHAPTER FIVE

Back To Misery

Things were going great, so I thought. Out of the blue I got a call from my mom and she wanted me to come back to live with her. I asked her if I could stay, she said no. I asked if I came home to visit for Christmas if she would let me come back, she said no. I asked Papaw what he thought. He said it was time for me to go back to live with my mom. I didn't understand. I thought we were getting along great. He made it sound as if he wanted me to leave. If he wanted me to leave I wasn't going to argue with him, so I made arrangements to go back to Missouri. I got a call from my grandma and she was coming with me so I spent what money I had left to buy us bus tickets. I had broken a couple fingers playing football a week earlier and the nail on my pinky was falling off so I ripped it the rest of the way off. This made for an uncomfortable trip. We had an eight hour layover in St. Louis and as soon as we got there I got sick. I guess it was the flu but I was puking my guts out in a greyhound bathroom on my seventeenth birthday. I called my mom and told her we were in St. Louis and I was sick. We were two hours away with over eight hours to wait on the next bus. I asked my mom to come get us because I was sick. She said no. She left me there puking in a bus station on my birthday because she didn't want to drive the two hours to get me after it was so important to her that I come home. This did not start our relationship off on the right foot. I came home with an attitude that didn't go away.

Not long after I got back into town, I was hanging out with my old friend Devin and he showed me a car that his neighbor had agreed to sell him. It was a 1976 Mercury Marquis. It was an ugly brown color and had a white cloth looking top. It was a big car with a big engine and it ran. The guy was only asking $100 for it because his wife was throwing a fit about how ugly it was sitting in the yard. Devin and I were each working at different fast food restaurants. I waited a couple weeks to see if Devin was going to actually buy it or not but when it was still sitting there I asked the guy if he would sell it to me instead. I didn't think it was wrong at the time. I figured if Devin really wanted it he would have put some money on it. I was wrong and Devin was upset about that for years. He had every right to be and I feel bad about it now but like I said, at the time I didn't see the wrong in it. I put a few parts into it but it didn't need much and it ran great. I drove that thing all over the place. I even won a couple drag races with it. (Illegally of course)

Now that I had my own car, I made the decision to try to find some of my fathers' relatives to learn more about him. I was almost an adult and had no contact at all with his family since he died. The only information mom would give me was his mothers' name and the town where she lived in Tennessee. Devin said he wanted to come along and asked if we could stop by to visit his dad on our way home. I was glad to have the company so away we went. When we got there I tried everything I knew and finally found an address for my grandmother at the courthouse. She was living in an assisted living apartment complex and we were headed to see her. I was thrilled to finally get the chance to talk to someone about my father. I had so many questions; what type of man was he, how did he feel about me, what did he like or dislike, was he close to his family, all these and so many more that needed answered. As I pulled into the parking spot in front of her apartment, it took all the courage I could muster to get out and walk up to the door. She wasn't home. I drove around and killed some time and went back. This time she answered. As soon as she opened the door a strange look came over her face. I didn't want her to be startled or afraid so I immediately told her who I was. She said "I know exactly who you are. You look just like your father." I felt chills running all over my body. She invited me and Devin in and was as nice as she could be. She showed me photo albums and told me a little about my sister. She obviously had fond memories of my father but didn't talk about him much. We visited for a short time and the phone rang. She was hard of hearing so the volume on the phone was extremely loud. I heard every word of the conversation. It was one of her daughters. My grandmother was excited to tell her daughter that I had come to see her. The daughter was not impressed at all. She made it clear that she thought the only reason I would have come to see her would be to ask for money. I pretended not to hear it but she knew I did. I finally got the chance to get to know something about my father and his family thinks I'm some kind of beggar. I was devastated. I politely ended the visit shortly after she hung up the phone.

Devin and I started to head back. As we got to the last gas station at the edge of town we decided it would be better to find somewhere to sleep for a little while and drive home when we woke up. It had been a long day and I was emotionally exhausted. We pulled into the large parking lot behind the gas station. I lied down in the front bench seat and Devin got in the back and I was asleep in seconds. It seemed like I had just closed my eyes when someone was tapping on the window by my head. I reached for the large hunting knife between my legs as I looked up. I saw an officer with a flashlight and slid the knife back under my leg. I sat up and rolled the window down. He gave us the third degree and I was sure we were about to be arrested for something. He said the gas station employees had called them because they were afraid we were going to rob the place in the middle of the night. He was asking a lot of questions very fast and I was half asleep. After about a thousand ridiculous questions he said "you see that road?" I said "ya." He said "It leads out of town and that's where you need to head if you don't want trouble." As angry as that made me, I knew this was not a battle I could win. We left and I drove as far as I could until I was falling asleep at the wheel. Devin said he would drive and get us to one of his relatives house that he knew lived close by. I agreed and I know we stopped somewhere to sleep that night but I was so out of it I barely remember anything after Devin started driving. The next day we went to see Devin's dad. I had no idea where we were and it seemed way off the route home. I had just enough money for the trip and Devin was broke. On our way back we realized we didn't have enough gas to get there and

I had no money left. I made the decision to pump gas and leave without paying. I was so ready to be home that I was willing to take the chance. I felt terrible for doing it but we made it home. The curiosity about my father and the feelings I had never left my mind but I didn't talk to anyone from my dad's family for years after that. I had gotten my sisters' address from our grandmother and I eventually started writing her. She responded and seemed very nice. We wrote for quite some time and I went to see her once but she wasn't home.

I started to feel differently after the trip to Tennessee. I was very angry that mom had made me move back to Missouri after living with Papaw, where I had pretty much taken care of myself. Instead of missing my father, I started to become angry that he wasn't there. By this time I was drinking and smoking pot on a regular basis and sleeping with any girl who would let me. My friends and I would see how many people we could fit in my car and go party somewhere… anywhere. I was always ready to party or fight it didn't matter to me. One night I was cruising around town with a car full of people and we saw some friends we had just been to a party with the night before. We stopped and made plans to meet a little later after we had gotten some alcohol. I got sidetracked and ended up not making it back to meet them. I found out the next morning that four of the people I had planned to meet died in a car crash that night. It was the biggest shock I had ever felt. I had no idea what to do. All of my friends were blown away by the news. For me I think it dawned on me that life could be over in a second, no matter what age you are. None of us handled it well at all. I got so drunk it's a wonder I didn't have alcohol poisoning. That was a rough week. The principal of the high school wouldn't excuse the absences of anyone who missed school to attend the funerals. The manager where I worked was bad mouthing my friends, saying things like, they were losers anyway and he wasn't letting anyone off work to attend any services. I quit my job, threatened the manager and skipped school to attend each of the services. It's not that I was really close friends with all of them but this felt extremely important. They were my age, I went to school with them, one of them I had been friends with since middle school and I had just seen them hours before they died. It was unreal. After the last service a bunch of teens got together to cruise around together in our own type of memorial. Half way through I was running out of gas and I was broke. I didn't want the night to be over so I pulled into a gas station, filled my tank and left without paying. We were headed out of city limits when we got pulled over. I was arrested for stealing gas and apparently one of the girls in the car had not told her mom where she was for two or three days. The officers were about to charge me with kidnapping until she admitted that she had stayed away from home on her own and I was just giving her a ride. I had no idea she was reported missing or that she had not been home. The police went to my house and told my mom what I had done. She paid for the gas and they let me go and dropped the charges. My mom yelled at me when I got home. She said having an officer come to her door right after those other kids had died in a car wreck scared her but there was no punishment. She just yelled for a couple minutes and then let it go. That is a time when I should have been set straight. Instead of doing something about the way I was acting she let me continue to do whatever I wanted. I ended up ruining the car. It was bound to happen the way I was always hot rodding it around. I slid into a concrete barrier on a rainy night and totaled it. Nobody was injured thankfully and nothing was damaged other than my car.

Anna had started really noticing boys now and I wasn't so sure how to handle it. As a matter of fact I didn't like it at all. She was 13 and started dating an older boy. Mom allowed her to date whoever she wanted even though I protested. After a while Anna found out this boy, who was about to be 16 had been seeing another girl behind her back and she broke up with him. I was proud of her for not putting up with it. He and I had mutual friends and a few days later I heard him talking about Anna. I asked what he had just said. He replied "it's none of your business." I said "what?" He says "It's none of your business what I do to your sister." I came unglued. We were in a very public place and I didn't want to be arrested so I said if I caught him anywhere near my sister again I would beat him within an inch of his life. Later that day he showed up at my house with the same mutual friend I saw him with earlier. Our friend came up to me and said "he came here to fight you." I walked up to him and asked if he came to fight me and he nodded yes, so I lit him up. I punched him on the bridge of the nose so hard it knocked him backward and I ran up and kicked him repeatedly before he had a chance to get up. He went home and his parents called the police. I was a year and a few months older so it didn't look good and they could have had me arrested. The officer I spoke with agreed that he shouldn't have been messing around with a girl that young but he told me the boys' parents were debating on taking him to the hospital because they couldn't get the bleeding to stop. They finally calmed down and dropped it. My sister on the other hand never forgave me for beating up her boyfriend, even though she had broken up with him. She and I didn't talk much after that.

Mom was still working at the same restaurant and I needed another job so I went back to work there with her. I started back as a dishwasher and worked my way up to the buffet and then to grill cook. I met a few new friends and my lifestyle started to get more dangerous. One day a friend of mine who lived across the street from us asked me to give him a ride. I wasn't comfortable going into the neighborhood he wanted me to take him but he said if I was with him it would be ok. I drove him there and waited in the car while he talked to whoever it was he needed to see. Another guy gets in the passenger seat and starts reaming me about being where I wasn't supposed to be. He was telling me how if he ever saw me there again he was going to kill me just because I was white. Maybe he was bluffing but at the time I believed him. The weird part is that I wasn't afraid at all. There was no fear left in me. I was angry that I felt like I had to sit there and take being talked to that way and had to control my temper. I just agreed and didn't say a word because I wasn't about to take on the whole neighborhood by myself. I was brave but not stupid. A few of my friends and I got tired of being outnumbered and thought we were going to start our own gang and be thugs. This was an ignorant idea but nothing ever came of it besides sitting around getting high together and walking around bad neighborhoods acting like we were tough. We were lucky we weren't shot. I remember breaking up a fight at the carnival when about 25 or 30 black teens were chasing a friend of mine around. They got him on the ground and started beating him. I pulled him out of the pile and got between him and the group that was after him. We didn't stand a chance but I distracted them long enough for the cops to show up. I had been in some minor trouble several times so the cop came up and called me by name. I explained what happened but not a single person was arrested and the cop acted like he didn't believe us. A few days later a friend of mine who kind of looked like me got jumped by five guys a few blocks from my house. They made it clear they thought it was me. It was supposed to be payback for helping my friend in that fight.

Over the summer I noticed my sister Anna hanging out with people I knew. Knowing what they were involved in I assumed she had started smoking pot. I told her if she was going to do that she had to do it with me so I could keep an eye on her. She said she wasn't but I didn't believe her. I introduced it to her because I was afraid she was going to try it with someone who might take advantage of her. I was wrong for doing this. I introduced drugs to my little sister. She couldn't have been more than 13 or 14 years old. I was so scared she would be pressured into sex but I found out later she was sneaking around doing that anyway. I only offered pot to her that one time but I should never have done this.

CHAPTER SIX

To Go Or Not To Go

That fall I played my senior year of high school football. During football season everything else stopped for me. I didn't smoke, drink or party during the season. It was important to me to be in great shape and play at my best. I started lifting weights more seriously and wanted to play. We had a great season but lost in the playoffs. After the season ended I started to hear some of the other seniors talking about ACT and SAT scores and what colleges they were planning to go to. I had good grades but I knew there would be no possible way I could afford college. I needed a plan to get myself out of the mess I called a life. After I turned 18 I went into the Marine recruiter station and enlisted in the delayed entry program. I passed the physical and I passed the ASVAB with an overall score of 77. The recruiter asked why I wanted to enlist. I said if I stay in this town I'm going to end up in prison or worse. He asked why the Marines? I said "I want to be the best." I thought

I had found a way to a better future. I wanted to make something of myself and I thought this was the way. I started spending my Saturdays with the recruiter getting into shape and doing activities like playing paintball with other recruits. I was working at the restaurant part time and they said if I wasn't going into the military they would make me a manager. There's no way I would give up the Marines to be the manager of a restaurant but it felt good to know that I still had a great work ethic and it was noticed. I was on the right track for a while but I started to hang out with friends again and started missing the Saturday training sessions.

I had connected with the defensive backs coach, during the season. He came up to me one day in the high school gym and said "you're headed down the wrong path." I still don't' know exactly what he meant but I had gone back to my wild ways now that the season was over and I thought my future was set in stone. I wasn't worried because I thought I had it made. I had good grades and I was on schedule to graduate. I had a plan for my future but I was headed down a dangerous road. I was spending my spare time getting into trouble instead of getting into shape. I had done so many things that he could be referring to that I wasn't sure which one he was talking about. Was it the mailbox baseball I was arrested for? Or maybe someone found out I was smoking pot? Was it one of the many fights I had been in? Did he know that I had enlisted? I wish he would have explained himself. I wish someone would have taken the time to explain to me what I was doing wrong in a way I would understand. I knew I was doing some bad stuff but I didn't think it would stop me from achieving my goals. I thought I had it all under control and I was going to have fun while I was here because once I left for boot camp, I didn't plan on ever coming back.

I suppose my mom was getting worried too. Dean came to see me at work one day. We hadn't talked much and for him to show up out of the blue was obviously my moms' doing. She hadn't set any guidelines for me since they spit up. I pretty much didn't have any rules to follow at all. He had always been the strict one. She let me do whatever I wanted and never said much of anything to me. It's not that we argued a lot, we just didn't talk. I would go out and party for two or three days straight and when I came home the only thing she would say was "nice to see you're still alive." I'm not blaming her for my mistakes. I knew the things I was doing were wrong and I did them anyway. I will admit that I believe if I had some structure during this time and had maybe been told not to do some of the stupid things I was doing it may have helped. Maybe I'm fooling myself but I should not have been allowed to run wild. I was not yet mature enough to handle that much freedom. I could tell Dean had been sent on a blind mission without all the facts. He tried to talk to me like he was throwing darts at the wall trying to hit an unseen target. He asked how things were going and why I had started smoking cigarettes. I had allowed a girlfriend to talk me into trying them and most of my friends smoked. I hate to admit it but it was mostly peer pressure. Still my choice, I could have said no but I didn't. He didn't say much, he asked what my plans were and I told him I had enlisted. I could tell right away this was some sort of intervention attempt but like I said, I had it all figured out. He and I had never got along well but I was glad to see he was showing an interest in me. At the time, it just didn't feel like it was genuine.

The High School had an open campus which meant students could leave at lunch to go eat wherever we wanted. I got free lunches at school so I would eat my free lunch and then walk a block away to the gas station where kids hung out at lunch. It was the smokers or the pot heads, poor or troubled teens like me. It wouldn't have been out of the ordinary to see small time drug deals or a fight in the parking lot. I was there one day and Devin came walking up and said he and a friend were walking to McDonalds for lunch and I tagged along. There was a new employee being trained at the counter when we walked up to order. Her nametag said Jessica and Devin's friend knew her. I flirted with her and she got nervous and messed up my order. The next day there was a fight at the gas station. After the fight was over I was walking back to school and a girl got out of a car and came up to me. It was Jessica. She asked who was in the fight. She turned to go back to her friends' car and I asked her out. She said maybe. A day or two later Devin and I skipped school to go hang out with her and one of her friends. She lived about 20 miles away. She was working at McDonalds after dropping out of school and getting fired from a couple jobs in her hometown. These would have been huge red flags if I was looking to start a relationship but I wasn't. I was leaving for boot camp in a few months and I just wanted to get laid. Once I saw how easy she was I decided to keep seeing her. I thought it would be a steady piece until I left. I'm not proud of this fact but it's the truth.

I asked her to go steady and took her to a school dance. When I went to pick her up, her mom and who I was told at the time was her aunt, kind of made a big deal about us going to this dance. Sometime later Jessica asked me to come over. When I got there her mom said there was someone on the phone that wanted to talk to me. It was Jessica's father. I thought this was extremely weird because I hadn't been in a relationship serious enough to have this kind of talk since I stopped seeing Emma. He asked what my future plans were. This really took me by surprise because my plans were to sleep with his daughter until I left for boot camp but I couldn't say that. I told him I had enlisted in the Marines. He said he had been a Marine and it was no life for a family. I was speechless. I stood there like a deer in the headlights. This guy thinks I'm going to marry his daughter?!?! My first thought was to run away screaming. They told me he lived across the country so I wasn't too worried that he was going to hunt me down or something but this should have been the red flag I needed to end the relationship. I didn't because I figured I was being honest with them by telling them I was leaving for the military. I had no plans of taking her with me or marrying her and I never let on that I did. I'm not sure why people thought this. The only agreement we had made was that we weren't going to see other people, which I had already broke and she knew it.

My mom had met a few of the girls I dated and never had a problem with any of them until now. She hated Jessica from the very first time she saw her. Again I'm not sure why. My Aunt Tina came up for a visit and my mom had me sit down with her and Tina for a talk. They asked about my relationship and wanted me to break up with Jessica. I didn't get it. Why does everyone but me think this is serious? I had not caught on yet but Tina brought it to my attention that Jessica's mom and "aunt" were actually lesbians. I knew they lived together in the same house but I was oblivious. My mom and Tina had a huge problem with this. Tina was extremely religious and I had been to church with her many times throughout my childhood. I knew what she believed and I respected that and believed all the same things she did. She asked me a question that shocked me "would you want to raise kids with lesbians as their grandparents?" I thought, KIDS?!?!? You're joking right? I asked them why they thought this was a serious relationship. They just looked at each other confusedly. They asked, "Aren't you planning to marry her?" I said "no, I'm going to boot camp in a few months why would I get married?" They acted like they didn't know what to say. I have no idea what was going through everyone's mind or what caused this to get so out of hand. I continued to see her because I still didn't get why people were so set on this idea. Looking back the only thing even close to an explanation I can come up with is that Jessica had been in a lot of trouble herself. She had dated a guy who was a dropout and a drug addict. He would abuse her and send her home with bruises and black eyes. I think her parents were so excited to see her date what they thought was a decent person that they pushed her towards me to keep her from going back to that other guy. I wasn't worried about what other people thought of me or who I was seeing so I didn't feel the need to stop the relationship but I still wasn't thinking of it as serious as everyone else seemed to be.

I worked out a deal with a guy to buy a car so I could get back and forth to see her. We dated through Christmas that year and my mom made it clear that she still didn't agree with it but didn't try to stop it. On New Years' Eve Jessica and I planned to go to a party at a friend's house whose parents weren't going to be home. I scheduled off work a month in advance but when the day came the manager said I had to work. I went in but argued with my boss to get off early enough to make it to the party. I ended up having to walk out just to make it to the party right at midnight. I was angry that I didn't get the day off I requested and other people did so I didn't go to work for a couple days. This obviously cost me the job. Not long after New Year we went to a birthday party for a friend of mine that was turning 21. It was at his moms' trailer out in the country north of town. He made it clear that there would be a bonfire and drinking and we could stay the night so no one had to drive home. Jessica and I got really drunk. As the party was winding down the guys mother said everyone she didn't know had to leave. This included us. I had been misled but I wasn't staying where I wasn't wanted. We got in the car and started the drive south to drop her off but I was having a lot of trouble driving. Jessica had already been puking and I didn't think I could drive the 40 mile round trip to her house and back to mine without passing out at the wheel. I decided to go to my house and take her home in the morning. Everyone was asleep when we came in. I told her she could sleep in my bed and I would sleep on the couch. I didn't want my mom or sisters getting the wrong idea before I had a chance to explain. Jessica begged me to come into my bedroom and sleep with her instead of on the couch. I started to argue with her but didn't want to wake my mom up knowing how angry she would be so I just went with it. I shut my bedroom door and planned to make the drive in the morning. When I got up my mom had left a note on my bedroom door for me to pack my stuff and be gone by the time she got home from work. I always slept with my door open so when it was closed she knew I had brought "that girl" home. I thought she would cool down by the time she got home and didn't think anything about it. I took Jessica home but first we stopped by the truck stop where her mom worked. She needed to tell her where she had been all night. She was impressed that I actually came in to talk to her and own up to the fact that I kept her daughter out all night. She was still plenty upset but just said not to let it happen again. I was a little confused because Jessica knew this was going to be an all night party but didn't tell her mom.

I went back home around the time my mom should have been getting home from work. She had taken off early and when I got there she had already packed all my things and had them sitting by the front door. I explained to her what had happened and she didn't care. I told her there was no way I could have gotten her home and made it back without having an accident. She still said I had to leave. I asked her if she would rather I had an accident and died from drinking and driving? She didn't answer me. I asked her "You want me to die?!" She just stared at me and wouldn't answer. I took that as a yes. As much as I wanted to finish school and knew my chances were slim that I would make it on my own without a job or place to live, there was no way I was staying there after that. I went to talk to Dean. I didn't go into a lot of details I just told him mom had kicked me out and I needed a place to stay so I could finish school and get to boot camp. He was living alone at the time and let me stay in the extra bedroom. I figured since I wasn't living at home anymore I could have my girlfriend spend the night now. The first time I had Jessica stay the night I got a surprise. Dean knocked on the bedroom door and said if I was going to move her in we had to keep the place clean. Again with this relationship talk? I did not want her to move in. I had no plans for her to move in but he said it right in front of her and she instantly got excited. She started talking about having one of her friends help her go get her stuff. I didn't know what to say. I knew what I wanted to say. I wanted to say she's NOT moving in! She started talking about how mad her mom was going to be that she had stayed out all night again. I didn't know she had not told her mom where she was. She said her mom was probably going to kick her out too and she wouldn't have anywhere to stay either. I felt bad for her so I just let it go. It started to snowball and I was feeling like I was no longer in control of my own life. People were making decisions for me and it happened so fast I didn't know how to handle it.

I was still going to school but I wasn't working and I still owed money for the car I was driving. I had put some money into fixing it up but couldn't keep making the payments so I let the guy come get it. Dean was driving me to school on his way to work but he wasn't happy about it. He said I needed to find my own way around. He told me that now that I was 18 the social security check mom was getting was now coming in my name instead of hers. I knew this was true because I had cashed it once while she was out of town with her truck driver boyfriend and bought myself a pair of shoes. She was angry that I had used some of it to buy something for myself. I told her I thought that's what it was for. She didn't agree. She said it was for her to pay the rent with. Dean's suggestion was for me to go get the check and use it to take care of myself while I was still in school. It was only $320 per month but I didn't need much and didn't have any bills. I thought it seemed reasonable so I went to talk to my mom about it. I walked in the house and she snapped off with "What are you doing here!?" I asked where my check was. She got agitated and said "it's on the table, why?" I figured she wasn't going to want to talk with the attitude she was already talking to me with so I said "I'm taking it." She got furious and said "That money is to put a roof over your head!" I said "Exactly, you kicked me out. You're not putting a roof over my head anymore." She jumped out of the chair she was sitting in and said "Fine, I'm moving to Florida then." That's where her current truck driver boyfriend lived. She had wanted to move there with him for weeks anyway and I had talked her out of it. She started packing her things right away but didn't have a way to haul her furniture so she was going to put it in storage. I came back the next day and offered her a deal. If she really wanted to go to Florida I would stay at that house with her furniture and live there until I graduated. She wouldn't have to pay a storage bill and that gave her a few months to get a place and a way to haul her stuff. At the time she couldn't afford to pay the storage bill so she agreed. She left everything as it was, even the utilities, all I had to do was pay the regular bills. I moved back to the house and mom left for Florida with my sisters.

Jessica tagged along with me of course but I told her she needed to get back into school and get her diploma. She was way behind but could still graduate if she tried. Jessica's mom had started to dislike me now that her daughter had moved in with me but this opened her eyes to see that I wasn't a bad guy after all. She had been trying to get her back into school for a while and couldn't get her to go. We went to school every day but we didn't stop partying. We were at a friends' house one weekend and the guys decided to play some backyard football. I tried to tackle a guy who was much heavier than I was and he slammed his elbow into my forehead as we collided. I blacked out for a second and for the next three days I could barely open my eyes because of the pain and light sensitivity. I still went to school but I nodded off in my English class and the teacher asked what was wrong since I was normally a really good student. I told her what had happened and she suggested I get it checked out and she would help me catch up any school work I missed. I had no idea how or where to schedule a doctor appointment so I went to the emergency room. They performed a CT scan and told me I had a severe concussion and blood had pooled in my sinuses. The ER doctor recommended I see a neurologist. This was out of the question considering I had no insurance and no money. I stayed home a couple days and returned to school when the pain went away. When I went back to school I took the slip from the ER in to the principal. He said he wasn't going to excuse the absence because I had already missed a lot of days this year and the slip I brought in wasn't an actual excuse it just showed that I had been to the ER. This was all true. I had skipped school several times that year but still had great grades and was on schedule to graduate. I explained what the teacher had said about helping catch up on missed work. He said he had kids come to school with injuries all the time. He gave a specific example and insinuated I was weak for not showing up. This really ticked me off. We started yelling at each other and he just simply stated I'm not excusing it and I walked out.

This principal and I were not on the best of terms anyway. Before all the turmoil with Jessica and my mom started there was an incident at school. I had an auto mechanics class that started at 7am, an hour before the rest of school started. These classes were two hour blocks that were offered this way to make them fit the school schedule. The students who took these classes got an extra credit towards graduation for being there an hour early. I didn't get out early at the end of the day and I still had a full class schedule. I was late for this class one morning and when I got there everyone had already changed clothes and was in the shop working. I went to the classroom area, changed my clothes and went to the shop. As soon as I got started the teacher told me to change back into my regular clothes and go to the office to speak with the principal. I sat down in a chair across from the principal and he asked me a simple question. "Where is it?" I said "where is what?" He instantly became irate and started yelling at me. He said I knew what he was talking about, but I didn't. The teachers' grade book was missing and because I had been in the classroom alone I must have been the thief. I told him over and over again that I had no idea what happened to the grade book. He searched my locker and then threatened to have me arrested. He was yelling, screaming and acting like I was the worst criminal on earth. He made me sit in the vice principals office with the boys basketball coach watching me like a hardened criminal for over half the day. Eventually he walked in and said "you can go." That's it, just you can go, not we found it or I'm sorry for accusing you and calling you a thief. No explanation at all. The next day the auto mechanics teacher said a former student came in to visit him that morning and took the grade book as a prank. He said I shouldn't have been treated like that but he never told me he was sorry for telling the principal it was me that stole it. A day or two later the teacher told me he had a project for me. He pulled the principals car in the shop and told me to change the plugs and wires on it and if I refused or didn't do the job right I would fail the class. This was a true test of my resolve. I had been at school early all year. They made a false accusation towards me and because they were proven wrong I was being punished for it. It was demeaning but I didn't want to fail so I did the job exactly right. Then I noticed an open pack of peanuts in the console. I took it out and urinated into the package, just a little, but enough that he wouldn't mistake what it was. I thought surely he would see something in the package and throw it away but one of the other students said they saw him turn the package up when he was leaving that day. I felt avenged but I still had one more to go. The teacher was constantly leaving us in the shop to go get coffee so I waited by the wash station one morning and as he was walking back to the shop I hosed him down. He was angry but after considering the situation he actually laughed it off and said I wasn't the first senior to pull a prank on him.

All of this had taken place just a couple months earlier so there was some left over resentment when the argument over the concussion took place. The day I walked out of the principals' office was the last time I set foot in that school. After a week of sitting at home I was ready to get back in there and finish what I started. I needed my diploma. That was also when the truant officer knocked on my door. I was 18 and living on my own so there wasn't anything he could do about me not going to school but he said he had a message for me from the principal. He said if I wasn't in school the following Monday not to bother coming back at all. I was ready to go back but after everything that happened there was no way I was going back based on an ultimatum. I gave serious thought to showing up on Tuesday just to get under his skin but I knew that would lead to more fighting and it wouldn't do any good anyway. Since I was the only reason Jessica had gone back to school, she quit when I did. It still hurts to drive by there and know I was three months from graduation when I dropped out.

It wasn't long before my recruiter was at the door wanting to know why I hadn't been showing up for the weekly training sessions. I had been spending all my time with my friends and hadn't been doing what I had agreed to. I told him about not going to school so his superior got my transcripts and took me to a neighboring school. The principal of that school took one look at my records and said they were so good that if I just showed up and didn't do a thing for the rest of the year he would hand me a diploma. The problem was I had no transportation to get to that school. The Gunnery Sergeant who had taken me there said I could go back to the school I had before and ride the bus but I refused. My pride wouldn't allow me to walk back in there and let that guy think he had me where he wanted. The way I had been raised and the influences I had on my young life led me to believe that the way that man had insulted me could not be forgiven. That mindset was so strong that I didn't consider the damage I was doing to my own future. Not finishing high school was the biggest mistake I ever made. That single decision sent my life on a completely different path.

CHAPTER SEVEN

Limbo

I was now in limbo. I wasn't sure what the right thing to do was anymore. There were no future plans, no job, no family for at least 400 miles and no one to tell me how bad I had screwed up. It was just me and a girlfriend who was also a dropout. I started feeling like the world was against me and I became very hard and jaded. I had spent most of the last year partying so that's what we continued to do. Devin had gotten kicked out of his moms' house and was looking for a place to stay. He had a job and was willing to pay the utilities so it worked for me. Devin was the only person I could come close to calling a best friend. We had known each other since kindergarten and had been friends since that day Jimmy and I saw him at his house years earlier. We had a few disagreements over the years. Like when I bought the car he wanted or the time I had sex with his ex-girlfriend when he still liked her. I even punched him in the face once for talking about me behind my back. I punched him because at the time there wasn't anyone I trusted more than him and I felt betrayed when someone told me he had been talking trash about me.

When Devin moved in he not only had a job but come to find out, he had also started selling weed for one of the local dealers. He was kind enough to share some of his overflow with us so now we had free weed. Devin had another bad habit he shared with us. He had gotten quite good at shoplifting. We asked him where he was getting some of the things he was bringing home and he showed us. I was completely against it at first but Jessica took to it like a duck to water. She had zero problems with stealing. This bothered me but they were getting away with whatever they wanted and made it look easy. After watching them do it for a while, I decided to try it myself. I got really good at it very fast. I could take anything I wanted from any store I wanted. I didn't think I was hurting anyone because these were large companies we were taking from, not real people. I was no angel but I knew this was wrong. I was angry at the world for the hand I had been dealt. I had watched my family drink themselves stupid, fight each other and waste their lives until I thought this was normal. I was jealous of every kid I had been to school with who had more than me and rubbed it in my face. Now I was fighting at every turn and stealing everything that wasn't nailed down. I was so offended by the principal who had called me a thief and yet that's exactly what I had become.

Devin came home one afternoon and showed me a handgun he had gotten from the guy he was selling drugs for. This made me nervous. He didn't act like he had any idea how to handle a weapon and he was bragging about it to everyone. A few nights later a guy from the neighborhood came by and asked for Devin. I told him Devin would be home from work any time. He said he wanted to wait for him because when he got there he was taking Devin's gun from him. I let him stay and wait for Devin. I figured it would be safer to have this happen here, where I knew what was about to happen and could help Devin, instead of it happening on the street when he was by himself. Devin walked in the door a few minutes later and they started talking. The guy asked to see the gun and I didn't say anything because I thought "there's no way Devin is dumb enough to hand over his gun to this guy." Devin took the magazine out and gave him the gun. Then the guy asked for the magazine and before I could say anything Devin handed it to him. I never thought that he would have actually given it to him. In less than a second the guy snatched the magazine up and the loaded gun was cocked and pointed right at Devin. He said "this is my gun now." I opened the front door and pushed the guy outside. Devin quickly followed him but as soon as we stepped out the door the gun was right between Devin's eyes. I was hoping that Devin would take the gun back from him but he just froze. As I saw the guys arm twitch I jumped in front of him grabbed the gun and pried it out of his hand. When I ejected the bullet, I noticed it had lodged crooked in the chamber. It was a miracle that Devin was not shot. I may have jumped in front of him and taken the gun away but God saved Devin's life that night. I turned and told them both to go in the back yard and fight it out and I would give the gun to the winner. I hid the gun and followed them into the back yard. I had every intention of making sure Devin won. I couldn't believe what I saw next. These two wouldn't get within ten feet of each other, now that neither of them had a gun. They stood on opposite sides of the yard and mouthed at each other. I had enough. I lost it and went after the guy. He had almost shot my best friend right in front of me. This couldn't be allowed to stand. He saw me coming at him and ran away. He disappeared into the dark of the night. By now, I'm completely full of pure rage. I couldn't contain it. I walked over to Devin and all I could think was how stupid he was for giving that guy his gun and how much of a coward he had been for not standing up for himself even after I took the gun from the guy. I wanted Devin to kick this guys' butt so badly that I could feel it pulsing through me. Devin had been running his mouth again about how he was going to get me back someday for that time I punched him. I told him if you want to get me back for the time I punched you, now is the time. I stood there and offered him a free shot to punch me. He just stood there so I offered again. He kept standing there and I just unloaded on him. I hit him with everything I had. He flew backward off his feet and landed on his back. As Devin hit the ground the other guy raced out of the darkness and tried to kick him while he lay on the ground. I ran after him but again he disappeared into the night. Devin got up and started to come toward me. I asked if he wanted some more and he turned away and left. He came back with a friend to get his stuff and move out. I told myself that Devin deserved that punch for some things he had been saying about Jessica behind my back. The truth is I wasn't a very good friend to him. I had bought his car, had sex with his girl and punched him in the face twice. The funny part is that, this is one more person who couldn't stand Jessica. I seemed to be the only one willing to put up with her.

Some people might wonder why the cops weren't called while

all this was happening. If you recall, this wasn't a nice neighborhood. I had seen 12 year olds selling weed and crack cocaine and walking around carrying bankrolls bigger than I've ever seen anywhere else. Some arguing in the yard wasn't even a blip on the radar there. No cops ever showed up but I hid the gun just in case. Devin came back the next day and asked for it. I was afraid something like this would happen again and he wasn't brave enough to defend himself so I lied and told him I hid it and someone stole it from the hiding place. I was trying to protect him from himself. I was afraid he would end up dead if he kept carrying that gun around. The truth is I sold it. Devin and I didn't talk for a long time but we actually had one big thing in common. We were both scarred on the inside and we were overcompensating for the enormous insecurities we didn't want anyone to see.

Jessica's mom showed up to the house a week or two later and told us they were moving to Illinois. They asked her to go with them. They said we didn't know what we were doing and we were just "playing house." They were right and I knew it. I couldn't take care of myself and I had no idea how I was going to take care of her. We weren't getting along that well either. She was violent and unstable. She would get extremely upset and not be able to tell me why. She would hit me and throw things at me. I wanted her to go with her mom but she turned and looked at me and said she really wanted to stay. For some reason I can't explain, I couldn't tell her no. It would be easy to say I was used to getting sex whenever I wanted but I'm not sure that would be the right answer. I could go get that from any number of other girls. I had no idea what a good relationship was supposed to be like and I had started to have feelings for her. She didn't treat me well and nobody that I knew liked her at all but I cared about her. She stayed and I soon regretted that decision. There was the time she put a cigarette out on my leg. We hadn't even been fighting she just did it for the fun of it. She laughed as she was doing it. Another instance I walked into the bedroom and she had taken a kitchen knife and slaughtered a pillow. The entire room was covered in pillow stuffing and she was sitting in a ball in the floor crying with the knife still in her hands. Again, we had not been fighting that day. I have no idea why she did this. We were at a party a couple weeks later and she called me her ex-boyfriends name. I may not have had money but I treated her very well and I was putting up with all of her crazy antics just for her to call me the name of the boyfriend who had beat her and treated her like crap. I found out the reason he was on her mind was because she was asking her friends at the party how he was doing. I lost my temper, threw a bottle of liquor at the wall and stormed out. I went to a bar close by that I knew would let teenagers in and found some other people I knew. She came in after me and asked if I would go outside to talk. I did and she started punching me when I said I was done with her. I asked for my class ring back but she had already thrown it into a field (so she says). I tried to back away from her but she followed me and continued to punch me. I told her if she punched me again I was hitting her back and she stopped. She finally left when she realized I wasn't going with her. I wanted to make sure she knew I was done with her so I stayed at another girls' house that night. The next day Jessica gave me roses and a card and begged me to stay with her even though she knew I was with someone else the night before. I still didn't want her anymore but she wouldn't give up. She was relentlessly trying to make up so she could stay with me. I gave in and stayed with her knowing this relationship wasn't a good one.

We started hanging out with a different group of people after that. One of these was a guy in his twenties who moved in for a while and was supposed to split bills with us. He never paid a cent and moved out in a matter of weeks. For some reason he left with an attitude. He kept driving by and cussing at us and flipping us off. So I had a friend take me to his parents' house where he lived. I told him to come outside and settle this like men. We fought for about 45 minutes in front of his entire family and when it was all said and done he was crying for his mom to get me off him. Once again we had to find new friends.

Jessica signed up for food stamps and we got by on bare necessities. We had no idea what we were going to do or how to do it. I think the only reason I didn't get a job was that in the back of my mind I was still thinking I was going into the Marines. It was foolish to think this now but again I was extremely naïve. Another person that came to stay with us was the younger brother of a girl Jessica had gone to school with. He wasn't living with us but he had been spending a lot of time there. He came by one day with a car. He said he had borrowed it from a friend. It didn't have license plates or insurance but he said we could use it as long as I was willing to drive since I had a drivers' license. You may find this hard to believe but I really didn't know how much trouble I could get in by driving this car around. I knew it wasn't legal but my mom had driven cars around my whole life without insurance or proper registrations and she had never gotten in trouble once for it. I thought if she could get away with it so could I.

The next thing that happened was completely my fault. I saw

a magnetic dealer plate on the back of a car and took it to use on this borrowed car. I thought if the car had some kind of plate on it we would be less likely to get pulled over. I thought as long as we drove safely the police wouldn't have a reason to run the plate and they wouldn't know it was stolen. I was a moron. We had the plate for a day or two and decided to go out for a late night snack. We pulled up to the drive through and a cop pulled up behind us. Within seconds we were told to pull over to the side of the parking lot out of the way of traffic. The officer got out, pulled his gun, hid behind his door and yelled "get out with your hands up!" I got out and he pointed his gun at me and told me to walk backward toward him with my hands behind my head. I did as I was told and when he told me to stop I was in the middle of a mud puddle. He told me to lie down on my stomach. I tried to move out of the puddle first and he shouted for me not to move an inch, just to lie down right there. As I was lying there face down in a puddle they searched the car and found evidence that we had been shoplifting. They arrested all three of us and separated us immediately. When we got to the station our friend was allowed to call his mom since he was a passenger and he was only 15. The officers interrogated Jessica and she told them everything we had done for months but she blamed everything on me and Devin. She claimed she was an innocent bystander to everything. When the officer took me to my cell he looked at me in a disgusted way and said "Why did you drag her into all of this?" I was speechless. I knew right then, I was screwed. Devin and Jessica had started shoplifting way before I did. It was her friend who brought over the car. She had multiple chances to leave and didn't. I didn't have the guts to tell her to go and now I was stuck. She was putting on a show, making herself look like a damsel in distress and they bought every single word of it. Believe me when I say I know I did wrong. I was not innocent of any of the charges they accused me of. I had shoplifted and I had taken that license plate but I was the only one behind bars.

I spent the night in the cell and was brought along the next morning when two officers took us to the house so she could give them all the stuff "I" stole. She was only giving them my stuff and some of it wasn't even stolen. So I grabbed a few of her things and threw them in the pile. We were in the back of the police car together and she tried to hold my hand. I pulled away and she forcefully grabbed my hand and pulled it toward her. The officers looked back at us and I knew they'd never believe me anyway so I let her hold my hand. She said she would bail me out as soon as she could. I was locked back in a cell and she was released. I'll admit I was afraid. I kept asking to make a phone call and after a few hours someone finally felt sorry enough to let me. I got to the phone and it suddenly dawned on me, I couldn't think of anyone I could call that would care. I called my recruiter and told him I'd been arrested. He asked why I didn't call my mom. I told him she had moved to Florida and even if I had a way of reaching her she probably wouldn't care. He told me there wasn't anything he could do.

The next morning I was taken into a detectives' office where I was shown the statement Jessica had made. It was as thick as a paperback novel. I read a few pages of it and quickly got the drift. What I couldn't understand is why she threw Devin under the bus. He hadn't been around in weeks. Why did she bring his name up? The detective looked very aggravated and asked if I was willing to sign the statement admitting my guilt. I said no. He explained that there were only two ways this was going to go. He could go after all of us for everything she accused us of. He was going to try to get charges on me, Devin, Jessica and her friend. She would get her charges dropped in exchange for testifying against the rest of us and I knew she would be more than willing to cooperate to save her own hide. Then he started talking about how a local restaurant had been robbed and that it was an inside job. He wanted to pin that on Devin since he worked there and had been named in this statement. I defended him saying I knew he wouldn't do something like that. The detective said they would figure it out and whoever did it would get caught. I looked through the statement one more time. He told me if I sign it he would drop all interest in everyone else and I would be the only one in trouble. I knew I had done wrong and deserved to be punished. I reasoned with myself thinking I was doing the right thing by taking the blame and letting the others off. I signed the paper and was transported to the county jail where I was introduced to the public defender. She said there wasn't anything she could do since I had admitted guilt. I was then locked in a cell with a bunch of scraggly looking guys who were a lot older than I was.

I spent the night there and when I woke up the next morning the reality set in. I was locked up, my future plans were gone and I didn't have a soul that cared about me. As big and bad as I had acted for the past year I was terrified. I asked the guard if anyone had come to bail me out. When he said no, I started to panic. This couldn't be happening. I had a future. I had a plan. What had I done? Just as I was about to lose my mind the guard came up and said someone was here to get me. As he took me to change into my street clothes I tried to peek around the corner to see who was bailing me out. It was Jessica. I was mad about the statement but she was the only person willing to get the money to bail me out of jail. I couldn't help but think she was the only person who cared about me even a little, although I knew she would sell me out to save her own hide. We went back to the house to await my court date and find out my punishment. Within days of being out of jail our house was broken into. We didn't have much but they stole our food and cigarettes. I guess karma was already kicking in. I was done with stealing. I wanted no part of anything illegal. Jessica on the other hand, learned that crying and acting innocent would get her out of trouble so she kept doing everything we had before. Her and her friend from school went out together and brought home some brand new clothes. I knew she didn't have any money and I couldn't believe she had so little regard for what happened. I chewed her out for stealing after I took the rap for all of us. I told her we were never stealing again.

CHAPTER EIGHT

The Avalanche

My mom contacted me to let me know she was on her way back to Missouri. My recruiter had tracked her down in Florida and told her I had been arrested. Papaw gave her money to get back and bail me out. When she got there she told me she was upset with Jessica for bailing me out. She wanted me to sit in jail and learn my lesson. Probably the first time she had a good parenting tip but she was more than willing to keep the money my grandfather had given her. She moved back into the house and said she was staying until my court date. My grandmother heard about what was going on and showed up there as well. My grandmother, mother, two sisters and Jessica, none of whom get along with each other, all living in a small house. The last time I had to live with this many women I ended up in a psyche ward. Jessica and I both got jobs and tried to clean our act up. She worked at a local seafood restaurant and I worked fast food for a while. I couldn't stand working there, so

I got a job as a grill cook at a truck stop. It was strange working there because I would see ex- boyfriends of my mom who would recognize me and tell me to tell her hello. We were doing our part to get along but there was an extreme amount of tension. I was asked constantly by my family why I cared about Jessica. My mom just flat out asked me one day. "Why do you love her?" I answered "Why do you love your boyfriend?" I knew the answer before I asked the question. She didn't love him. She was with him because he had a steady job, paid her bills and was gone on the road a lot so she didn't have to put up with him often. She didn't answer the question and dropped the conversation. I didn't know what love was supposed to feel like. Jessica cared enough to stick around and bail me out. She was putting up with a ton of crap from my family and working alongside me to straighten this mess out. I had feelings for her and as far as I was concerned at the time, this was love.

The court date came and my mom drove us to the courthouse. We pulled up in front and she told us she would come back to get us later. I was really confused now. She had driven halfway across the country and stayed in a house with someone she hated to be at this court date and now she wasn't staying?! I asked her why. She said she had something to do and she would be back before they called me up. I wasn't going to argue with her so I just got out and she left. When my name was called I approached the judges' bench. He went over my charges and asked a few questions. I told him I had planned to graduate high school and had enlisted in the Marine delayed entry program and would like the opportunity to see that through. He agreed to drop the charges if I did what I said but warned me that if I got in any more trouble he was reserving the ability to bring these charges back up. I agreed and left a free man without a criminal record. An enormous weight had been lifted and now I had one more opportunity to get back on track. I was excited to get started. I had one more chance to make this work.

We left the courtroom and mom was still not there. We waited for hours and she never showed up. We started talking to an older couple who offered to give us a ride the 20 miles back to the house. When we got there no one was home and the place was almost completely cleaned out. The only thing left in the house besides our clothes was moms' water bed mattress that was being drained. I now knew why my mom didn't want to stay at court with me. I went from happy at the courthouse, to worried waiting on my mom, to instant rage when I saw what she was doing. I looked around for anything I could find. I found a fork in the kitchen and stabbed as many holes in my moms' water bed as I could. She got there seconds later and when she saw it, she charged after Jessica because she was sure that's who did it. Jessica ran out the back door and fled. She was not about to face my moms' wrath. I told my mom it was me and she called the police. Dean showed up at the same time as the officer. I went outside to explain what was going on and Dean came straight up to me and told me that if that cop wasn't there he would have "hurt me bad." I made sure the cop heard what was being said and the cop said he was just there to make sure nothing happened. I don't know what my mom told Dean or what he was upset at me for. I'm sure they were mad because I destroyed the water bed but I really don't know what the rest of the issue was. He was angry and there was no talking to him. I find this ironic because he was the one who gave me the idea to come over that day and take the social security check. That was what sent my mom to Florida and he acted like I was some low life degenerate that deserved to be beat in the street. Maybe I was. Maybe I was the person they seemed to think I was. Maybe this was karma rearing its' ugly head and I deserved all of it and more but whatever it was, I was screwed… ….. again.

Everyone left and I realized my mother had the electric and water turned off before she left to go back to Florida. She also tore the doors off the kitchen cabinets and told the landlord we were trashing the place in an effort to get us kicked out in the street. I fixed the doors and explained the situation to him when he came by. He inspected it and said we could stay. I called to have the utilities turned back on but they wanted several hundred dollars apiece for deposits. I had been working but didn't have the money to pay these amounts. I don't know what she told them but I tried to explain that I was the one who had been living there this whole time but they wouldn't budge. I lost hope and we lived there without water or electricity for weeks. I didn't go back to school, even though that was the plan. I had been ridiculed enough for being poor. There was not a chance I was stepping in that school without being able to at least take a shower. I didn't go back to work either. I didn't have a ride to the truck stop now and I hated working in fast food. I knew I could do more than that. I just didn't know how to get started. Jessica quit her job because I quit mine. We hung out at the house doing nothing. I felt betrayed and defeated. I gave up on the idea of being a Marine. I couldn't see how it was going to be possible any more.

Jessica called her dad for help. He told her if we could find a way to get there to him he would give us a place to stay and help us get on our feet. That task in itself was a mountain I wasn't sure how to climb. We took what money we had and the last social security check before they cancelled it and bought the cheapest car we could find. It took all the money we had to buy the car and we had nothing left to pay for the trip. We obviously didn't think this plan through. What happened next was extremely poor judgment on my part. I made the decision to steal anything we could before we left. Partially because we needed to pay for the trip and mostly because I was fed up and wanted to give a giant middle finger to my hometown as I left for what I thought would be the last time. Jessica was not against the idea. In fact she and one of her friends were thrilled to get to steal stuff again.

We went to the mall. We were going to hit several stores in a row which we had never tried. The girls went together and I went by myself. I got caught and I ran out looking for the girls. They had already taken off in the car and left me there. I ran across the parking lot to some restaurants nearby. The police caught up to me and I was arrested again. Jessica and her friend were arrested as well. They had been seen stealing and tried to speed out of the parking lot and were pulled over just down the road. The girl that was with us called her father to come get her out. Jessica called her mom in Illinois. She came to get her and I could hear them talking as they let her out of the cell. I had been acting tough up to that point but knowing she was leaving and I was truly on my own from that point forward, I lost control of my emotions and started yelling out to her. I begged them not to leave me there. Within minutes it went completely silent. I was in a tiny cell for what seemed like an eternity with nothing but my own thoughts. I'm sure it was actually only a day or two and then I was transported to the county jail.

This was a lot different than the first night I spent there. I had the past couple of days to get myself used to the idea of being locked up and I knew no one was coming to bail me out this time. Jessica and I started writing back and forth. I couldn't stand the thought of having no one at all in my life so I kept writing her but the feelings were different. I was alone and scared and needed a connection to the outside world. The longer I was in there the harder I became on the inside and eventually I told her to just move on with her life. I was constantly being confronted in one way or another in jail and I wasn't about to show weakness there. I fought a lot and it usually wasn't one on one. I was beaten by several guys at a time. Once for being accused of saying something I didn't say. Another time for watching television and refusing to let a guy change the channel. The other guys would just let certain guys get away with whatever they wanted to avoid fighting them. I never backed down but I paid for it every single time. I stood up to four or five of them at a time but it never ended well for me. I could take them one at time and I proved it one night. One of them came up to me to start a fight and I asked if they would let it be a fair fight. They agreed and I beat this guy so badly they had to carry him back to his cell. They didn't like that I won so another guy stepped up. I said I thought this was going to be one on one. They said, "ya, one on one but you still have to go through all of us." I woke up the next morning with knuckle shaped bruises all over my head. I decided I needed to stop fighting and asked the guards to move me somewhere safer. They moved me to "the hole." It was one cell with four bunks in it. Once you were in that cell the doors didn't open. You were in that cell 24 hours a day. It was me and three other guys. We all got along just fine until we were allowed to go out to the yard one day with the other inmates. One guy in our cell, hung out with the guys I had fought. They were playing basketball that day and when we were returned to our cell he tried to pick a fight with me. I told him if you can give me one reason why you want to fight me I'll fight you. He didn't have one. The other guys he was around earlier that day put him up to it. We both got moved to new cells after that. I did meet the guy who actually robbed the place Devin was accused of robbing while I was in there. His girlfriend was one of the managers and he hid at her place after he did it. I didn't get along with him either.

After a couple weeks they needed the cell I was now in so I was moved back with the rest of the inmates. Luckily they put me in the other cell block away from the guys I had been fighting with. I actually got along with a few people here. At one point, I even shared a cell with the guy I had wrestled in middle school. I also met a guy who was involved in the shootings the first night we stayed at that house when I slept in the car. Apparently the guys I was in so many fights with were involved as well but on the opposing side. Things went ok for a little while but I got pushed into picking a fight with a guy that I thought had disrespected me. I walked up and started swinging. It was a close fight but at the end the guy was screaming for the guards. I found out right afterward that the guy hadn't even done anything. I was hyped up to go get this guy by some people who wanted to see a fight just to pass the time. I felt manipulated. I had done to this guy what others had been doing to me. I told him later that I shouldn't have started that fight. For me, it was another lesson learned.

Dean came to visit me once, while I was there. We didn't say much but it was nice to see him. It was getting close to my court date when the public defender came to see me. She didn't have any good news. She said after the chance they gave me before, I shouldn't expect them to go easy on me. I understood. She also said that after looking everything over the only thing they really had on me was the statement Jessica made. I didn't quite get it so she explained that without that statement they couldn't have convicted me of anything. If Jessica had just kept her mouth shut we would all be free. She told them every detail of everything we did. The fact that the detective convinced me to sign it by making me think I was saving my friends showed my own stupidity. I developed hard feelings toward Jessica after this. Whether it was her fault or not, I felt like if I had not met her I would not have been kicked out and would have graduated and been in boot camp right now. Instead I was in jail with my fate in someone else's hands.

It really surprised me when my mom came to visit. Mom asked what my plans were when I got out. I said "I don't know but whatever I do, it won't have anything to do with Jessica." These words echo in my brain yet today. She said she was glad to hear that and she blamed Jessica for the whole thing. I knew I was just as guilty but wasn't going to argue with her. I started getting letters from my cousin who lived in Illinois, just outside of Chicago. We had gotten kind of close on the visits to Chicago when I was young and she offered for me to stay with her and her husband when I got out. She said they could get me a job and wouldn't charge me anything to stay there. I ran it past the public defender and on my court date we presented the idea to the judge. He agreed to give me five years probation as long as I left the state of Missouri and I never came before him in trouble again. It was now September and after four months in the county jail I was released on probation.

When I walked out of the jail I was surprised to see family there. My mom, Papaw and Aunt Tina were there. I asked why they were there and Tina said they were planning to come see me graduate high school but then all this happened. Nobody in my family had graduated high school and I was the one who got the closest. It would have been a big deal if I had but instead of a diploma I got a felony record. My mother didn't know about my plans to go to Illinois and got mad that I wasn't going to live with her. My sister was molested by a man at her school bus stop while in Florida. She was too terrified to leave the house after that and refused to go to school. Mom didn't know what else to do so she moved back to Missouri. I didn't know this when I made my plans. She just assumed that I would stay with her when I got out. She said she told the prosecuting attorney that one of the people I was going to stay with had a criminal record so they would cancel my approval to leave the state. It didn't work but it royally ticked me off! First of all I had no idea where she was going to be living when I made these plans and if I did know I still wouldn't have moved in with her after the way she left before. I told her she needed to stay out of my life from now on. I knew I needed out of Missouri or I wasn't going to have the willpower to change. I needed to start over and figure out what to do with my life.

My cousin and her husband took me to the house mom had rented to get some of my things she had picked up from the other house. All I had was some clothes, a few pictures and some cassette tapes. It was very uneasy but I got my things and left. It wasn't quite what I expected when I got to their house in Illinois. They didn't actually have a house. They lived in her moms' basement. It was like an apartment but it was the two of them and their baby and now me all living in this basement. Her husband was a daily pot smoker. The place he smoked was the room I was given to sleep in. So even though I was trying to straighten my life up, here I was with a guy smoking pot in my room every day. Even with that, they were very nice to me and I was grateful to have a place to go until I was ready for the next step. I got a day to rest up from the trip and started work the day after. I was changing oil at a car shop. I worked every week day and put everything I made toward paying off my fines and court fees.

Not long after I started working, I was looking at the calendar to see how long it would take me to pay off everything I owed. It dawned on me that it was Jessica's birthday. I hadn't made any friends and other than my cousin I didn't have any one to talk to. I started feeling nostalgic and lonely. I still didn't want a relationship with her but we had been through a lot together and didn't have any sort of closure when everything happened. I tracked her down through a friend of hers and got a number to reach her. She was living with her mom in Illinois. I called to tell her happy birthday and let her know I was doing well. She got very emotional and didn't want to hang up. We talked for a while and she wanted to see me. I was really uncomfortable with this and I said no at first. She started crying and begging me to come see her and I gave in. I talked my cousin into taking me to spend a day and night with her. When I first got there I could tell something was different. She told me she had been hanging out with other guys while I was in jail but swore she hadn't slept with anyone. I wasn't foolish enough to actually believe this but I had told her to move on with her life so I gave her the benefit of the doubt. We talked and she wanted us to start dating again. I told her she had to stop seeing other guys if that's what she wanted. We lived a good distance apart and had no way of seeing each other so it wasn't much of a relationship anyway. I didn't really expect it to go anywhere.

I decided to get a second job since I really had nothing to do in my spare time and needed the money. I started working as a grill cook. With two jobs I was going to have my fees paid in no time and be able to start saving. Right after starting my second job I had an accident in the car shop. I had just finished changing oil on a vehicle and reached in the car to start the engine. Someone else had driven the car into the shop and I didn't know it was a manual transmission. It was left in gear and when I turned the key the car took off. It crashed through a garage door and kept going through the parking lot headed for the building next door. I ran after it and jumped in to stop the car before it hit the other building. The car was supposed to be equipped with a safety feature to prevent that from happening but it had been left off due to factory defect. It was still my fault and I was fired. Because my cousins' husband worked there as well and he had talked his boss into hiring me, he was being scrutinized at work too. This caused a lot of tension at home. I couldn't catch a break. Everything I did and everywhere I went was a disaster. I kept working at the restaurant but that is not where I wanted my life to be. I still wanted more. I had no idea what to do. I sat down to talk about it with my cousin but her husband was very confrontational. I said maybe I should just go back to Missouri because I wasn't happy there and I was causing stress on their family. Her husband blew up and said if I tried to leave he would kill me. He said they had invested too much for me to just leave. After that comment, I definitely wasn't staying there. I got up early the next morning and left. I walked out with just the clothes I was wearing and $100 in my wallet. I left everything behind so I wouldn't start a fight about where I was going. I was going to the bus station and see how close to my hometown I could get with that $100 and walk the rest of the way. I stopped at a pay phone and called Jessica to tell her I was leaving and I wouldn't be back. She got upset and begged me to come to her moms. I knew her mom didn't like me and I said no. She said she would come all the way there to get me and her mom was ok with it. At the time it sounded a lot better than going back to live with my mom so I went.

CHAPTER NINE

A New Beginning

Jessica's "aunt" is a very reasonable and practical person. She took me around to put in some applications and bought me a few necessities. Two of the businesses I applied at offered me jobs so I took them both. I worked fast food from 5:30am to 2:30pm and a grocery store deli from 3:00pm to 9pm 6 days a week. I finished paying off my fines and started saving to get a place to live. Jessica's mom was about to move to a town a few hours away for her aunt's job. Jessica didn't want to leave and I didn't really want to quit another job. We stayed with a coworker of Jessica's for a short time while we looked for a place. As soon as we were out of her moms' house she quit her job and refused to work. She expected me to pay for everything. She left one night to go see an old friend. I found out the next day this friend was one of the guys she had been seeing while I was in jail. I got upset and jealous and left work at the deli to go check on her. This cost me the job at the deli. I told her if we were going to be together she couldn't keep doing this, she had to be faithful. I kept working all the hours I could get and it was just enough for us to rent an apartment. Things went well for a little while. We had our own place, I paid all the bills, she stayed home all day and did nothing but we were getting along so I was ok with it.

She started talking about having a baby. I knew we weren't ready for that but I thought maybe someday we would have kids. She said she was ready now. She stopped getting the birth control she was on and we agreed to have a baby if she got pregnant. That Christmas I bought an engagement ring for her and proposed. Her mom and aunt were excited for us, which is a lot better than being disappointed in us. We went to spend some time with them around Christmas. I had one drink at a family gathering and got extremely sick. It was so bad that I started hallucinating hours later when the one drink should have been out of my system. I thought something was seriously wrong. We went to a doctor a few days later and tried to figure out the problem. He couldn't pinpoint anything but said it could be a blood sugar problem. This scared me because of how my father passed away. About a week later I got a phone call from my grandmother. I hadn't heard from her in a while so this took me by surprise. She wanted to know how I was feeling. This was a weird question to start off with but I was honest and told her I hadn't been feeling too well. She asked if I had been drinking alcohol. I told her the truth, "yes, I have." She said "that's why you're sick." I told her I had been drinking for years and never had this problem. She said "yes, but I have been praying every day that you will get sick every time alcohol touches your lips so you will quit drinking. The same way I prayed for you to get in trouble so you would get kicked out of the Marines." I was shocked. I said "Why would you do that!?" That was my future! I don't know what your beliefs are but what I believe, I believe because I have seen it. I've seen things happen that someone was desperately praying for and it happen with no earthly explanation how it was possible. The fact that my grandmother prayed to keep me out of the military just so I wouldn't get hurt and now I was uncontrollably ill for what seemed to be no medical reason was not a coincidence. She had no regrets about it at all. She was glad I got in trouble and spent four months getting beat on in jail, if it kept me out of the military. I knew my mom and grandma were unhappy about my decision to enlist but this was a little crazy. I asked her to please stop praying for me. Above everything else this strengthened my belief in prayer. I know without any doubt my grandmothers prayers were heard and answered. I couldn't drink alcohol without getting sick for over a year after that and not a single doctor could tell me why. Be careful what you pray for.

It didn't take long at all for Jessica to start acting differently. We had been getting along so well and started to make plans like normal couples and then she started wanting to argue all the time again. I didn't understand. She would do everything she could to try and anger me. She would say things to get under my skin and try to get me to argue back with her. One day we were sitting in the living room doing nothing and she started an argument. I ignored her so she said "your mom is a whore." Without thinking, I jumped up from the couch and smacked her across the face. She had beat on me many times but this was the first time I ever laid a hand on her. We didn't talk the rest of the day. The next day she started another argument. She was pulling a pan of brownies out of the oven as I was leaving to avoid the argument. She said "ya, go ahead and leave, or just hit me again like Jeff used to." (Jeff was her ex boyfriend who beat on her) Then she threw the pan of hot brownies into my back as I was walking away. I turned and went back and smacked her across the face again. I went outside for some air. I couldn't keep doing this. Something had to change. I made a promise to myself I would never do that again and I didn't. Jessica made sure everyone knew about it though. I got a call from her dad about it. She even told one of the managers I worked with that I hit her. We talked about it and she said sometimes she felt like she needed someone to smack her around a little. It was like she craved it or something and you could tell she loved the attention she was getting from it. I should have wised up then but I thought I deserved it for hitting a woman. I told her that's not the type of person I am and that's not the type of relationship I want. Everyone looked at me different after that but nobody knew how psychotic she had been acting behind closed doors.

I got a call from my mother saying she wanted to come see me. My grandma had called her to tell her I was sick a lot. I said ok but when she got there she said the real reason she came was to convince me to go back with her because she was worried about my health. I figured we needed a change of scenery after what had been going on recently so we agreed to go. We got there and I got a job at another fast food chain. It wasn't but a couple weeks and mom kicked us both out in the street. I was clueless again. I asked her why did you go through all the trouble to come get us and bring us back here if you were just going to kick us out? She said "I wanted you to come without her. I don't want her here." I said "then why didn't you tell us that before we gave up our apartment and came all the way here?" We left and now we were homeless and needed a place to stay. We went to stay with a friend of Jessica. I went job hunting right away. I was tired of working with food and looked for something that paid a little better. I got hired at a factory but it was a bit of a drive every day. It wasn't great pay but it was above minimum wage and it was full time. The day I found out I was hired, I found out some other news. Jessica was pregnant. This was the day my life really changed.

I went into sort of a panic at first because I knew I needed a good job with insurance to provide for her and the baby. I spent my entire life longing for a father figure and I was going to be everything for this child that I had done without. I made a decision at that moment. This child's life was more important than my own and I was willing to spend the rest of mine making sure his was good. I stopped doing drugs right then and put that baby before anything else. If I didn't do anything else with my life I was going to be a good father. My life had purpose now and someone was depending on me. Jessica called her parents to tell them the news. Her mom told her she needed to abort the pregnancy. I came home from work that night and she said she had decided to get an abortion. I looked her in the eye and told her "If you kill that baby, I'll kill you." We went back to my mother's to get our stuff and she wasn't going to let us have it. It turned into a screaming match and I told her Jessica was pregnant and we needed our things. She said "so you're going to marry her?" I said yes and we took our stuff and left.

Jessica's father came for a visit and helped us buy a car and get an apartment. Jessica didn't want to work so I went to work during the week and she stayed at the apartment. She dropped me off at work one day because she wanted to spend some time with one of her friends who lived a few blocks away from the factory. I was suspicious so I left work early and went to the house she was supposed to be at. The girls' brother was the only one home and said they had been there but they left to take Jeff home. I said Jeff who? He said I think it was Jessica's boyfriend because they had sex in my sisters' bedroom. I instantly got sick to my stomach. I was working all the hours I could to provide for her and this is how she acts. She was messing around with her abusive ex boyfriend while she was pregnant with my child. There wasn't a worse thing she could have done in my mind. I was finally done. Every feeling of love I ever had for her was gone. She didn't care about me and I had been blind to it. I had fallen for lies this whole time and I was done. I called to tell her mom why we were breaking up before Jessica got a chance to put her spin on it. I walked back to work and waited for her to pick me up. When she got there she knew I was angry. I told her to take me to get my stuff and drop me off at my moms'. When we got back to the apartment it was clear she had him there too because there was an empty liquor bottle on our living room floor. She was caught and still tried to lie her way out of it. We started arguing and I busted the bottle on the wall and the neighbor called the cops. I calmed down enough to satisfy the officers and she dropped me off at my mother's. I would have rather put up with my crazy mother than her.

I tried to set up a ride to work but couldn't get anyone to take me that far so I lost another job. I was so trapped in my own mistakes I couldn't see a way out. Jessica showed up and wanted to talk. I said no. I wanted nothing to do with her. She left and came back crying and saying that she thought something was wrong with the baby because of all the stress. I drove her to the hospital and they said she was dehydrated and gave her an IV. When we left the hospital she said she was scared to stay alone and wanted me to stay at the apartment with her. I was trying to get her to leave me alone but I was afraid my mom was going to hurt her if she didn't leave so I went with her. I slept on the couch and didn't even speak to her. She wouldn't leave well enough alone. She kept apologizing and throwing it in my face that she was pregnant. I knew I wasn't ever going to be free of her and I was afraid of what kind of life my child would have if I left. I told her this was it. I couldn't take any more. If she really wanted to be with me she needed to prove it by being faithful or I was gone.

I worked for the landlord in exchange for rent. A couple weeks went by and a car full of guys pulled up in front of the apartment. It was dark and I stepped outside to see who it was. I walked about halfway down the sidewalk until I could see everyone in the car. It was Jeff and his brother and a few of their friends. He stuck his head out of the back seat and asked if Jessica was there. Can you believe this? He had the nerve to pull up and ask a pregnant woman's fiancé if she was home. She came to the door. She knew exactly who it was. I wanted to run up and drag him out of that car and beat him until I had nothing left. I didn't, for two reasons. There's the obvious one that there were more of them than me and I was barefoot. But more importantly, I wanted to know what her reaction was going to be the first time he wanted to see her after she swore to be faithful. He asked her if she wanted to go with them. She put her head down and shook her head no. The car pulled up to the next set of apartments and stopped. He yelled from inside the car "Coward!", and they sped away. He was calling me a coward when he was the one with a car full of back up and I was standing there barefoot willing to face anyone who stepped out of the car. I could tell right then that we would never make it if we stayed in that town and I knew exactly what kind of life my son would have if I left Jessica there. I walked back inside and told her that if she wanted us to stay together we were moving and starting over fresh somewhere nobody knew her. She agreed and not long afterward we packed the car with everything we owned and drove to Tennessee. I had to ok it with my probation officer to leave the state again but they didn't have a problem with it.

We moved and stayed with my Aunt Tina. I got a job at a furniture factory. We started going to church and started to get along again. Tina and our pastor talked with us about getting married. We had originally planned on getting married even before we knew she was pregnant and I didn't want my son being born out of wedlock. I wanted to do the right thing. I don't think anyone in my family wanted me to marry her. When we had counseling sessions with the pastor he seemed to think we should wait as well. We knew nobody was going to agree with our decision so we went to the courthouse and took care of it there. When everyone found out they decided to support our decision and the church and my family threw us a wedding at no cost to us. I was surprised at how many people showed up considering none of them liked her.

They treated us nicely but it was cramped living with Tina. She had a husband and four kids of her own and she started to get a little stressed out. I didn't want to overstay our welcome after they had been so kind to us. Jessica looked for places to rent while I worked and we took the cheapest one we could find. The place needed a lot of work. It was a trailer with holes in the floors and walls and we had to get rid of an ant infestation in one of the bedrooms. We agreed to rent to own it so that any money or work we put into it would be somewhat worth it. My Uncle and Papaw came over a couple times to help us get the place livable. We moved in and kept working at it. I would work during the day and spend our evenings at home working on fixing up the place. We spent almost every weekend at Papaws'. We fished and played poker and just spent time with him or Jimmy or Ted and his family. I was actually happy. We were never going to make much money this way but I was happy. I thought she was as happy as I was but Jessica was by far not used to living in these conditions. She was pregnant, it was a hot summer and the place was a dump.

Jimmy came by one night and asked if he could crash there for the night. He was high on something and Jessica said she didn't want him coming around on drugs after the baby was born. It would be a bad influence and we should let him know now that we won't allow it. He was like my little brother and we were finally living close enough to hang out and she's telling me not to let him stay. As much as I hated it, I couldn't argue with her point. My child was more important than anything else going on. She was right and I made him leave. The worst part is that Jimmy was always getting high so he hardly ever came around after that. My relationship with Jimmy was never the same after that night. I was torn on the inside. I didn't want drugs around my kids but I wanted a relationship with Jimmy. He wouldn't stay off the drugs long enough to do anything positive. He was high every day. I knew it was the right decision but down deep inside I resented Jessica for not being able to see him.

Jessica was talking regularly to her family and she had told them how bad the living conditions were. Her dad asked us to come up for a visit on July 4th. I didn't think her car would make the trip so Papaw drove us up there. We had a great time but her dad wanted to know if we would to move closer to him so he could be of more help to us. I appreciated the offer but I wanted nothing to do with living in a city. We went back and we got a call from her "aunt." She wanted to talk to me. She tried to convince me to move back to Illinois. I gave her a bunch of reasons why not and I told her we were happy there. She said Jessica had told her what kind of place we were living in and asked if that's how I wanted to raise my kids. She hit a nerve. I remembered back to my childhood and I had no argument left. She said there were better schools and my son would have a chance to go to college. Jessica's mom got on the phone. She told me there was a factory that was hiring people starting out at $20 an hour. This was a lot more than the $7 an hour I was making. She sold me on it and we packed our stuff in a U-Haul and drove to Illinois. All of my family was upset that we were leaving. My grandfather cried when we left. That was the only time I ever saw him cry over anything. I almost turned around and stayed for that reason alone. I had finally been happy and satisfied but I wanted a better life for my kids so I had to at least give it a try.

We moved in with her family and I got a job at a factory in less than a week. The big surprise was that the factory they told me about was shutting down and not hiring. I started out making barely over $7 per hour. I worked as much as I could to save up to rent a place of our own. Jessica was close to her mom so she was happy. It got close to her due date and she started getting worried because she didn't handle pain very well. She went into false labor a couple weeks before her due date and they told us she wasn't ready but the Braxton Hicks contractions freaked her out so badly that she panicked. She had herself so worked up that she started puking and got dehydrated. They tried to calm her down but she just kept freaking out worse and worse. They couldn't let her go home like that so they sent her to a larger hospital to have the baby right away. She had a C-section and Michael James Williams was born in September of 1997. I gave him my name and his middle name was after my cousin Jimmy. He was healthy but underweight from being born too early. He was 4lbs 4oz. They kept him in the NICU for ten days to make sure he was going to gain weight before they sent him home. I still remember holding that little bundle of wires with a blue stocking cap on his head. I had no idea what I was doing but I knew I had to make this little guys life better than mine.

CHAPTER TEN

The Inevitable End

Shortly after we brought Mike home, we rented an apartment. I worked all the hours I could get so I could take care of them and she could stay home with him. It wasn't long before she completely lost interest in him. I would get off work anywhere between midnight and 3am and come straight home. As soon as I got to the door I could hear him crying. I would walk in and she would be lying in bed just letting him cry. I would make him a bottle and feed him and get him back to sleep. Sometimes I would just sit in a rocker and hold him. I asked her why she didn't take care of him and she would say she didn't hear him or he just woke up. She made it seem like he woke up as I came in every night because he knew it was me. I didn't mind taking care of him but I worried about how well she was taking care of him while I was gone to work.

That Christmas Papaw and Jimmy came up for a visit. Jessica

and I argued a little bit while they were there but overall we had a good time and when they went home I missed being around them. The following weeks after New Year were stressful. Jessica told me she had been to the doctor and found out she was pregnant again. I was ecstatic! I loved being a dad and wanted to have a big family. Jessica flipped out. I thought now that our son was here, she had gotten used to the idea but she admitted that she didn't want to be a mom. She wasn't happy and definitely didn't want another baby. Things were pretty miserable for a while. I tried everything I could to make her happy. I did as much of the baby stuff as I could while I was home. I fed him, bathed him, changed him and spent time with him. Mike and I were bonding really well but she hadn't made a connection with him. We decided to try going back to church. We still weren't getting along and now she had lost all interest in me. The church we went to offered counseling so we gave that a try. The counselor was one of the pastors of the church so I felt comfortable seeking his advice. We explained our feelings toward each other and she told him she had lost interest in sex. He asked how long it had been since we had been intimate and she laughed and said four months. He got very serious and said this isn't funny. He said it's natural for a married couple to be intimate with each other. For one to withhold from the other for that long would definitely lead to more problems. He offered ideas to try to resolve our issues but the therapy didn't help much and she wouldn't go back to church after that. She continued to be depressed. The best way I can make sense of this is that sex is what got her pregnant and she was boycotting it all together now. I tried to understand but I needed to release tension too. I started going out with the guys after work. We would go to one of their houses or drive out by the lake. We would have a few beers and then go home. I told her where I was and what I was doing but she started thinking I was cheating on her. I can see why she thought that but I wasn't. Stress continued to build and I tried to remember the last time we were happy. It was in Tennessee. I asked her to move back there with me and she said yes. Her family didn't take the news well at all. They had become proud to be grandparents and angry that we were leaving. Her mom acted like a child. She came over and stole Jessica's purse to try to keep us from leaving.

We got back to Tennessee and rented a much nicer mobile home and I went back to the same low paying job. We started going back to church and I was asked to fill in as a Sunday school teacher. Everything was completely different this time. The nicer trailer came with higher bills and we were really struggling to keep our heads above water. The church people made it really obvious that there was something about Jessica they didn't like. I don't know what it was they saw in her but it got uncomfortable and we stopped going. We realized this wasn't going to work and moved back to Illinois. I got my job back at the same factory and we moved back in with her family until we could rent a house. By now my mother-in-law didn't try very hard to hide the fact that she didn't like me and we didn't get along at all. After we got our own place, Jessica started wanting to buy things we couldn't afford but refused to get a job to help pay for anything. I worked all the hours I could get and she would complain that I was gone from home too much. I tried everything I knew to make her happy and she made it clear that nothing about this was going to be easy.

Matthew Williams was born in September of 1998. Jessica went into a deep depression right after he was born. The doctors said she was having post partum depression and she would come out of it. I'm not an expert but it seemed much more serious. She was jealous of the relationship I was developing with Mike and she overcompensated by babying Matt. She was trying to make him attach to her like Mike did to me. She spoiled him and he did nothing but cry all the time if he wasn't held. I would come home from work and he would be crying worse than Mike used to. Jessica and I hardly even slept in the same bed by this point. She would find reasons to make me sleep on the couch or she would sleep on the couch to avoid me. We tried to make it work but it just kept getting worse. The mother-in-law was constantly bad mouthing me. Jessica would always side with her mom and there wasn't anything I could do that was right. I started to get attention from other women and I liked it. All she ever wanted to do was argue and it made it hard to turn down other interests. This doesn't make it right. I was wrong for cheating on her but I'll admit there is only so long I am willing to go without sex, especially when it's being offered. She was suspicious but didn't act like she cared at first. When I was at home, all of my time was spent with the kids. I would play with them in their room or take them out to play in the yard or watch kid movies with them, anything to spend time with them. With everything else going on I still tried my best to be a good father.

I saw a flier for an event going on at bar. It was a tough man contest. It was a boxing style fight but with fewer rules and you could use your legs as well as your fists. I had a lot of frustration I needed to get out and I was still in good shape. I thought this would be fun and I could test myself and see if I still had what I thought I had. I hadn't been in a fight in a couple years and this was going to be in front of hundreds of people but I wanted to do this. I need a battle to fight from time to time, it's in my nature. When we got there I was really nervous. The whole production was more than I expected. There were television cameras and people were being interviewed. Once all the hoopla was over, I ended up fighting two fights. The first was a draw and I won the second one. There were six fighters left including me, out of the thirty or so fighters that we started with. I was so nervous all day that I hadn't ate much and after that second fight I was completely drained. I didn't want to get back in the ring as weak as I felt. I backed out before my third fight and then I realized, I probably only had one or two fights left to get to the end but I was satisfied with my performance. Jessica had more fun that night than I think we had in our entire relationship. This was a little insight to her state of mind. The time she was the happiest was watching people beat each other. She was screaming obscenities from my corner, making herself look like an idiot.

Everything went back to status quo for a while and then I received a phone call that my grandmother had heart failure and wasn't expected to live but a few days. We went to Kentucky to see her, thinking this would be the last time. The car Jessica's dad bought her broke down while we were there and we had no money to repair it. It was obviously something serious and I knew it was going to be expensive. We arranged for someone to haul it away and started looking for a way home. Papaw agreed to let Jimmy borrow his car to drive us back to Illinois. While we were waiting for him to pick us up, Jessica made it very clear she didn't want to stay there another second. I'm not sure what she was upset about but she made a huge scene and alienated the last members of my family willing to give her the benefit of the doubt that she wasn't as bad as they had heard. We made it home safely and I knew that I had probably seen my family for the last time in a long time. My grandmother pulled through and lived for several more years but I didn't see her many times after this.

After that, I went out drinking more often and started cheating on Jessica somewhat regularly. She found out about it and I quit pretending to hide it. I came home from work one day and she said she needed to tell me something. What she had to say was the last thing I expected to hear. She said she didn't know why but she found herself with Mike pinned down on the bed with her hands around his neck. She claimed she felt like she couldn't stop herself until her hands were actually starting to squeeze. I had so many questions that I didn't know where to start. Basically she said she was miserable and she blamed her messed up life on Mike because she didn't want to be a mother. She said if I had let her abort him she would have been happier. By this time I was just trying to stay with her for the kids so I could be a part of their life but now I had to worry about their safety when they were with her. I made her see a doctor and they said she was bipolar and prescribed her some medication. I thought it was worth a try if it was going to help her. This didn't go over well at all. She faked taking a bunch of pills one night while I was at work and blamed it on me for cheating on her. She regretted doing it after they pumped her stomach. At the hospital, the nurse told me they didn't find any pills in her stomach and she just did it for attention. She had the kids with her when this happened so now I was worried for their safety again. I convinced her to go to a mental health facility for some help. We got there and as we were waiting for them to check her in she got up and walked out. I told her she needed to get some help but she refused to go back in. For the last year we were together I checked out mentally and emotionally. I just couldn't figure out how to leave physically without hurting my kids.

She decided she wanted to get a job so she could get out of the house a little more. I thought this was a great idea and hoped it would pick her spirits up. She worked for a few weeks and seemed to be a little happier. She was making friends and had started smoking pot again. I told her I didn't mind and even tried it with her but I told her not to do it in front of the kids. This became an ongoing argument because I kept catching her doing it around the kids. I had ended my relationship with Jimmy over her decision to not let him around the kids when he was high and now she was getting high right in front of them. I was angry and she acted like she didn't care. She refused to stop doing it in front of the kids and it was a constant argument. She came home from work on the afternoon of my birthday and wanted to go out with some girls from work. She didn't even say happy birthday. She wanted me to stay there with the kids while she went out to a bar. I didn't like it but I agreed because she had stayed home with the kids while I went out so I really couldn't argue with her about it but then she didn't come home that night. I had to call off work the next morning because she wasn't there to watch the kids. When she finally came in, she was so drunk I don't know how she got home without wrecking the car I had recently bought. She had spent all night drinking and left the bar with the male bartender at closing time. She couldn't even remember coming home. I was upset but I knew the relationship was over so there wasn't any reason to get in a screaming match over this. I started trying to figure out how to get out of this marriage. I was stuck and my actions weren't making it any better. I stayed there with her and the kids but I tried to stay away as much as possible. I went out drinking a lot. More than once I came home to find my clothes out on the front lawn. One night I was at a co workers house for a party. It was a few blocks from where we lived and Jessica knocked on the door. The guys' wife answered the door and Jessica literally threw my two boys in the house through the hole in the screen door where there should have been a screen. It was December, freezing cold outside and she had walked these babies in a stroller for blocks in nothing but their diapers. They were screaming and crying and cold. I had to find a way to get away from this crazy woman but I didn't want to leave because I felt like I had to protect my kids. I told her that kind of stuff couldn't happen and she had to think about what was best for the kids. She didn't care. She knew the only thing that got to me was the kids and she used that against me every chance she got.

Right after Christmas we were arguing and she told me that she didn't love me. She said she never was in love with me, she just knew I was willing to work and take care of her. I looked her in the eye and didn't know what to say. I think this was the first time in our entire relationship she had been truly honest with me. I finally saw her the way everyone else had when they tried to get me to break up with her. I felt like she had manipulated me this whole time. I just stood there trying to come to terms with what she just said and then she tried to knock the Christmas tree over onto me. She missed and it hit Mike instead. That was the final straw. I made sure Mike was ok then I walked out and Jessica followed me. I tried to leave and she opened the door of the car and wouldn't move out of the way so I got out and started walking. It was cold and there was snow on the ground. I had spent the night in my car to get away from her before but now I was on foot. I needed somewhere to go and I remembered the secretary at work had told me if I ever needed a place to go I could stay with her. I knew she was interested in me and we had flirted but I needed a friend right now. I walked to her house across town and she let me stay with her.

She was a divorced single mother and her and her daughter lived alone. She told me I was welcome to stay with her as long as I needed. She was very supportive and helpful. I hired a lawyer and explained the situation. My lawyer told me she would help me through this as cost efficiently as she could. Jessica and I agreed right away that I could see the kids every other weekend. At first everything went ok. We got along and agreed to things, probably because I was still paying the bills at Jessica's house. She was being nicer to me than she had in a very long time. She started showing interest again and we even fooled around once. That was a big mistake. She had assumed that if she could get me to have sex with her I would come back. When I didn't want to continue the relationship she got angry and called to start trouble with the woman I was living with. She was a very smart and reasonable person. We had started to develop a relationship and this hurt her very badly. She understood that the divorce was not final and we were still working out the details but this obviously caused a lot of issues.

I dropped the boys off one afternoon and Jessica had her cousin there with her. Jessica came out to the driveway and grabbed Matt out of the car and told Mike to go in the house as she hurried to go back inside. I said "can I at least tell them good bye?" She stood in the doorway and said do it from there. Something was weird. She hadn't acted this way until now and I wasn't going to leave the kids there until I knew what was going on. She made it seem as if someone was there that she didn't want me to see. I walked in the door and she tried to step in the way but I brushed past her and checked inside the house. They both swore that nobody was there and nothing was wrong so I left. I didn't make it very far and I was pulled over by a police officer. He told me to get out and he started shoving me around and then slammed me into the back of the car as he said "Why'd you do it?" I said "do what?" He said "you know what you did." I was arrested and after sitting in a jail cell for hours, I was released. I asked why I had been arrested. Not one officer acted like they wanted to talk to me. Finally one of them said Jessica had accused me of beating on her when I dropped the kids off. The only thing that saved me was that her cousins' story matched mine exactly and Jessica's story was completely made up. I asked if I could get a ride back to my car and they said "no, you'll have to walk." I couldn't believe this. I had been proven innocent and these guys were still treating me like a scumbag.

I started finding out more and more things she had lied about while we were together. She had gone back to stealing and gotten arrested. She didn't want me to find out so she had to call a friend to bail her out. I had been working the whole time and we had money to buy things we needed. As a matter of fact the day she was arrested she had enough money in her pocket to pay for what she stole. She just did it because she wanted to. There was absolutely no reason for her to steal something. She had weaved a bundle of lies and it was starting to unravel. Over the next weeks she tried her best to get under my skin. She would call thirty times a night and if I answered she would just scream and cuss at me. I got letters left on my car from both her and her mom. She was back to partying. Every weekend she was with a different guy and several of them told me she tried to get them to pick a fight with me. Only one tried and he backed down when I confronted him. I would drive by to see what was going on while my kids were there and it was always a house full of people. I hired a private investigator to see if anything illegal or dangerous was going on. He watched the house and said there was suspicious activity but without knowing what was going on inside he couldn't say for sure. I couldn't afford to keep paying him so I had to let him go before he found any evidence. I reported everything to the police but they acted like they didn't believe me. She had fooled them into thinking she was a helpless victim like she did that night when we were teenagers. It was starting to look like there wasn't much I could do. I felt handcuffed and I was forced to watch as my kids were stuck in the life I tried to protect them from.

I got a surprise call at work from Jessica. She said, "Come get these kids if you want them." I asked what she meant. She said, I want to live my life and party and I don't want to take care of these kids anymore. I didn't hesitate. I love my kids with all my heart and soul. I dropped the phone, ran to my car, drove to her house, picked up my kids and went straight to the lawyer's office to get something in writing. I almost lost my job for leaving without telling anyone but I wasn't about to miss this opportunity. The lawyer told me that if she stuck to this it would make everything easier. We worked out all the details and she only asked for regular visitation and that I didn't move out of state with them. I agreed and we went before a judge to get the divorce finalized. I know it's not a common thing for a dad to step up and be willing to be a single father but this judge didn't want to give me custody of my kids for some reason. He told Jessica if she wanted to postpone this he would. She said no. He said if you want your kids you can have them. She said no. I looked at my lawyer and she motioned for me to not say anything. I kept my mouth shut but I was very upset that this judge was flat out telling her I would have no chance if she wanted to fight for custody. He tried to push her into changing her mind and she started crying, stood up and yelled at the top of her lungs, "I don't want them!" Then she stormed out of the courtroom. The divorce was final but the only way I was given custody is because she literally did not want her own children. This judge had no idea the mistake he would have been making if he had given those boys to her. He would have been sentencing them to a life of misery. I was legally bound to stay in the state of Illinois where I had no family to help me but at least I had my boys.

CHAPTER ELEVEN

What To Do Now?

My new girlfriend had no problem letting Mike and Matt move in with us at her place. We had originally agreed that I would stay there until after the divorce and then I would get a place of my own. We started developing feelings for each other and tried to start a more serious relationship. She was a good woman with morals. She worked, was very responsible and took good care of her daughter. She didn't do drugs and she wasn't an alcoholic. She was so much better of a person than Jessica had ever been. After being with Jessica for so long this seemed like a Godsend by comparison. She showed me that a woman can be independent and work and take of herself.

Most of my family had pretty much decided to disown me when I was with Jessica. I had been to visit my mom a few times but it was always very uneasy. I thought now that we were divorced I could try to repair the relationships that had been torn apart. I visited a couple times and took the new girlfriend to meet my family. On one of these visits, my mom told me my sister Anna was running wild and I needed to say something to her. While I was there, a man called to talk to my sister. I asked who it was and my mom said it was a 32 year old man she had been sort of dating. My sister was only 17 at the time and I about lost my mind. I got on the phone and cussed him out and told him if he called her again I would find him and he would regret it. My sister was furious at me. She said it was none of my business what she did and told me to stay out of her life. She said it was my fault her life was so messed up because I left home and left her to deal with our mother. I told my mom she needed to be stricter with my sisters and not allow them to do whatever they wanted like she did with me. She said it was out of her control and she didn't know what to do. I tried giving advice but it always started arguments.

My current girlfriend wasn't the only coworker I had slept with and this caused some issues at work. I had a very bad temper and cussed out my boss. I brought it on myself but I had to get a different job. I had worked at that factory since I moved to Illinois three years earlier. I got hired at another factory and worked there six months until I was laid off. Over time, everyone started feeling a little cramped in the two bedroom mobile home we lived in. It was nice but three kids sharing a bedroom, was not working. Her daughter had been an only child her entire life and now there were two rowdy little boys tearing up her things. We tried to be understanding of each other but we started arguing over small things and I realized I had overstayed my welcome. I needed to get on my own and concentrate on being a dad. I found a small house to rent and moved out. We didn't want to stop seeing each other but she was mature enough to realize this was a step backward not forward. I had just been laid off so she helped me get a job with the trash company in town since she had worked in the office there in the past. We didn't talk for a long time after that but I'm glad we were able to split up amicably so that we could still be friends in the future. I needed that time to set myself straight and I am grateful for her kindness to me and my boys.

After the breakup I needed to get away for a little bit so I decided to go visit my mom and sisters. Mom had started dating another truck driver who was willing to work and let her stay home and get drunk while he was on the road. My sister Anna had been allowed to move back with mom after spending some time in foster care and she started dating a guy and was trying to keep it a secret. This made everything very awkward. I had learned by this point to not get involved if it wasn't absolutely necessary. Moms' boyfriend was just another dumb alcoholic truck driver. I didn't think it would last long but I underestimated my mothers' willingness to let someone else support her drinking habit. They drank themselves stupid every time he came home from the road. They would get drunk, argue, fight, make up and then he goes back on the road. I don't know why anyone would want to live like that. My mom swore she was happy with him so I left it alone.

When I got back to Illinois, I was completely on my own. I was a single dad with two boys, 2 and 3 years old. I would drop them off at day care first thing in the morning and be at work by 6am to pick up trash all day. After work I would take them home and spend every evening with them. My focus was always on my kids. I loved playing with them and spending time with them. I read to them every night and started teaching them the alphabet. I was determined to make sure they had a better life than I did and that starts with knowledge. I started trying to toughen Matt up because Jessica had spoiled him so badly. He wanted to be held and cried all the time. It was tough to be the only one and feeling like I'm being mean to my kid by not picking him up. I used to look back and wonder if I was too tough on them but I have to believe I did the right thing. I love them and sometimes love is tough. You have to do what's best, not what feels good all the time.

I got a letter in the mail that said I was going to start getting deductions from my pay for child support. I went to sort things out and the lady wouldn't believe me that I had custody of my kids, even after showing her the divorce papers. Jessica had gotten an apartment in the government housing and signed up for every program she could by telling everyone she was a single mother and that she had custody. The lady did everything but outright call me a liar. I had to prove that I actually had my kids every day. I was raising the kids by myself and didn't ask for any government assistance but she was trying to get every benefit she could and she only had to take care of herself. It finally got sorted out but Jessica was proving more and more how deceitful she could be. She was supposed to pick the boys up every other weekend for her visits. It was regular at first but as time went on she started missing a weekend here or there. She would say she had something to do. One afternoon, Jessica's "aunt" stopped by to say hi. I had always gotten along with her. She was smart, respectful, responsible and honest. She didn't mind telling you how it was but she was much easier to get along with than Jessica's mom. Her visit was more informative than social this time. She asked if I had seen Mike's back yet. I looked and there was a scratch and a bruise on his back. She told me Jessica had gotten into a fight with her boyfriend and they knocked a shelf over on Mike. This was the second time Mike had been hurt during her visits. The first time he had to be taken to the emergency room for broken fingers because something fell on his hand. I asked her to watch the boys and I drove to the housing where they lived. Jessica wasn't home but her boyfriend was. He invited me in and I didn't waste any time with pleasantries. I told him if he ever hurt my kids again, even by accident, I'd beat him to death with my bare hands. He got up and went for the phone. I wasn't about to lose my kids by going to jail over this so I stopped him. I told him this was a warning but it was the only warning he was getting. I told him if my kids ever come home with a mark on them again I was coming after him. I left and he never spoke to me again.

Through the week, I worked very hard to make sure the boys were provided for. They were my world but I started to get lonely and stressed out when the kids would be gone for the weekend. When they were home I was centered and grounded and had purpose. When I was alone I worried if they were ok and I felt the weight of everything on my shoulders. I started going out and looking for adult companionship when they weren't home. I didn't have many friends and the ones I had were the party type. I would go to bars and blow off steam by drinking and looking for women to hook up with. The people I hung out with were into some hard drugs and I tried cocaine a few times. I had a whole in me that I was trying to fill but I decided that this wasn't for me. I still hung out with them but the drugs were just not what I wanted in my life.

One lonely night, back when I was 17 years old, I cried myself to sleep. I had just prayed the most sincere prayer of my life. I asked God for one thing. I asked him to send someone into my life who would love me. Someone who would love me the way I loved them, no more, no less. I knew this person had not shown up in my life yet because I had always felt so alone. I had been a single father for a few months. Not long, but long enough to understand this wasn't going to be an easy task. A guy I worked with had been telling me about a girl he thought I should ask out. While working with him we stopped for lunch. There was a pretty girl working the counter and after we got our food he told me that was her. I made up a reason to go back to the counter so I could ask her for her phone number. She seemed a little unsure but she gave me her number. She later told me she thought it was funny that a trash man with a mullet asked her out but she gave me the number because I was cute. We set up a date and when I showed up she backed out. She said her parents were over the road truck drivers and had to check on her little brother who was left home alone. I was pretty disappointed. I was so excited about this date that I had cut my hair short for the first time in years. She was very attractive so I wanted to give it another try and set up another date with her.

Our first date was just us riding around talking to get to know each other. Her name was Marie and she was 18 years old. I was 23 and the fact that she was 18 almost scared me away. I had originally thought she was older. We spent half the day talking but she had to work that afternoon. We hit it off fairly well so I asked if I could see her again after she got off work that evening. She said yes and that night we went back to her house and I met the two roommates she shared the house with. It was another young couple. Her friend saw the tattoo on my arm and asked what it was and who the names were. "It's a cross with a rose and a banner with my kids' names on it." I was nervous to see what Marie's reaction was going to be when she found out I had kids. She was a little surprised that I hadn't mentioned it yet but she didn't mind. I ended up staying the night with her. The next morning she said she needed to go to her moms' and asked if I wanted to go. I needed to make a decision right then where I wanted this to go. If it was going to be a one night stand then I needed to just leave. If I was going to try and start seeing her it wouldn't look right if I said no. I asked her if she wanted to keep dating and she said yes. I went with her and met her mom and her 15 year old brother. They seemed really nice but I got the feeling her mom didn't appreciate her daughter bringing home a guy my age. She made it a point to bring up Marie's ex boyfriend and how much she liked him. It didn't bother me, in fact I understood.

Now that we were officially a couple I was curious how she felt about me having two kids. She immediately wanted to meet them. I pumped the brakes a little. I liked her but meeting my kids was serious. When I thought about it, I came to the conclusion that if I was going to start a relationship with someone, I didn't want someone who wasn't mature enough to handle my kids. I had her come over to meet the boys and they were more excited than I was. Marie brought two of her girlfriends with her to make her feel a little more comfortable. It was pretty funny to see the boys running around the living room showing off for these teenage girls. They stole the show and Marie hit it off with them right away. When she got ready to leave Mike asked her if she would stay the night. She turned and looked at me like it was a setup. I swore to her that I didn't put him up to that. It was really funny though. He said "You can have my bed if you want." She didn't stay that night but we started dating regularly after that. We had dinner at her house soon after and she got a rude call from a guy who was interested in her. He was mad at her for dating me. I got really upset and almost broke it off right then. I wasn't going to get involved in another dishonest relationship. She explained to me that just because she was only 18 didn't mean she had been innocent her whole life. Her parents had divorced when she was little and her dad enlisted in the Marines and moved away. Her mom had remarried to a truck driver and they were on the road a lot. When she still lived with them, they left her at home a lot to take care of her younger brother. She rebelled when they were out of town by throwing parties and getting pretty crazy. She admitted she had done drugs and slept around a lot. She was adamant that no matter what happened in the past she wasn't a cheater. That's not something she would do. The guy who made the call was only upset because she had told him she wasn't going to have anything to do with him any longer because she was seeing me. I wanted to believe her and I kept seeing her but it was extremely difficult to trust anyone after the life I had lived to this point.

Marie offered to keep the boys one day instead of taking them to day care. I was very uneasy about this at first. I wasn't sure how it would go but she insisted it would be fine. She had an old convertible and she rode them around with the top down and they loved it. She took them to meet her mom and they fit right in. When they got ready to leave the boys told her mom, "Bye grandma." She didn't know what to say but they didn't think anything of it, so she let them call her grandma. She was "grandma" from day one. She was extremely nice to my kids. She was too nice in fact. I actually had to ask her to stop spoiling my kids. I wanted them to be strong and tough and she was babying them.

CHAPTER TWELVE

First Impressions

Jessica found out I was seeing someone and asked to meet the person who was going to be around the kids. I talked to Marie about it and she was more than willing to try and be friends with Jessica. She wanted every part of our relationship to work and she wanted to do as much as she could to help. I warned her it might not be a good experience but she was confident it would be ok even though she was a little nervous. Jessica tried to act like she was nice and easy to get along with but she got a little too comfortable and said some things that threw up a red flag. She made the comment that she couldn't handle being around the kids unless she was high. This upset me because I knew I couldn't get out of letting them go to see her but I knew that she was stoned the whole time they were there. I had no way to know they'd be safe. From this point on I would get even more worried and upset every time the boys would leave for the weekend.

We had a few more dates. I had her over for a cookout where we played volleyball with friends and on another date we went fishing. We hadn't been dating long but it was starting to develop into something more. She was staying at my house almost every night and I had given her a key. I decided to take her to meet my mom and sisters. I thought this would be the real test. If she meets my family and doesn't run away screaming then this might work out. The visit went fine and I started to take our relationship a lot more seriously. About a week later Marie found out she was pregnant. She asked me what we were going to do. I asked her "Is it mine?" She was offended that I even asked that question but I had a real hard time trusting anyone and I wanted to know if she had any doubts. She was absolutely positive. I told her we were going to raise the baby. She said ok and we started making plans to move in together. I wanted her to move in with me but she didn't want to move. The house she was renting was owned by her mom and step dad and it was bigger but she had roommates and I was not a people person. She convinced me to give it a try. It was strange living with other people in the house but I tried to be ok with it.

Marie told her mom she was pregnant and had to break the news to the rest of her family as well. We went to her moms' for dinner and met her grandparents. Her grandmother made it clear she didn't like me right away. She threatened to call child protective services on me because I made Mike and Matt finish their supper before they were allowed to have snacks. She said that was child abuse and that kids should be allowed to eat whatever they want. I was a confrontational type of person so I plainly told her these were my kids and I was raising them to eat healthy. She never did come around to liking me and we just didn't talk to each other. Her grandfather was nice but didn't say much at all.

Meeting her father's side of her family was even more interesting. Her dad was living out of state but came over for a visit to meet me. He came to the house where we had a short conversation about how I was a trash man only making $9 an hour. He also mentioned how weird it was having roommates when we were starting a family. I couldn't argue with any of the points he was making. He was right and I knew it. We met for dinner at his parents' farm. I was about to have a talk with the family of the 18 year old girl who I had knocked up. I was a little nervous. I wanted to be respectful and honest, yet confident and show that I was going to take care of her. None of that happened anything like I wanted it to. When we got there we sat in the living room and talked. Marie and I sat together and her grandmother sat in her recliner. Her father and his wife sat on a couch with a picture of him in his Marine uniform on the wall behind him. I had wanted to be a Marine so badly and here I was being confronted by my girlfriends' father who had spent over ten years in the Marine Corps. I would love to say I was confident and handled myself well but that didn't happen. He asked me what our plans were. He wanted to know if we were going to get married. I had asked Marie to marry me but I didn't have a ring and I wasn't exactly romantic about it. When I asked, she said no. She said she didn't want us to get married just because she was pregnant. If we were ever going to get married it had to be because we loved each other and knew it would last. I didn't want to tell her family this so I stumbled for the right words. Marie's grandmother had a few drinks before we got there and was visibly upset about this whole situation. Before

I could come up with something to say, she tried to say the old phrase "Why buy the cow when you get the milk for free." She was slurring her words and couldn't quite get the whole thing out. I knew what she meant and I was a little offended that she would talk about Marie like that. I wanted to respond to her comment so I finished her sentence for her, thinking I could explain. Before I could even start the response she cut me off and very angrily said "Don't you talk about my granddaughter that way!" I couldn't believe it. I felt like I was set up. There was nothing I could say the rest of the evening that could recover from that.

The night was just beginning. After dinner Marie and her family started to loosen up a little and talk more plainly. I was still reeling from the initial conversation and needed to calm down. I walked outside to have a cigarette. Her grandmother smoked and wouldn't have minded if I smoked in the house but I needed to get away for few seconds. I didn't want to look disrespectful by smoking in someone's home and I also didn't want to give them the opportunity to lecture me about smoking around a baby. I finished the cigarette and started to calm down. I needed to take a leak so I walked to the side of the house. It was pitch black outside and at the corner of the house there was a gutter extension. I stepped over it around the side of the house to be completely concealed in case someone came out looking for me. As I stepped, there was no ground on the other side. I fell into pure darkness. I had no idea what was going on or how deep of a hole I was falling into. I frantically reached my arms out for anything to grab onto. My right hand hit something. It shattered and cut my hand. I hit hard on the ground and I felt something prickly poking into me as I tried to stand up. I found my way back into the house and headed straight for the kitchen sink to wash out the cut and see how bad it was. As I rushed past everyone they started bombarding me with questions about what had happened. I really wasn't sure. At first I told them I don't know. Then I told them I knew I fell and broke something that sounded like glass. Marie's dad and grandpa went outside to investigate while I washed the cut. It was bleeding but looked worse than it really was. I had annoying little stickers all over my hands and cat feces all over my clothes. I had never been there in the daylight and didn't know there was a drop off that led to the walk out basement. The glass was a basement window I had put my hand through. Once I gathered myself I tried to explain what happened but now all they kept asking me was, "Why did you lie about it?" Are you kidding me? Now they were accusing me of being a liar because I was too flustered to know exactly what happened. This night had to be the worst family meeting in history. By the time I got to work on Monday morning, the coworker who had told me I should ask Marie out had already heard about it. He said I can't believe you told her grandma "Why buy the cow when you get the milk for free." No matter how many times I explained, there was just no recovering from this. For the next several years when we visit her grandmother, I would be told how disrespectful I was that first meeting and that she has indoor plumbing so I wouldn't go outside to pee. It became a running joke in her family and Marie thought this was hilarious.

At home, living with other people was getting under my skin. They were trying to make us comfortable but I wanted to have a family and a home and this wasn't how I pictured it. I like things to be my way and when they're not I can be difficult to get along with. I started arguing with her roommates and they moved out to find a place of their own. Marie had been friends with them for years. They didn't talk much for a while but continued to be friends after they moved out. Marie and I were both working and had our own place now and we started making our life together. We had the house to ourselves and it was nice. We were getting closer and learning more about each other. Marie was great with the kids. They stayed with her during the day while I worked and she worked in the evenings. The boys loved her right from the start. They bonded and everything seemed right.

CHAPTER THIRTEEN

Could This Be Real?

Marie and I had a great relationship. We connected in a way I had never felt before. The kids adored her and she treated me better than anyone ever had. I asked her to marry me several times and she kept saying no. She explained that we had both looked at that first night as a one night stand and she still didn't want to rush into it. I respected that and I dropped it. For a while, I pondered the notion that maybe she kept me around just to tick her dad off. It was clear that her family thought she could do better than me. Her dad even said those words to her. I couldn't argue with that. She's a beautiful, kind and caring young woman who puts everyone else's needs above her own. She was responsible and worked to support herself. She was also carefree, fun loving and hardly anything stressed her out. She was level headed and fun to be around. She made everyone around her laugh and feel better about who they were. I couldn't help but feel like I didn't deserve her.

Where I worked there was a lady that worked in the office who was selling an engagement ring. She showed it to me and it was beautiful. So beautiful in fact, I thought Marie has to have this ring. It was expensive but less than what I could have bought it for new. I went to the bank and refinanced my car to buy it and I held on to it for a little while. My sister Anna came for a visit with her fiancé and I thought this would be a good time to propose. I went to where Marie was working and asked her to come out into the lobby. I got down on one knee in front of a restaurant full of people and showed her the ring. I was nervous but this time she said yes!

I started to bond with Marie's younger brother. He was into lifting weights so I would lift with him. It became a competition and we pushed each other to get stronger. It was really nice to have someone to work out with. We had fun hanging out together. We would watch football or play paintball. He started wanting to throw parties while his parents were out on the road. They would be gone for weeks at a time sometimes. He asked me to buy him alcohol and I knew from my own experience that if he wanted to party he would find a way. I thought if I did this for him I could set some ground rules and keep it contained. I told him to limit it to just a few friends and once they started drinking nobody was allowed to leave. He and his friends agreed and I would hang out there with him to make sure nothing got out of hand. This was a little strange having a twenty something guy hanging around a bunch of teenagers drinking but I didn't want them doing any of the crazy things I had done to get myself in trouble. There was a time or two when I started feeling younger than my age and we did some childish things but nobody got in trouble. He and I got along great. He bonded with Mike and Matt too. He would rough house with them and they loved it. When he was little, Mike used to say that he was his best buddy. We hung out all the time for quite a while. He got a job and started working to save up for after high school. He met a girl he really liked and started spending his free time with her. They got pretty serious and started making plans for after high school and decided where they were going to further their education.

There are a few things that I'm ashamed to admit but they cannot be left out or I would not be being totally honest with you. When Marie and I met I was an emotionally damaged person. I constantly accused her of cheating on me. I would check to make sure she was at work or check on her in general. I knew there were guys interested in her but she swore they were just friends. There was a local cop who had asked her out around the same time I did. She chose to go out with me instead of him but he would still come up to her work and talk with her. I went up there one night to check on her and she was in the parking lot talking to him after closing. I stopped and asked if she was coming home, in a very accusing sort of way and then peeled out. She talked the officer out of giving me a ticket. I found it very hard to believe someone this good was interested in just me and wasn't leading me on or messing around behind my back. One night she was having a dream and talking in her sleep and it sounded like she was talking to a guy. I asked her about it and she said she didn't remember what she was dreaming about. The next day she had been asked to fill in at the restaurant in another town because they were short handed. I spent all morning thinking about her dream. My mind started coming up with all sorts of scenarios that might have happened. I couldn't handle it. I drove to the town she was supposed to be at to make sure that's really where she was at. She was there and they were really busy. I walked in and told her to give me the ring back. She got upset and asked why. I said "just give me the ring." She said "What did I do?" I was causing a scene and figured I better leave before they called the cops. I walked out and she followed me. I saw three guys standing outside and asked them if they wanted a three thousand dollar ring. They said yes and I said "if you can get it off her finger you can have it." She was obviously pregnant by this time and very upset. She left work and got in her car to leave because she was afraid they might actually try to take it from her. I've done some pretty terrible things but this was despicable. I hate that I have to write this but it happened.

I had been cheated on by several of the girls I had dated. Until now, every time I suspected someone of cheating it turned out to be true. The one that hurt the most was when Jessica cheated on me while she was pregnant with my son. I couldn't take that kind of pain again. I had no proof and no real reason to suspect anything was going on. Marie was nothing like Jessica. In fact, she was the exact opposite. I still had so much pain inside from so many people doing me wrong that I didn't know how to trust Marie. She had done nothing to deserve being treated like this. I went to blow off some steam at a bar and when I got home that night we talked and worked things out. I wanted a real relationship and she was willing to try to understand after what I had done. I couldn't walk away from someone this wonderful.

Marie threw a party for my birthday that year. She knew I loved to play pool and got me an old pool table her grandma had in her basement. She put it in the garage and we bought a keg of beer. I didn't know a lot of people in this area so I invited the people I had partied with before her and I met and a couple people I knew from work. They brought drugs with them and I caught them doing them in our house. I wasn't happy about it at first but then I figured, it IS my birthday, and the kids aren't here, so I did it with them. Marie was very unhappy about this. This was the first time she had really gotten mad at me. She said it's not like I haven't tried that kind of thing but we have a family now and I'm not going to watch you throw it away. I knew she was right. I never did drugs around my kids but now I saw that doing them at all wasn't right for our family. I needed to be an example my kids could follow and I stopped doing anything that I wouldn't want them to do. I even tried to quit smoking but that took several years before I was able to put them down for good. Marie showed me yet again that she was the right person for me.

Marie's mom let us use her video camera to record holidays and birthdays. The first one we recorded was Mike and Matt's 4th and 3rd birthday party. They got their first swing set and within a few weeks Mike fell off it and broke his arm. He swears Matt pushed him off. Watching videos of the kids swimming through wrapping paper to unwrap Christmas presents made me see something I hadn't noticed before. I would fill the living room with as many cheap toys as I could. There were many years I would take out a small loan just to buy presents. I didn't want my kids to feel like the poor kid I felt like. I think back and I know this was not the right way to handle this. I was overcompensating for being poor. I made sure my kids never felt like they had to do without. The first Christmas we were together (and pretty much every year after) Marie proved that she was way better at giving gifts than I was. She always got me something nice that I really wanted and I usually got her something that was useful instead of thoughtful. There were a few times I got it right but not often.

A new year rolled around and we had decided what to name our baby boy. Alexander Williams made his appearance in February of 2002. I stayed the night there in the hospital room with Marie but I was so excited I couldn't sit still. The day they were being released to come home I went out to get some flowers and I had Alex added to the tattoo on my arm with Mike and Matt's names. When I got back Marie and Alex were ready to go and waiting on me. Marie's mom was there with them and none of them looked happy that they had to wait on me. We went home and settled in. I was afraid that now that Marie had a child of her own flesh and blood that she might feel differently toward Mike and Matt. She never acted any different at all. She treated them just like they were her own. Mike and Alex seemed to bond right away. Mike had a natural protector instinct but Matt was not happy to have a new baby in the house. We had to keep a close eye on him when he was around Alex to make sure he didn't play too rough. Alex was an excellent baby. He didn't cry much and was a very happy baby, always playful and laughing. He loved when his big brothers would play with him and he would try to follow them around.

After Alex was born we started talking a lot more seriously about getting married. We decided to get married one year from the day we started dating. On April 29th 2002 we went to the courthouse and said our vows in front of a judge with Marie's mom, step-dad, brother and our baby Alex in attendance, while Mike and Matt were at pre-k. We couldn't afford an actual wedding or a party or a honeymoon. We went back home afterward and one of Marie's friends came over to congratulate us. I made a complete idiot of myself by flirting with her friend. I couldn't give her a wedding, a reception or a honeymoon and then I ruined her day by flirting with another girl. I didn't mean any harm but it really hurt Marie's feelings, obviously. There were so many times she had good reason to give up on me but she didn't and I can't be more grateful for that. I had found someone who actually loved me.

The summer before Mike started kindergarten we signed him up for T-ball. This started many years of bonding for our whole family. I would practice with the kids in the back yard. We would play catch or I would pitch to them. Mike was very smart but pretty average at sports. Matt excelled at sports right away but didn't like school as much. This led to competition between them that made them both work hard to get better. I loved spending time with the kids in this way. I knew it could be a positive way to help them make friends and keep them doing something constructive instead of getting in trouble when they got older. We let them sign up for most of the things they wanted to try. After T-ball they played soccer. They both enjoyed playing sports and meeting new people. It was so much fun playing with them and teaching them. I spent pretty much all of my spare time playing with the kids and this made everything feel like it was worth it.

I would work long hours and often volunteered to stay and help other people for the overtime. Pretty much every day I would come home to Mike and Matt meeting me at the door with their happy little voices yelling "Daddy's home!" It made me feel great to be so warmly welcomed. Before I could get my nasty boots off they would be all over me wanting to play. I loved that they were so happy to see me but at the same time I was tired and covered in filth from picking up other peoples' trash. By the time I got my boots off and settled them down, Marie would be waiting to unload the stress of her day. She was 19 and had two toddlers and an infant. That alone could be enough to make someone pull their hair out. She wanted to go back to work after Alex was born but I begged her to stay home and keep the kids. It would have cost us a fortune in daycare and I would much prefer to have my kids with someone I trusted.

Marie needed to get out of the house during the day and her mom and step-dad needed a hand with their trucking business. She would go to their house and basically work as a secretary, paying bills and making sure the fuel was paid for and learning how to handle the taxes. She was able to bring the kids with her and come and go as she needed to. It fit what she needed and they paid her a small amount to handle things while they were on the road. There were some drawbacks. She had to be on call pretty much 24-7. If they weren't home and needed something she was expected to do it. Marie would complain every day about having to deal with her parents. I would go into protection mode. I told her to stop going over there if she didn't like the way she was being treated. This would start an argument. I cared about her and didn't want her to be stressed out so I would try to fix the problem. To me this meant cutting the stress off at the source. After months of arguing about it, she explained that she didn't want to stop working for her parents. She wanted me to listen to her daily problems when I got home from work. She hadn't had anyone but toddlers to talk to all day and needed to vent. This was not easy for me to understand. I'm not a great listener. I'm a fixer. If there is a problem I want to jump right up and fix it, not sit around talking about it. I finally got it and we started getting along a lot better.

Now that we were married and had a child together I wanted Marie to meet the rest of my family, so we took a vacation to Tennessee. The first place we stopped was my Papaw's house. I tried to explain to Marie just what to expect but nothing could have said it better than when we turned off the main highway onto a back road that led to "The Bug Hole." This is the name for that particular area. In fact, Papaw lived on Bug Hole Road. Just off the highway on our way to Bug Hole Road, was a fenced in area with several dumpsters where everyone in this small community would drop off their trash because the roads were too small, hilly and curvy to safely drive a trash truck on. At the gate of the fenced dumpster area were two old men sitting on folding chairs and one was playing a banjo. They seemed to be having a grand ole time. About a half mile down the road we pulled into Papaw's driveway and he of course met us at the door with his signature outfit on, cutoff jean shorts and no shirt. We had a nice visit and then went to see my aunts and Uncle. It was a good trip and we had a good time but after describing my family to Marie, seeing it was much more revealing than just hearing about it.

Later that year we found out we were going to have another baby. This made Marie pretty nervous. She was on birth control and we hadn't planned to have another baby just yet. We already had three kids and Alex wasn't even a year old yet. She said "this one better be a girl because I'm done after this one." I was excited. I loved the idea of having a big family. I found a great woman, had a steady job and the kids were happy. I had stopped doing anything that could get me in trouble and was walking the straight and narrow. Marie and I talked about what we wanted our future to look like. She wanted a girl first of all. I was scared to death of having a girl. I knew how to handle the boys. What do you do with a girl? Second, we decided it would be a lot smarter to buy a home rather than renting. Marie's mom owned the house we were renting and was extremely nice to us. We knew if we ever had trouble paying rent she would help us out but we needed to move forward. We talked about where to look. I was open to living pretty much anywhere but Marie refused to move out of her hometown. She made it clear that she wanted to stay there. This narrowed the search right away. She also wanted to live outside of city limits so we could have animals some day. She loved animals, especially horses. I wanted to live in the country my entire life so I agreed to shoot for that goal but I wasn't picky. Our budget was small, very small. What we wanted and what we needed to provide for four kids was going to be a hard thing to find. Or so we thought.

We started looking and right away something jumped out at us. Marie found a house a few blocks away. It was a huge two story house with four bedrooms and a big yard. It wasn't out of town but it was cheap and we thought this would be a good place to start looking. It needed a ton of work but the important stuff was in decent shape. While we were looking and asking questions we found out that it was owned by a local church that was in financial trouble. We had walked into the house through the back door. After seeing all of it, we liked it but didn't know if we should jump on the first thing we looked at. We were about to leave and we walked out of the front door. As we turned back toward the house from the front porch, I saw something that changed everything. There was a small, square, brass plate over the front door. It stated "As for me and my house we will serve the Lord." I got chills all over my body. I knew God was speaking and for the first time in a very long time, I was listening. I explained to Marie what I was feeling and that I believed this was meant for us. It wasn't our dream home but it fit all of our needs. She understood and was completely on board. This was going to be where we raised our kids until we could find that perfect place in the country for Marie to have horses.

I went to the church that owned the house to speak with the pastor. He seemed much more interested in inviting us to church than talking about that old house. This was the same type of church I had gone to many times growing up. I didn't want to start attending while we were negotiating the purchase of the house but I did feel drawn to this place. Marie and I talked it over and she was completely against it at first. She had a couple bad experiences with one or two of the local churches when she was a child. The pastor and some of the members of those churches had acted like they were better than her and her family and she had zero desire to go back and be treated that way again. I started explaining to her the experiences I had as a child and that I really wanted to give it a try as a family. I wanted our kids to know about God and have the opportunity to learn about the Bible. She agreed to give it a try. When we did we felt very welcomed.

CHAPTER FOURTEEN

The Horror

Now that I had started a new life together with Marie, I tried to continue repairing the relationships with my family. We made a trip to Missouri and one of my cousins was there. He was a teenager and was having some trouble at home. He was visiting my mom for the summer and trying to decide if he wanted to live there. My mom was back to drinking very heavily and I couldn't see this being a good place for a troubled teen. My mom, sisters, my wife, and I were all sitting around the kitchen table and my mom asked me to tell my younger cousin "how I messed my life up" so he wouldn't make the same mistakes. I started telling my story to him and my mom kept cutting me off and saying that I wasn't telling the truth or telling the story right. I finally turned to my sister Anna and said "you were there, have I said anything that is untrue?" She replied "no, everything you said is true. Mom just doesn't want to admit her part in it." I knew then that my mom was in complete denial that she had done anything wrong at all during our childhood. This really upset me but I tried not to let her see that. She got angry and confrontational so we left.

My cousin went back to Tennessee and a short time later I got a call from his mom. She asked if her son could live with us because she couldn't handle him anymore. I talked it over with Marie and she said yes. He came to live with us and we gave him the room in the basement that had been Marie's when we met. It wasn't anything fancy but he had a huge bedroom with his own full bathroom. We did everything we knew how to make him comfortable. We took him to church with us, helped him make new friends and got him involved in the youth group. We helped him get a part time job to make his own spending money. He started high school and joined the football team. Everything went ok when it was new and he was getting all the attention. When things settled down and got more normal he started acting very differently. He started making up stories to draw attention back to himself. It started out as harmless little white lies but it escalated. We planned a trip to Six Flags and we couldn't figure out why he didn't want to go. We found out that he spent the entire day at his girlfriends house and I had to force him to come back home. I thought we worked it out and got things settled back down but I was wrong. Marie got a call from a lady at the high school saying that he had been in to talk to the counselor. He told the counselor we treated him so badly that he was contemplating suicide. She accused Marie of being a bad mother and said she could get our kids taken away for the things he had accused us of. She wouldn't tell Marie what had been said but we were extremely disturbed by this. Marie told the woman that this was not our child and in fact she wasn't that much older than him herself. I took my cousin to see a counselor and I don't know what he told them but the counselor told me that he needed to be admitted to a mental facility. They said if he didn't go willingly that they would force him and I would be responsible for the bill. We were floored. We had people threatening to take our kids away and we were in the middle of buying a home. This was not what I expected at all when I agreed to help him. We were way out of our league so I took him home and called his mother to come get him. I told her everything that happened and she said she would take him back to Tennessee and get him some help.

For the next couple of months we got phone calls from multiple family members asking questions about his time with us. He had continued telling lies about what happened while he was here. Even people at our church were asking us why he said the things he did. He accused us of locking him in the basement and treating him like an animal. While at work I got a message that I needed to call my mom. This was out of the ordinary because even though we were on speaking terms again we still didn't quite get along. I figured it was probably more questions about my cousin. When I called her back, she had some of the worst news I'd ever received. Papaw was dead. He shot himself with a 30-30. The cousin who had stayed with us and his little brother had gone to visit and found him lying on his living room floor. As troubled as this kid already was, I can't even imagine what this did to him. We have only spoken a few words to each other since this. I have no idea what to say to him.

Up to this point in my life, this was the most difficult thing I had ever experienced. I'm sick to my stomach still as I write this.

Papaw made it clear that when he decided to go, it would be on his own terms. He told us years before exactly what he wanted and we had tried to talk him out of it but honestly nobody thought he would actually do it. He had already paid for the cremation and left very specific instructions as to how he wanted everything handled. I know he didn't expect it to be as hard on us as it was but this traumatized the entire family. The authorities came in and took the body away but no one cleaned up the mess. I'm sure there are companies that do this sort of thing but nobody in my family could come up with hundreds of dollars at a moments' notice. When we got to Tennessee everyone was trying to figure out who to have clean up the house before the family went in to pick up his things. We all decided mutually that the only two people there that were not blood related would be the best choice. When they left, an uncontrollable feeling came over me. I couldn't just sit still and let them go do this. I went after them. Maybe I shouldn't have but I needed to see what happened to someone who had been so important to me as a child.

They had just gotten started as I walked in. I could feel the cold emptiness of death. There was a small amount of whiskey left in the bottle he had been drinking. It was still sitting in front of the place where he ended his life. The house was an open floor plan between the living room and kitchen so there was blood everywhere. The cushion of the chair he had been sitting in was completely saturated in bodily fluids. The mirror behind the chair, the bathroom adjacent to the living room, the kitchen floor, the walls, everything was splattered with dried blood. There were palm size chunks of his head on the floor that had to be picked up. During the cleanup I actually held a piece of my grandfathers' head in my hand. It still had the hair growing out of it. I saw the hole in the ceiling where the bullet passed through. The look of a full length mirror streaked in the real blood of someone you care about is a horrific sight. It was winter and there hadn't been any heat on in the house for days, so you could see every breath you took. It truly was a scene from a horror movie. I choked back all the emotion I could. It was like swallowing a burning ember. I started wiping down the blood splatters and tried to think of it as something it wasn't. Anything but what it really was. After the cleaning was finished, we went back to tell the family it was safe to go to the house. Marie was very upset at me for going. I had lied and told her I was going outside for a walk because I knew she would stop me from going. Jimmy was mad at me for going without him. I knew he wanted to go but he was obviously on drugs at this time and I knew he wasn't emotionally strong enough to handle it.

I went back to the house with my family and I was appalled that they immediately started arguing over who was going to take what. They argued over who got his car or who got this or that. My mom even raided his refrigerator and took his beer so she could drink it. Maybe because I had actually seen what happened here before it was cleaned or maybe I just saw it in a different way in general. Possessions were the last thing on my mind and taking something of his didn't seem right. They finally decided that each of his grandkids should pick out one souvenir to keep. I chose an old worn out deck of cards. Everyone tried to get me to take something that had some value but I refused. I was positive these were the same cards we had played many nights of poker with. For years I could open the lid on that deck, close my eyes and put my nose up to the cards and breathe in the smell of Papaw's house. For just a moment, I was a teenager in his house one more time.

There was a service at a local church, which Papaw did not want but the family thought it was important. It was very simple and quiet, just a few photos and some friends and family talking amongst themselves. The next day we gathered at the site where he wanted his ashes spread. My stomach was in knots. I was feeling so bad that I convinced myself it was the flu. It was more likely the stress I was under and trying to act normal in front of everyone. After following Papaw's requests we were headed to our cars to leave and deciding who was going where. Papaw's brothers and nephews were going to their childhood home to get drunk and his kids and grandkids were going home. Jimmy rushed to his car to leave but as soon as he put it in gear he passed out. He had been a basket case for days and this was proof that he wasn't ok. We heard his girlfriend screaming from the passenger seat and I ran to the car that was now slowly rolling away. I jerked the door open as the car stopped on an embankment and asked what was wrong. She screamed that she thought he had overdosed on something. I tried to wake him up but I got no response. I yelled at Marie to bring our car around so we could get him to the hospital. I slapped his face and screamed "don't do this to me!" I couldn't even contemplate losing Jimmy too. I was trying to pull him out of the car onto the ground to start CPR when his mother ran up and started screaming at me to leave him alone. She got between me and him and said she would handle it. Then all of sudden everyone claimed that he hadn't taken anything and he did NOT overdose. It was clear to everyone around that he had been on something. Whatever drugs he was on added to the stress of the situation and was more than he could take. His body shut down for a minute or two. He woke up and his mother continued to be in denial that he had taken any kind of drugs. She would rather have risked his life than take him to an emergency room where she would have to answer questions about his drug use.

We had planned to stay a couple more days to visit with everyone but that night something strange happened. We were staying at my aunt's house and I took some Nyquil because I was still assuming that I felt bad because I had the flu. I went to bed early and Marie came to bed after me with Alex. Marie woke me up the next morning and said she needed to tell me something. She said she had an experience she couldn't explain. She woke up in the middle of the night but she wasn't really awake. She felt as if she was floating above the bed. She could see herself and then Alex and then me. She said it was like someone else was looking through her eyes at me and Alex from over the top of the bed. She told me she felt an overwhelming feeling of regret. She absolutely believed that Papaw had used her to see us one last time. I have no doubt that she was telling the truth. It freaked her out so bad that she refused to stay another night there. I can't explain what happened but it didn't upset me. It might seem a little weird but I felt honored that he chose me to see for the last time. We got ready and headed for home that morning.

We got back to Illinois and tried to go right back to normal. I went back to work and tried to act like I was fine. We moved forward with buying the house and getting moved in. This was our first time dealing with realtors and buying a house. It was a trying ordeal. We even thought we might not get the house at one point. It needed a few big things before we got the sale finalized. The church allowed us to start working on it before we officially owned it so it would be ready to move in right away. We didn't have any money and Marie's mom allowed us to use her credit card to buy materials and we did most of the work ourselves. We charged her card and agreed to make the payments. We were approved for a first time home buyers loan that allowed us to not have a down payment. We purchased our first home for $40,000. Our house payment, including escrow was less than we were paying for rent. It needed a lot of work but it was ours. This is such a huge milestone in my life. During my childhood my mom had never owned a car or even our own appliances, much less an entire house. We had done something that I hadn't even been sure was possible. All of my hard work was starting to pay off. It wasn't long after we moved in that Marie's mom got really upset with us. We missed a payment on the credit card. I hated owing someone so I got a small loan to pay it off in full. We were officially in charge of all our own finances again.

Everything seemed to be going great but on the inside something was still very wrong with me. I was working long hours to stay ahead and I started going to bars after work. I would shoot pool and have one or two beers and then go home. It seemed harmless to me but Marie got tired of it. She didn't mind if I stopped off once in a while but I had started doing it two or three times every week. She said either I start coming straight home from work or she was leaving. I knew she had a right to be upset. It wasn't that I was doing anything she didn't know about but she could see where this was headed. She was right but I begged her to not be upset with me. I tried to explain to her the pain I was feeling inside. I felt as if I had a baseball size hole in my chest where my heart should be. I was very confused about what my life was supposed to be. I knew I was on the right track to having a better life than how I was raised but there was a yearning deep in my soul to do things like my grandfather had. Being wild, carefree and doing anything and everything without hesitation was the way other members of my family seemed to live but this did not fit with the life we were trying to create at all. I had to step back and look at the choices I was making. I saw that the people that were living carefree were also not great parents and not even very good people in general. Yet again Marie saved me from myself. It took some time but things went back to normal.

CHAPTER FIFTEEN

Trying To Find "Normal"

In July of 2003 Amber Williams was born. With all three of the boys it was clear in the ultrasound that they were boys. Amber was the only one that was a surprise. We waited anxiously in the delivery room for the big moment. When she was born we all yelled "it's a girl" so loudly that Marie's family heard us in the waiting room. She didn't cry at all at first. The doctor laid her on Marie and the nurses took her to clean her up. The nurse handed her to me and as I held her nervously in my arms, she looked right into my eyes and smiled the prettiest smile I have ever seen in my entire life. I said "she's smiling at me" and the nurse said "it's probably not really a smile, let me see." I knew it was a real smile though. I didn't just see it, I felt it. When she looked at Amber she said "I think you're right, she is smiling at you." At that moment my heart melted. Every piece of emptiness was filled with joy and love for this little girl. She was an angel sent from Heaven to heal my soul.

When we left the hospital we went straight to have her pictures taken before we even took her home. I was wrapped around her tiny fingers right away.

Amber cried every night for months. She was nine or ten months old before she slept through the night. Marie would get up with her so I could sleep, since I had to be up so early for work and she was getting very frustrated. Eventually we had to just let her cry through and she finally started sleeping all night. Having another baby in the house was an adjustment for the boys. Alex loved being a big brother. He was still a baby himself but he wanted to help take care of his little sister. When she would cry he would jump up and run to get her bottle. He was just learning to talk so he would say bobble instead of bottle. In his mind that became her name "bobble" because every time she cried he ran to get the "bobble." This nickname for Amber stuck with her and for years we called her bobble. As soon as she was big enough to walk, she started finding her way into our bedroom at night and would crawl into bed with us. Marie complained every night about how Amber kicked and tossed and turned. She got away with more than any of the boys did. She also pressed her luck a lot more than they did. She knew she was doing wrong and would do it anyway. It got to the point that Marie would come into the room to check on her and if she was doing something she wasn't supposed to, Amber would smack her own hand and say "no no." It was funny to see but she was a handful. There was one time she got into the cabinets in the kitchen and poured an entire box of cereal out on her head and played in it. When she started Pre-K, she actually believed her name was "Bobble No Williams", because the phrase you heard most around our house for quite some time was "Bobble

NO." I know some of it was because she was allowed to push the limits and that's my fault but I also think part of it is really her own personality.

All the while, we were attending church services regularly. Sunday mornings and Thursday nights we could be found at church. The church wasn't only in financial trouble but they didn't have a lot of people attending and they needed help. We were asked to help the youth leaders handle the large number of kids coming in. We were more than happy to help. I had felt a calling to help youth ever since I was one myself. The kids were coming in with not a lot of structure and being allowed to run wild. They were having fun but nobody was learning anything. They came to have fun and meet up with boyfriends or girlfriends. They were getting out of control and disturbing the services for the adults. Marie and I were asked to help get things under control. We did but that didn't sit well the current youth leader. She thought the kids should be allowed to run wild and do what they wanted. She left to go to another church and we were asked to take over the youth program. I was thrilled to get this opportunity. We started putting together classes and dividing up the age groups so they could learn at their own pace. We kept it fun but structured and did fundraisers to pay for everything the teens needed so as not to be a burden on the church. After a while the youth fund had more than the church fund. We took trips to Youth Explosion and Momentum every year. There were a few kids who stopped coming because they weren't allowed to run wild anymore but overall the program was a huge success. We met some wonderful young people who were looking for guidance and we are still friends with some of them to this day.

We were led there for a reason and I hope we were able to make some positive influences on some kids who may not have gotten that anywhere else in their lives. It was a lot of fun and I took this calling very seriously. I loved the work we were doing. Marie is so creative and friendly that the kids absolutely adored her. She had been through many experiences herself that made her a great asset to help troubled teens with emotional problems. I worried at times that my lack of education would hinder me from doing the job as well as I should but I found that just being willing was the number one thing kids are drawn to. Live a Godly life in front of them and be there. Be willing to listen, to participate, to help or to just be an example. Kids need to feel like they have someone in their corner. Marie had given her life to the Lord and she was baptized with several of our teens. Everything was going in such a positive direction and we continued to grow in the Lord and grow in our marriage.

Mike and Matt came up to me one day with very serious looks on their faces. I was worried that something was wrong when Mike said he wanted to talk to me. They wanted to know if they could call Marie mom. Alex and Amber were calling her mom and their mom hardly came around anymore. She would miss visits or not show up when she told us she would and the boys were hurt every time she did this. I wasn't sure what to say at first because I didn't want them to feel like they had to call Marie mom but here they were asking me for permission. I talked it over with Marie and she was touched. She said she wouldn't have a problem with it at all. I told them it was completely up to them. If they were comfortable with it and wanted to, then they could. From that day forward Marie has been "mom."

Marie's family pressured me to get my GED. I didn't feel a need for it at the time but it triggered me to try and better myself. It was extremely easy and I realized that I had the ability to further my education and it would set a good example for the youth and my own children. I started taking night classes after work at a community college. I wasn't great with computers but the classes were very easy. One night Marie called me at school and said Jessica had just called and needed to talk to me right away and it sounded important. Right after class I went to the address she gave me. When I walked in it looked like a flop house. It was her and three guys. There was hardly any furniture and nothing on the walls. She said "can we go somewhere and talk?" I said yes and we went for a drive. I parked and she pulled a note out of her pocket and began to talk. She looked strung out on something. Her hands were shaking and she was pale and skinnier than I remember seeing her before. She said she needed to work on getting her life together and she couldn't be a mother right now. She said she wasn't going to be coming to see the kids or picking them up for visitation. She wanted me to take care of the kids but she wanted them to know she still cared about them. I dropped her back off and went home. The next day I had to sit Mike and Matt down and tell them that Jessica wasn't going to be coming to see them for a while. I didn't go into a ton of detail because they were not old enough to understand. We didn't hear from Jessica for a while after that. The boys would still ask about her on the weekends that she was supposed to pick them up. I would try to be as honest as possible without traumatizing them with the reality of the situation.

Things went smoothly for a few months. Without the constant

stress of dealing with my ex-wife, life was great. I worked all the hours I could get, I was going to classes at night, we were having fun as youth leaders and I had even been asked to coach the boys' summer league baseball team. I knew very little about it because I had never played on an organized baseball team myself but it was a lot of fun and we continued to meet new people. It was very busy during the summer. There was not a day that we didn't have something going on but we loved every minute of it. Marie was a huge help. She handled all the paperwork for the baseball team and the youth group and she is great with people one on one. The areas that I'm weak in are the areas she's strong in and vice versa. We make a great team, not only in coaching but as youth leaders and most importantly as parents. We talked about how we wanted to raise the kids and what type of people we wanted them to be when they got older and what the best plan was to reach those goals. I made a decision early on that I wasn't going to lie to my children. They would know what it's like to work for what you want and that there are always consequences to your actions, good or bad. We matured a lot and very quickly. Marie and I worked so well together that I don't feel like there is anything we couldn't take on, as long as we were doing it together with the blessing of God.

Jessica showed back up and made a huge deal about being able to see the boys. She took me to court multiple times and made it sound like it was my fault she hadn't been to see them. I agreed to follow the visitation rules set forth and she started seeing them again. It didn't take long before she started to not show up again. It tore the boys' hearts out every time she flaked on them. She wouldn't even bother to call and say she wasn't coming. They would just be waiting by the door to see their mom and she wouldn't show up. I agreed to meet her at McDonalds once to visit with them and I let them play for three hours while we waited for her and yet another no show. Then out of nowhere she just disappeared. We didn't hear a word from her for six months. She had moved to Missouri and not bothered to tell us. She didn't even contact the kids on their birthday. I didn't mind her being gone but I was fed up with watching her hurt my kids. She showed back up out of the blue again and took me back to court over visitation. It made no sense at all. She was the one who left and she was telling the judge it was my fault she hadn't seen the kids. I explained this to the judge and he didn't believe me at first but then I mentioned that her current boyfriend was sitting in jail at that very second for a violent crime and he finally took my side. Because of the violent nature of her living situation we got an order of protection to keep her from taking the kids where she lived. She wasn't happy about having to follow the rules of visitation and wanted to come and go as she pleased. When I wouldn't let her walk in and out of their lives how she wanted to, she got upset and took them from elementary school one day. It was a day she was scheduled to visit with them but didn't bother to tell me she had picked them up. When we found out the kids weren't at school, we spent the rest of the day frantically looking for them. We had to meet her at the police station to pick them up because she was afraid of what I might do when I finally saw her. Of course she told everyone I was a horrible person who was keeping her children from her so the police did nothing about her taking the children without permission. Jessica was a constant nuisance for years but I did my best to protect my family from her erratic behavior. Eventually, Mike and Matt took it upon themselves to stop talking to her altogether.

We supported them for making this decision but always let it be up to them if they talked to her or not. She would call and cuss me out or accuse me of things that didn't happen. She said I was pushing the kids not to talk to her. That's not true. I made a vow to myself that I would never lie to my kids. If they wanted to know something I found a way to tell them the truth, even about me and my past. I didn't want them growing up thinking everything was always perfect and getting blindsided when they found out it's not. I was always honest with them about every situation and they were smart enough to tell her themselves to stay away. Once they did, I kept her away the best I could. When she would come around or call them they would get upset and start doing poorly in school. Mike would almost always end up in a fight at school within a week of seeing Jessica. It was so regular that it was very easy to spot the source of the problem. When she stayed away they hardly ever got into trouble.

Mike and Matt played baseball and soccer for a few years. I coached their baseball team for two years and their soccer team for two or three years. I wasn't experienced enough to be a great coach but it was so much fun to be a part of helping them learn and grow as athletes. We met new families and started developing friendships. Some of the kids I coached have graduated high school now and still call me coach. It's a great feeling to know you had a positive influence on a child. When Mike was entering 4th grade and Matt 3rd they started playing football. It was flag football until 5th grade. I volunteered to help coach and the boys and I loved it. They both found positions they were good at and football became a huge part of our lives for a long time. We spent many weekday afternoons at practice and our Saturdays were at the field watching the games. I would be coaching one sport or another and Marie would be watching from the stands with Alex and Amber tagging along. It was a great way to get them to exercise, stay out of trouble and keep their grades up. Mike never had any trouble with his grades but Matt hated doing his homework. Marie or I would spend hours at the kitchen table trying to help him or waiting for him to finish and he would complain and cry that he didn't want to do it. We were adamant that an education was the key to their future.

I tried to make the drive to Missouri a few times a year to visit my mom and sisters. Some years more than others but when I did, there was always some sort of drama going on. There was a time my sister Anna was in foster care and Lucy had gone to live with her dad. Another time that Lucy wanted to move back to moms' after Anna got out of foster care and I tried to tell her she was better off with her dad. She didn't listen of course and ended up pregnant and dropping out of school. Anna dropped out, got married and had a daughter. Mom was always drinking and fighting with someone. There was one visit that moms' boyfriend hit his grown daughter in the face. I ran outside and pinned him to the ground until we figured out what was going on. It became clear that he was the type of man who would hit a woman. I told him that if he ever hit my mother, I would take him back out in the front yard and we were going to fight it out like men until one of us wasn't getting up. About a year later my mom called me in the middle of the night. She was very upset and said she had gotten into a fight with her boyfriend and was scared of him. I got up and called off work and we drove the three hours right then. When we got there mom had a black eye. Her boyfriend had passed out and she was up waiting on me. I was fully expecting to beat this guy within an inch of his life when I got there but he was out of it and it didn't seem right to attack a guy when he couldn't defend himself. I told mom to pack her things and come home with us. My sisters had already moved out by this time so mom grabbed a few things and we left.

We made room for her at our house and the next day we had a talk. I told mom she could stay with us until she could get on her feet but she needed to get a job and support herself. She agreed and we rented a u-haul to go get her things. Her boyfriend left when he found out we were coming. Once we got mom moved in, Marie talked to someone about giving mom a chance at a job close by. She got the job and it went ok for a couple weeks. We were sitting on the front porch talking one night and she made a comment that knocked me for a loop. She said "yup, you definitely married into money." I couldn't believe she said those words. She saw the shock on my face and said "don't get upset I'm just telling you what I see." I wanted so badly for my mother to be proud of what I had accomplished and to be able to help her accomplish something in her life. She couldn't wrap her mind around the fact that I worked 60 hours a week, mowed lawns in my spare time and bought my own house. I told her that Marie and I did this on our own and nobody had done it for us. She had no idea how distant Marie's relationship was with her father or that her grandmother treated her like trash or that her mom and step-dad were barely hanging on to the business they had started. She looked around at the nice houses in our neighborhood and even though ours was not nearly as nice as the other houses around us, she assumed that I couldn't have done this on my own. We had guidance from God in choosing the house that was right for us but nobody bought it for us. I wanted so badly to set a good example for my family to see. It was staring her in the face and she couldn't see that you can do something about your situation and change your life without someone handing it to you. I was so broken hearted that night. It destroyed my view of the example I thought I was setting. My mother completely dismantled my confidence with one sentence.

I made the mistake of letting my mom drink alcohol. I knew she was an alcoholic but I thought asking her to quit cold turkey was going to be too much for her so I limited how much she could drink. Mom started sleeping in later and later and eventually started missing work. She had been walking to the gas station and buying more and more alcohol. She decided she wanted to go back to Missouri and move back in with the boyfriend I had just rescued her from weeks before. I told her I strongly disapprove but she was a grown woman so there wasn't anything I could do to stop her. I've been in many fights and confrontations where I was trying to defend the honor of a woman who was being mistreated and every single time the woman goes right back to the guy she was saved from. It's sad but I started to think there was no point in getting involved. Why help them if they are just going to go running back? We didn't talk for a while after that. The same thing happened when Lucy called and said she needed to get away for a couple days. I jumped into action and drove down to pick her up. I thought something was strange right away when she didn't bring her son along. She said she was thinking about leaving her babies' father and wanted to stay with us for a while. It only lasted a couple days and she went running back to him. He wasn't physically abusive, as far as I know but it bothered me very badly anyway. I didn't know what the real situation was like. I was only getting one side of each story and when I try to help, I end up being the bad guy for trying to get them out of the situation. I became stressed out and had what I thought was a migraine. I was in uncontrollable pain for days. I went to the doctor and then to the ER two different times. The ER gave me a shot of something that finally took away the pain. I woke up the next morning and Marie asked what was wrong with my face. Half of my face was drooping. It had become paralyzed. I went to the doctor and he said it would go back to normal in a few days. I felt better but now I looked deformed. Thankfully, it subsided in about a week and I looked normal again. We're not completely sure what the cause was but we assumed it was a side effect of the shot I was given.

Lucy started seeing a doctor and for years she claimed to have so many health problems that I started to believe she was becoming a hypochondriac. Anyone who had an injury or illness around her, she would suddenly have all the same symptoms. After a while I stopped taking her seriously. I'm not sure what was really wrong with her and how much of it she was making up. She left her boyfriend and moved back in with our mom for a short time and then got a place with my old friend Devin. They ended up getting married. This was a little weird for me but I was beyond the point that I felt anything I had to say would matter to her. They only lasted a few years and got divorced. Right after her divorce she moved in with a guy she met on an online video game and they got married. I thought she had absolutely lost any sense she had but they seem to be happy so who am I to judge.

My sister Anna and her husband seemed to have a good relationship from my point of view but secretly it was rocky from the start. They came to visit us in Illinois a few times. We hung out and had fun. We went to the St. Louis Arch and spent time together hanging out with the kids. She was always very secretive so I don't know exactly how things started or escalated but I found out she was taking prescription pills. Her and her husband began arguing a lot and ended up divorced. He went to prison not long after they split up. Anna started going further and further into drug use and refused to talk to anyone about what was really going on. I didn't see her much and when I would come for visits it felt like she was avoiding me. I think this was because she knew I would lecture her about the things she was doing and she felt guilty. I wanted to help her but I didn't know how. Any time I tried to talk to her about anything serious she pushed me away.

CHAPTER SIXTEEN

Roll With The Punches

We were doing well at home and we decided to get a couple credit cards for emergencies. This was a terrible idea. We started using them for things we wanted instead of actual emergencies and it didn't take long to realize we were headed into a debt that wouldn't be easy to get out of. We refinanced the house, paid off all the cards and made some repairs and upgrades. The roof needed work, we put new windows in the house, a new furnace and we put up a privacy fence around the backyard. We now owed more toward the house but I was making a little more at work so it was still affordable for us. The house was in better shape and the only debt we owed was the house and vehicle loans. After a while of sticking to our budget, we actually got ahead far enough that I was able to make a purchase just because I wanted it. I had been talking about it with Marie for quite some time and I finally found something I liked that we could afford. I sold my car and bought an '85 Chevy pickup with a 4 inch lift and 35 inch tires. It was a mud truck. I loved this truck and it was so much fun to drive. The kids loved riding in it and I think secretly Marie really liked it too. I drove it every chance I got. I felt like we were getting somewhere now that we could do something other than just pay the bills.

Things were going great. That's when you know something is about to happen. I got news at work that our division was being shut down. We were all sat down and told we had a week before this happened. I was furious. Things were going too well in my life to have a major blow like this. At first they made it sound like we were all being let go. Then, they said they would transfer us to another division to work. This meant I had an hour drive to work instead of ten minutes and at the same rate of pay. I had just sold my car and bought the truck which got terrible gas mileage. This was going to be a lot more expensive just to get to work. I knew there was a division that paid a much higher wage for the same job I was doing. It would be about the same distance if not maybe a few minutes closer. I demanded to be sent there instead. The manager agreed to send me and one other driver there under the condition that he reserved the right to fire us at his discretion if we couldn't handle the job.

When I started out as a trash man I made $7 an hour. I got my CDL and bumped up to $8. I would always keep my eyes open for better paying jobs but every time I tried to put in a notice to leave they offered me more money to stay. I was able to work during the day and be home with my kids at night and I was outside all day instead of being cooped up in a factory, which suited me great. I worked hard and always came to work. I was willing to work anywhere they needed and as many hours as they needed. I tried to make myself not so expendable. In less than three years I made my way up to $11.50 an hour. Now that I was transferring, I would be making over $15 an hour.

Even though I got the transfer I asked for, I still looked around for another job closer to home. I put in a few applications but in the end I decided to give it a try and see where it led. I was confronted one day by a fellow driver who had been with the company longer than I had. He made it clear that I and the other driver weren't welcome there. I made it clear to him that I wouldn't put up with any of his crap. They tried to play mind games with us by holding back our raise and seniority for over a month. They also had me picking up trash on some of the biggest and nastiest routes. I even got a letter in the mail saying I was getting my health insurance cancelled. They didn't hide the fact that they were trying to break us. What they didn't know is, I don't break easy and I won't back down. Within a year we had to go through a contract negotiation. It was stressful and looked like we may have to strike at one point. It worked out and I got yet another raise and cheaper health insurance. They also decided to give me and the other driver credit for the years we had worked at the other division toward our seniority. This was huge. It allowed me more vacation time, put me much closer to my next raise and more job options within the company. What started out as a temporary job as a trash man, now had the potential to be a decent career path. The biggest problem I faced now was time. I had a 45 min drive to and from work each day. I had to be there by 6am and I had no set time to get off work. I could work 8 hours and be sent home or have to stay for 12 hours to help other routes. I was still taking night classes, running the youth program and coaching sports teams. I finished the classes

I was currently taking and didn't sign up for any more. This gave me more time at home in the evenings. I juggled everything else to make it work for a while.

I wanted a big mud truck and a motorcycle for as long as I can remember. I had my big mud truck but the cost to drive it to work and back every day didn't make sense. I saw a used motorcycle for sale and fell in love with it. Marie saw how excited I got every time I looked at it and she told me I should buy it. I really wanted to but I wasn't sure it was something we should spend money on. Marie said if you don't get that bike you're going to regret not doing it while you had the chance. I knew she was right so I went to take it for a test ride. It only took a short ride around the block to know that this was going to be mine. I bought the bike and rode it to work as often as the weather would allow. I absolutely loved it. Being able to take a ride on a nice afternoon and feel the wind blowing across me made all my troubles seem trivial. I felt something I had never felt before and it was exhilarating. There was something about it that made me feel centered. It pretty much paid for itself in the money it saved me on fuel each week during the summer.

In 2006, I decided I wanted to try and meet my sister in Tennessee. Not that my moms' side of the family didn't already have enough drama to deal with but I still felt it was necessary. I wasn't sure where it would lead but I needed some kind of closure to the feelings I had about my father. I had stayed in touch with her off and on over the years and the time felt right. I drove down by myself and found the address she gave me. She is divorced and has two sons. They were living the same way I had grown up. They lived in a small town and their home was a trailer in a mobile home court. They were simply surviving. I hit it off right away with her and my nephews. We got to know each other a little and I played catch in the yard with them. The more we talked the more I realized she had just as hard of a time growing up as I did. She got to be around our father when she was young, before he passed. This gave her a different outlook on who he was and what he was like but she didn't know much more about him than I did. Her mother was living with her at the time and I got to hear her side of how things happened. She didn't have a very good opinion of my father but it was also clear that she had been no angel herself.

My sister got a phone call that night just before I left for my hotel. I could hear her talking about me to whoever it was. She handed me the phone and said your aunt wants to talk to you. After the time I had visited my grandmother, I was really nervous about what this lady was going to have to say to me. She said her name was Robin and she wanted to meet me. I agreed to meet her the next morning for breakfast. I sat in the restaurant waiting nervously and a lady walked in. She took one look around and walked right up to me and said "you're Michael." I had never met this person but she knew me right away. She said I looked like my father. We talked for a while and it was clear that she had good intentions. She was a very sweet lady who had nothing but nice things to say about everyone. She was very enthusiastic to get to spend more time with me before I left and to have me visit again. She was divorced and had one daughter. She wanted me to meet her daughter and her mother, who was my father's step mother. My grandfather had passed away a few years earlier.

This was the person I needed to tell me the story. I had so many questions for her and she answered every single one the best she could. She was my father's youngest sister. She was the only living child from my grandfathers' second marriage and she adored my father. He was the closest sibling to her age and she loved him. She tried to make him sound like a good person but she told me the truth about everything I asked. The more I learned the more I wanted to know. She asked if I wanted to visit his grave. I jumped at the chance because I had never been to his grave. By the time we got the letter saying he had passed the funeral was over. We visited two graveyards that day. My grandfather was in one and my father in another. There had been a rift in the family when my grandfather divorced and remarried. He was in a graveyard with his second wife's family and my father was in the one with the rest of the family.

It had been a great trip so far. I met family who were glad to see me and I had a few questions answered but nothing could have prepared me for the emotion that took over when we got to the graveyard my father was in. Robin had not been there in a long time and couldn't remember where the grave was. We searched for a while and it felt strange. I got more and more determined the longer we looked. I started to panic. I was not leaving without seeing it. Then I wandered off in a different direction from the group. Something was pulling me toward it. When I saw my fathers' name on a stone, I started to tremble. My knees started shaking and gave out. I fell on my hands and knees on top of his grave and started bawling. Robin and her daughter came running up to check on me. Once I had collected myself, she said "I wasn't expecting that kind of reaction." I said "I wasn't either." My father died when I was 7 and I was now 28. I had been pushing all those feelings deep down inside for 21 years. When I finally got to see it for myself the emotions burst out like a volcanic eruption. I felt better but at the same time it solidified the idea that I couldn't let my children go through the things I did growing up. I could never make them feel like I did at that moment. I was more determined than ever to give my kids a better start in life than I was given.

I brought Marie and the kids on the next visit and we had a good time. I met Robin's mom, who everyone called "Big Momma." I also met her brother from her mom's previous marriage, who everyone called "Bubba." Bubba had been close friends with my father and was able to give some insight to my fathers' personality that no one had before. Between Bubba, Big Momma, Robin, my sister and her mother who had been married to my father, I was able to put the picture together. He was a partier and a drinker, a fighter, a woman abuser, a thief and always in terrible health. Big Momma told me very sternly that I had turned out much better without him than I would have if he had been a part of my life. I fully believe her but it didn't change the yearning in my heart. I also found out that some parts of me weren't so original. My love for riding motorcycles was something I had in common with him along with my looks. My temper and desire to fight didn't come only from my mom. There were other similarities and it baffled me to think that I could be so much like someone I never spent any real time with. I also learned that through all the bad, Robin still loved my father whole heartedly. He was her big brother and nothing would change that. She bonded with my family and stayed in touch. We visited each other a couple times a year and she treated me like a member of the family. I tried contacting my fathers' other sisters but there wasn't any interest in talking to me. To them, I was just their dead brothers' illegitimate child.

I spent my vacation time to bring my niece and nephews up for a visit over the summer. We had our four kids and three nephews and a niece for a week. It was a blast. We had a week of fun and everyone got along for the most part. I wanted to spend time getting to bond with them and also show them that life has options and they can make something out of it if they really set their mind to it. The sister I had met seemed normal at first but over time she seemed to change. She started to call and ask me for money and wanted to know when I was coming for another visit. She didn't seem to understand that I didn't have money to just throw around. I could relate to how she felt. When I was a kid I thought anyone who owned their own house must be wealthy. As an adult with a mortgage, I realize that's not true. She didn't quite understand that the five hour drive it took to get from my house to hers wasn't something I could do every weekend. It became evident that even though she had graduated high school, she had a learning disability. Some common sense things didn't register with her. She would call and ask me to stop by for a birthday party for my nephew later that day. I would have to explain over and over again that I couldn't just jump in the car and be at her house in a couple hours. It was a long drive and I had to save money for trips like that. We stayed in touch and I tried to be a good influence on her boys but the distance made it difficult.

The pastor of our church retired and a new pastor was hired. Marie and I didn't seem to mesh well with the new pastor. I felt uncomfortable around him and his wife. They seemed much more well to do and they just didn't quite seem to be the right fit. We found out they were stretching the truth at times and other times it felt like they were flat out lying about some things. Small things but it was not a good sign. Marie and I talked it over and decided to quietly leave the church. I met with the pastor and told him he needed to find someone to run the youth program soon. He tried for weeks to get us to stay. He offered me the title youth pastor, an office and a small salary to stay but something felt wrong about it. I declined the offer and we started teaching Sunday school to our own kids at home on Sunday mornings. It was very important to me that our kids learn from the Bible and be taught right from wrong and about Gods power and grace and mercy. The kids were doing well with it and we were in control of everything they were learning.

I got a phone call out of the blue from my cousin Jimmy. We hadn't talked in a long time and I was glad to hear from him. Unfortunately it wasn't good news. He said he had stabbed a guy in a drug deal that went wrong and he was afraid there may be people looking for him. He was desperate for a place to go. I thought this would be the perfect opportunity to help him change his life. I said he could come and live with us under some conditions. I told him there would be absolutely no drugs of any kind. He had to be clean and he couldn't bring any drugs at all into my house. Second, he had to get a job and start saving to get his own place. I told him I would help him start over if he was willing to leave his old life behind. He agreed to everything I said and he said he was ready to change. He came on a greyhound bus and brought his girlfriend with him. It was great to be around him again but that feeling didn't last long. It only took a week or two before we ran into a problem. He wanted to stay up all night and drink on days that I had to get up early for work the next morning. He would try to pressure me to stay up and get drunk with him. I tried to help him see that I had a family to take care of now and that was my priority. I wanted to set a good example in front of him and show him he could achieve a better life if he just gave up the drugs and was willing to work for it. He wanted to hang out and have some fun and I thought I could show him that it was ok to have a few drinks in moderation without getting completely drunk. We went to a bar and shot pool but he spent the whole time talking to other people in the bar. I made a huge mistake by taking him there because he met people who were into the drugs he wanted and everything went downhill after that. He had his girlfriend get a job as a waitress but he didn't even try to find work. He would claim to be going out to put in applications or going for a walk and I found out later that he was going to a guys' house to get drugs. He refused to work but was using his girlfriends' money to buy drugs. Now, she wasn't innocent in this. She was using drugs as well. At the time, I wasn't sure yet if they were using drugs in my house but I could see that something needed to change in a hurry. One night after we put the kids to bed I heard arguing coming from upstairs. I told them to be quiet because the kids were asleep. I heard yelling and a loud thump. I'm not sure what happened but I told him to settle down or he had to leave for the night. He went outside and I locked the door behind him. He disappeared for a little while and I heard a loud bang outside. He showed back up on the porch and I went outside and asked him what the noise was. He claimed to not know what it was. I went looking around the area I heard it come from. He had stabbed Maries' car tire with a knife and cut one of the plug wires on my truck. The loud bang was my truck hood slamming down. I went upstairs where he was already arguing with his girlfriend again. I asked if he had done it. He said no. I couldn't believe he would stand there and lie to my face like that. I was giving him the opportunity to admit it and face me like a man and he claimed to not know what I was talking about. I went downstairs, told Marie what happened, and told her that we had two options. I fight him or we call the cops to get him to leave without a confrontation so the kids don't have to see what's about to happen. She said he was my family and it was my decision. I wanted to beat his head in. I did nothing but try to help him and this is how he repaid me!?! I really wanted it to happen. There's only one reason it didn't. Years before, I had given my word that I would never hit him again. I was older but Jimmy was bigger and stronger than me. However, every time we got into a scuffle I won. There was once that it got a little too serious and I punched him into submission. He got really upset and held it over my head. He said we were supposed to be close and I shouldn't have hit him the way I did so I gave him my word that I would never hit him again. I take my word very seriously. If I give you my word, I will do my very best to keep it. I went to the kitchen to think. As I was walking back to the living room, Jimmy came in the front door. He was facing away from me and had one of my kids' baseball bats in his hand. He asked Marie where I was. He hadn't seen me yet so I jerked the bat out of his hand. Thinking about what he was about to do hurt me deeply. The look of shock on his face when he saw me with the bat was all I needed to see. He was about to beat me with a bat and now I had the bat! I asked him why he had it and he started trying to come up with a story. When he saw I wasn't buying it he just stood there. I took the bat and put it away. It took everything I had to resist the urge to bash his skull in with it. By now I'm fully enraged and having a hard time controlling it. Next to my kids and my wife, Jimmy was the person I loved most in this world and I just couldn't understand why he was acting this way. I decided to call the police. I thought maybe they would send him to a rehab facility and he could get the kind of help he needed. I had Marie make the call while I kept an eye out for Jimmy. The cops showed up and I showed them the slashed tire. They were headed to the door just as Jimmy was about to come out the door. They told him to stop where he was. He reached in his pocket for his knife and the officers drew their weapons and told him to freeze. They arrested him and as they cuffed him he was screaming at me that I had done him wrong again by calling the police. What he didn't realize was that if I had not called the police, it could have been a lot worse. I don't know how bad the fight would have gotten if I exploded on him but it was not going to end well. He was much safer in police custody, that I'm sure of. We took his girlfriend to the bus station and told her she needed to go home. We made sure she had a ticket and left her there. She found a way to get Jimmy out of jail the next day and they both left on a bus. Quite some time later he called me in the middle of the night drunk or high or both. He was blubbering and trying to apologize. I could barley understand anything he said. I listened to what he had to say but really I couldn't care less about his apology. The more you care for someone the deeper the pain is when they do you wrong. I loved Jimmy unconditionally and he treated me like I meant nothing to him. I was done with him. Marie and I had a good life and we weren't going to let something like this change that. The next time I saw him was at our grandmothers' funeral and we didn't speak to each other.

It wasn't too long after this that one of my Aunts contacted us. She said her son needed help. He had started using drugs and had a drinking problem. He wasn't an alcoholic necessarily but couldn't control his temper when he drank. He had been in trouble his entire life. He had not had a very good example from his father and it showed in his actions. He had gotten his girlfriend pregnant and wanted to settle down and start living right. Once again I felt the need to open our home to a family member in the hopes that I could show them how to turn their life around for the better. It was another short lived attempt. He and his girlfriend argued constantly. They couldn't get along at all so he sent her back to Kentucky and told her he would get a job and save enough to get a place and come get her when it was ready. He got a job and went to work every day. After a few weeks we helped him look for a vehicle. He spent all he had on the car and didn't have anything left to put towards his insurance. I told him I would pay his insurance for him so he could get the car completely legal to drive as long as he agreed to pay me back out of his next paycheck. He agreed so I paid the $400 it cost to start his car insurance. He had started taking classes at a technical college and it seemed like he was really on the right track. Payday came and he disappeared. We didn't see or hear from him for days. I called his mom to ask if she had heard from him. She sounded nervous but said yes, he's here. He had taken the car and his paycheck and drove the 6 hours back to see his girlfriend instead of paying me back. He spent all of his money and showed back up a few days later like nothing was wrong. His mom told me, he knew I would be upset and did it anyway. He had given work some lame excuse and took a little vacation. I tried to let it go and let him keep staying there so he wouldn't lose his job or his spot in school but after a few days I couldn't stand it any longer. I told him he needed to find somewhere else to stay and he left the next morning. I didn't hear from him for a long time but apparently he lost his job for punching out his supervisor and wrecked the car on his way to school. He moved back to Kentucky and I still get calls about the student loans he never paid off. I guess he gave them my cell number because he didn't have one. He ended up having four kids. Three of them with the girl he brought to our house. His mother is raising those three children for him because he can't get his act together and the girl didn't either. Over the years, I've gotten random calls from him asking for money or advice but he never takes any of the advice and he still hasn't paid me back the $400 he owes me.

Marie and I talked about it and decided that we had been through enough drama from my family and started to distance ourselves from them. I would still answer their calls but the visits got few and far between. When we would visit anyone I would get very emotional on the ride home. I missed my family and wanted to show them that there was more to life than being drunk or messed up on drugs all the time. Nothing I could do or say made a difference to them though. Once we were home it was like a new awakening each time. I saw the life Marie and I had built and it was so nice that I wouldn't trade it for anything. Seeing the contrast of where I had come from to where I am now helped me to stay focused on my goals.

CHAPTER SEVENTEEN

Ups, Downs And New Experiences

I got the opportunity to make more money at work but it required me to basically be on call. I was trained to run any route, operate any truck and could be called in at any time throughout the week, day or night. To take this position I had to agree to do it for a full year. It was terrible from the start. I knew it wouldn't be a cake walk but it wasn't anything like they had described it. As soon as the year was up I put in for an easier position. I worked a pretty easy route for a couple months and then a new position opened up that really piqued my interest. It was a roll-off route. This meant hauling large dumpsters every day but the catch was that this would be a night shift job. I didn't want to work nights again but this would be steady hours and a foot in the door to a better position later. I took it with the understanding that I would be expected to work 60 hours every week. Anything over 40 hours was time and a half so the pay was nice and I liked being on my own at night when there was hardly any traffic. I was pretty much running completely on my own most of the shift. One problem with this is that a lot of the time I was in a very dangerous part of the city picking up dumpsters in the middle of the night. There were many times I would hear the news over the radio and they would be reporting on a shooting that happened blocks from where I had been the night before. I was confronted by people more than once who were up to no good and had someone try to sneak up behind me a couple times but thankfully I was never involved in anything serious.

I liked the job but this was an extremely stressful time for Marie and me. I was still coaching baseball and this made for a long summer. I would work from 11pm until sometime between 11am and 1pm then drive the 45 min home, eat shower and be in bed between 1 and2pm. The kids would wake me up almost daily by being loud. They're kids, of course they are loud. I know it was unintentional but it made it very difficult for me to get any sleep at all. Marie went out of her way to try to let me sleep and keep the kids quiet but I admit there were times I actually thought she woke me up on purpose just to tick me off. Maybe she did it to spend time with me since we hardly had any time together but that never worked out in anybody's best interest because I would wake up in a terrible mood and end up yelling at her. I would usually have to be back up in 4 hours or so to be at a baseball practice or game. If the game was a late game, I would have to go straight from the game to work that night. I was always grouchy. I would try to spend time with Marie and the kids but I was always so exhausted. She was taking care of the kids and the house and needed to get out once in a while so I would grudgingly go out with her on the weekends to get her away from the kids for a bit. I would try to have fun but I felt like an old man trying to keep up with a much younger crowd. I just didn't have the energy. I would complain and get on her case about the house not being clean or supper not being done when I wanted it. She was a wonderful mother, a great cook and she was good to me. She was terrible at keeping the house clean but that wasn't a good enough reason for me to treat her the way I did. I started yelling at her a lot and she hated it. There were times I would completely lose my temper and be screaming at her for really nothing at all. By the end of the summer she'd had enough. She took the kids and went to stay with her mom. She said she wasn't going to be treated the way I was treating her. She was right and I knew it. I was working so hard to provide for my family that I had forgotten that they need attention from me too. I didn't argue with her or beg her to stay because I knew all too well what it was like to be forced to stay in a situation you were miserable in. If she really wanted to leave I wasn't going to stop her.

The house was deafeningly silent everyday when I got home from work. I tried to take advantage of it and catch up on my sleep but it was no use. I couldn't have any peace at all without my family. I spent all my free time with the kids. I would still see them every day but just for a short period of time and they were gone again. Marie and I continued talking but she wasn't coming home yet. She wanted to know I was going to change. I didn't know how to make her see that I needed her in my life. Then one weekend I felt I needed to get out and blow off some steam so I could relax. I went bar hopping and after closing time a woman at the last bar I had been at tried to follow me home. I past my house and stopped down the road because I didn't want her to see where I lived. I stopped to talk to her and she tried to come on to me. That was about the time I noticed there was someone watching us. She had been followed and I knew the person watching. It was obvious that anything that happened was not only going to get back to Marie but also be exaggerated. I left and went straight to Marie's parents' house to talk to her. I knew right then that I needed to do whatever it took to get her back. Going back to the life I had lived before of partying and sleeping around was not what I wanted. I needed to tell her what happened before someone else distorted the story. She was not happy about it but I was right, the person who saw me, told their version of the story the next day and of course it was juicier than the truth. I was upset that someone was trying to intentionally cause more problems than we already had but it didn't matter. The important thing was putting my family back together. I asked Marie what it would take to get her to move back in. She said I needed to take some anger management classes or counseling of some kind. I agreed and found a place to talk to a counselor. The first visit was helpful. I talked to someone about why I thought I needed counseling. I got a few things off my chest and it felt better. The second visit was not so helpful. I just filled out some forms and answered some questions. The next visit or two stalled out. I tried to get my feelings out but I didn't feel like I was making any sort of progress at all. Marie had moved back in and that was my ultimate goal behind the counseling so I stopped going. It took time but at least now I was aware there was a problem and made a conscious effort to control my temper.

I was never violent with Marie or the kids but I had yelled a lot. I worked on getting that under control. Over time it got better but this is something I would struggle with for many years to come.

Marie would ask me often "Why are you so angry?" I started trying to find the root of the problem. I don't want to sound like I'm throwing a pity party but there were so many things I had held onto that were so hard to let go of. The feelings I had about my father, not finishing high school when I had been so close to graduation, the effect my mother had on my life, always struggling to make money, all of the times I had tried to help different members of my family, my time in jail, always feeling like I need to prove myself, the loneliness I felt from not being close to my family, trying to be a good father, all of these things and more played through my head constantly. I had a fire burning in my soul that I thought I needed to quench by confronting all these people who had hurt me. I realized that by holding onto these feelings I was allowing those same people to ruin my life. The only way I was ever going to have any peace in my spirit was to forgive everyone I had hard feelings toward. I had to just let go of it. I couldn't let them control my life anymore. The noise in my head quieted down after that and Marie and I were able to start making our relationship strong again.

In 2008 we were trying to decide on a family trip for the summer. Marie had her heart set on taking the kids to Disney in Florida. We had saved a little money but not enough for a vacation like that. I couldn't even wrap my mind around the idea of taking my kids on a trip like that. That was the kind of thing I still thought of as something for rich people, not people like us. Her mom and step dad said they would help us with the amount we were short so the kids would get to go. We agreed and made the drive to Florida the week school let out. Marie had moved back in not long before this and I was still working on my temper but overall the trip was a ton of fun. We spent a day at the beach playing in the sand and on boogie boards. It was the first time at the beach for me and the kids. Marie had been when she was younger. We got to Disney as it was opening the next day and we told all the kids that the better they behaved the longer we could stay. We told Amber, who was four at the time that we weren't carrying her all day. We said she had to walk and she agreed. We had a great time all day long. We checked out everything there was and not a single argument was heard. We rode every ride and picked out a few souvenirs. I rode Space Mountain with the boys as many times as they could handle. Amber got to see Cinderella, her favorite princess, and she walked the park without a single complaint. We watched the parade and the fireworks at the end of the night and when we started to leave Amber started crying. I asked, what was wrong? She had been good all day and had so much fun I thought she would be happy. The problem was she didn't want to leave. Somehow she had gotten the idea that she was going to get to stay the night with Cinderella in the big castle that they shoot the fireworks over. When she saw everyone walking toward the exit it broke her heart. We tried to explain it to her but that poor little girl cried all the way to the car. I felt bad for her but it was so cute at the same time. When we drove home I felt a sense of pride that we were able to take our family on a trip like that at least one time.

As soon as the opportunity arose I moved from night shift to day shift. I was able to continue driving the roll-off truck, which made me happy. The hours were still long but it was a lot more bearable. I had to be on the clock by 4am and I still worked 12 hours a day. This became the norm. I was home in time to eat supper with my family be at football practice in the evenings and go to bed with my wife. Marie and I had worked things out and life got really good now that we were getting along. We usually spent Sunday afternoons at her parents' house watching football. Her mom was extremely nice and loved having the kids over. It was around this time that Marie's step-dad asked me if I would work for him. It would be driving a semi over the road. He had started his own trucking company and needed dependable drivers. I thought if I took this job it could lead to an opportunity to run the business one day. The problem was that he was on the road a lot and expected his drivers to do the same. I didn't want to be away from my kids or my wife for weeks at a time like he was. I told him I appreciate the offer but I'm not going over the road until the kids are grown. He said he would be retired by then. I knew I was passing on an opportunity I might not get again but being with my family was more important. He continued having trouble keeping drivers and ended up selling several of his trucks to keep them from just sitting.

Marie's grandmother would call from time to time and ask us to come out to her farm and give them a hand with something. It was usually when a fence needed repaired or there was storm damage that needed cleaning up. She would always pay me for my time but I kept telling her that I didn't need her to pay me, that families help each other. She would never let me leave without a check for a few hours of work. I asked if she would mind if I brought the kids out to fish in her pond. I told her that would be payment enough. She let us come out and fish once in a while but still paid me if I came out to work. She liked when we came out to visit but she was very mean to Marie. She would insinuate Marie was stupid or call her fat. She constantly told her she needed to lose weight. I couldn't believe someone's grandmother would treat them this way. We started going out to visit less and less because Marie would be upset every time we left and I didn't like the way she got treated. Marie would blindly defend her grandmother to the point that she knew the things she said were wrong but put up with it anyway. I could tell she loved her grandmother but I told her that she needed to stop letting people walk on her. And that meant even if it was me that was doing the walking. She was so nice and forgiving that many people tried to take advantage of her kindness. She finally spoke her mind to her grandmother and we didn't visit for a while. When we finally did it was a little better but not much. Marie realized her grandmother was never going to change so she just let her disturbing comments roll off like she hadn't even said them. Her dad hardly ever visited or called. We really only saw him for a short visit once a year or maybe at Christmas. I didn't mind because he made it obvious he didn't like me and Marie didn't mind because she didn't really get along with her dad.

We found out that my ex-wife had another baby. She made it clear that she still didn't want to be a mother and this time the father had ended up in prison. She came to us to ask if we would be willing to adopt her son. Marie and I talked about it and we knew if she didn't want the baby it would not have a happy life. We already had four kids to care for but we were willing to help a child in need if it meant he could have a better life. We invited her over to discuss what the terms would be if we agreed. We wanted a legal adoption and for her to not have any contact with us or the kids. We would raise the child and let him believe we were his parents. We knew if she was allowed to be a part of the kids' life it would not go well. She didn't like that idea. She wouldn't agree to give up visiting the kids. She wanted to have us take on all the responsibility and let her come around whenever she felt like seeing the kids. We wouldn't budge on our stance and she wouldn't talk to us about adopting her son anymore after that. For years she used her son to try to get Mike and Matt to spend time with her so they could see their little brother. They cared about the new little brother they now had but hated putting up with Jessica to see him.

Marie had been having back pain and it was gradually getting worse. Once we were able to get in to see a specialist, the doctor told her she needed surgery. After some planning, Marie had surgery to replace two of the disks in her lower back. I took a week vacation from work to care for her and the following week my Aunt Robin came up for a week to help take care of Marie and the kids. Afterward Marie felt a huge relief and was glad she finally had this taken care of. I was pretty stressed out the whole time. I hated seeing her in pain. Taking care of Marie, the kids, the house and going to work was not a walk in the park. I wanted to be everything for everyone but I didn't handle it all that well. We got through it and luckily I didn't kill anyone.

The kids were a little older now and Alex and Amber started school. Marie was thrilled to get the chance to finally go back to work. She started out at a small department store in town. A position opened up at the local bank where a friend of hers was working. She went for the interview but didn't really expect to get the job without any experience. She is easy going and such a people person that she got the job right away. She loved being able to get away from home during the day and being able to contribute in a financial way to the household. It took her a little while to get the hang of it but she is so fun loving that almost everyone there loved her right away. She fit right in and made some new friends that prove to be better people than we could have ever imagined.

Alex and Amber were now getting old enough to start playing sports. I was excited to see them get to do the things their brothers had. They started off with t-ball and soccer. Marie wanted to coach Amber's t-ball team. She volunteered and it was fun but she decided to only do it the one year. Amber continued to play every summer and loved it. We met some new people when Alex was playing t-ball and became friends with several of them. Alex wasn't a natural athlete. He was shy and small for his age but he wanted to play and tried his best every time he stepped out there. I worked with him at home and he got the hang of it. He always gave it his best. That kid has a heart of gold and cares deeply about everything. I couldn't buy him anything if I didn't buy something for all his siblings at the same time. If I bought him a snack at the gas station he wouldn't take it unless I bought one for everybody and took it home to them. He would give you anything he had without hesitation if he thought you needed it or it would make someone happy. He might be the most genuine person I have ever met and I'm proud to be his father. He hardly ever got into trouble and when he did it was because he didn't know any better. He looked up to his older brothers and tried to do everything they did. They were great kids too but Mike tried to push the limits and usually had his brothers tagging along.

This was one of those breaks in the insanity when everything went according to plan and we were happy and healthy. I wanted to keep doing things with the kids that I had wanted to do as a kid but never got to. I had never been to a professional ball game so I got some cheap tickets to a St Louis Cardinals game. There were plans to build a new stadium and I wanted to be able to say we went to at least one game at the old Busch Stadium before it was tore down. The first time I took my family to a Cardinals game was my first time as well. We made it to two games at the old stadium and a couple times to the new one when it was finished. I was a Rams fan so we went to several Rams football games as well. This became our routine. Almost every year we would try to see a game around one of the kids' birthdays and that would be their gift. We all had different favorite teams so for whoever's birthday it was I would try to get tickets for games when their team was in town. I wouldn't necessarily call it a tradition but it's something I'm really glad we did. We have a lot of good memories rooting our teams on.

I was always wrestling with the kids or playing in the yard with them. We practiced sports or just roughhoused. We played board games and I taught them to play chess. We were all very competitive except Alex. He must have gotten that from his mother. He was the least competitive but he was the one who won the most when we played board games. He would also find four leaf clovers by the handfuls. He has to be the luckiest kid I've ever seen. We played a lot of video games as well. Of course that was also competitive. Mike was always the best gamer in the house so he would tick me off when he would beat me repeatedly. I even sent him to his room one time because I was convinced he was cheating somehow. We laugh about it now but Marie and Mike will never let me live that down. I always had fun spending time with the kids. It was never dull or felt like a chore. It was something I found to be purposeful and meaningful. I enjoyed every second we spent together.

Alex and Amber got put on the same soccer team. Amber decided right away that soccer was just entirely too much running for her. She didn't even finish the first game. Alex played soccer for several years and we ended up being good friends with the coach and his family. They invited us over to their house now and then and our kids got along great with their two boys. We seemed to hit it off great, even though the coach didn't always appreciate my sense of humor. We hung out with our new friends from time to time and I felt like I had found people I could have fun with now without getting into trouble.

Marie found a horse. I say it bluntly like that because that's exactly how out of the blue this was. We had talked for years about getting a place in the country and having horses. We had not started looking for a house in the country yet and she had already picked out a horse that she just had to have. It was a Belgian. If you don't know what this is, it's a huge animal. It's a smaller version of the Budweiser Clydesdales. It was broke to ride and also trained to pull wagons. It came with a saddle that fit this massive creature and Marie loved it. She couldn't stop talking about it. She was talking about it at one of Alex's baseball games and our new friend said her parents had horses and might be willing to board it for us. Marie got really excited and we talked it over. I wasn't sure this was something we could afford but if it was going to make Marie this happy then I wanted her to have it. We worked out the details and they even let us use their trailer to go pick up Marie's new horse. They gave us a great deal on boarding cost and without them it would've been several more years before we could have made this happen. They were extremely kind to us and we got closer and closer to their family.

I liked horses and always wanted one but didn't have much experience around them. Marie on the other hand was in love right away. She spent all her free time with her horse. She took me and the kids and taught us everything she knew and what she didn't know we learned together. This also started a love of horses in our daughter. We have photos of Amber lying on this massive creature bareback like it was a bed. She could lay completely flat and have plenty of room on this horses back. It was so gentle that she could lay there and it would just slowly walk around with her on it without a care in the world. It felt as if it was meant to be.

Marie found another horse that someone was giving away. We went to look at it and not only took the horse but bought a saddle and a horse trailer from them. Marie started looking for new places to ride so we could spend more time riding together. She found a horseback riding club and we started going and learning how to ride in the different events, like barrel racing and poles. It was a lot of fun and the kids all learned how to ride but Amber was the one who enjoyed it the most. The horse shows were on Saturday evenings which was the same day as the boys' football games at the time. I would take the boys to the games and me and Alex would watch Mike and Matt play while Marie took Amber to the horse shows. After the games I would drive straight to the show grounds and watch my wife and little girl ride that huge horse around the arena. It was so cute watching Amber control an animal that was 30 times her size. Horseback riding became a regular sport for us like any other.

We hadn't been to church for quite a while and we went out drinking and having fun when we had spare time. A lot of the time we hung out with Marie's brother and his girlfriend. They had moved into the house we had been renting from Marie's parents before we bought our house. We never got into any trouble but we cut loose and got a little crazy once in a while. I had to blow off steam somehow to keep my sanity. The crazier the dare the more I enjoyed it. I streaked through the bank parking lot one night when no one was around. I flirted with every woman I saw. I tried to have fun everywhere I went. Marie never got upset or jealous but she let me know what the boundaries were. We would have a wild adult costume party every year around Halloween. It was always exciting and fun and there were usually anywhere from 15 to 25 people there. This went on for a couple years. By the third year the excitement was starting to wear off.

Marie's brother proposed and he and his girlfriend decided to get married now that they were both out of school, living together and starting their careers. I was surprised and honored when he asked me to be his best man. I knew we had gotten close but I didn't know I had become that important in his life. I gladly accepted and they had a beautiful wedding. I had written a speech and as I was writing it I started realizing just how close he and I had become. Marie was my best friend and kept me grounded and sane but she was my wife and I needed that male friendship he and I had. He had become like a brother to me, not just my brother-in-law. After they got married, they bought a house of their own about 30 minutes away so they could be a little closer to where they were working. They had two boys and were living the American dream. They had careers, a home and kids and we had careers, a home and kids. Because of this, we started to see each other less and less. It's sad but the daily grind of our lives kind of pulled us apart and we didn't spend nearly as much time together as we once did. We tried to stay close, but to be honest it never really was the same.

I hadn't noticed just how far away from God I was starting to slip. Not really. Not until we got a letter from the church where we had been youth leaders. They had another new pastor and he had heard good things about us and wanted us to come back. Marie and I talked it over and we put it off for a while. When we finally decided to give it a try, I knew right away that God was speaking again. It was time for me to stop acting foolish and get back to what he had called me to do, helping young people. We started going regularly and right after we did, the church called a meeting. The pastor who had sent us the letter was leaving. I was a little upset that he was asking us to come to a church that he was getting ready to leave but I still felt like I should give it a chance. There was a decision made to combine two churches under the leadership of one pastor. The pastor of the other church would oversee both churches and handle all the services. I tried to be a part of the decision making but I was not where I should be with God just yet. I think that was more obvious to the pastor than I realized. I still had some things in my heart I needed to work on. We kept going to the church and found that we liked the new pastor a lot. We decided to change our life for the better. We kept going to church, stopped going to bars, started paying our tithes and tried to help out anywhere we could.

Jessica's father decided that he wanted to move to Illinois. He called us and asked if he could stay with us instead of with her until he could buy a house close by. He said he couldn't stand Jessica and it would give him a chance to spend more time with Mike and Matt. Marie had met him a few times and said she didn't have a problem with it. She showed me just how great of a person she was. Marie was raising our four kids, two that were not her biological children, putting up with all the craziness that comes along with me, my anger, jealousy, and insecurities. She had put up with my insane ex-wife and more troubles from my family than anyone should have to endure. Marie is beautiful, smart, confident, a great wife and a wonderful mother. She is incredibly good to me and the kids and is always trying to make me happy. She is creative, inventive and she always thinks of others before herself. When we met I was jaded and troubled. She has shown me the good in people and made me a better person. Now she is willing to let my ex-father-in-law move into our house for an undisclosed amount of time. She is absolutely amazing. She is far better than I will ever deserve. She is the answer to the prayer I prayed at 17 years old as I cried myself to sleep, when I begged God to send someone into my life who would love me. I asked for someone who would love me as much as I loved them and he gave me more than I could have imagined. I was so glad that everything worked out without any real problems with our new house guest. He found a house quickly and was ready to move out just as things were starting to get a little uncomfortable. You can only live with a house guest for so long before it becomes weird.

CHAPTER EIGHTEEN

The Smell

Right after we got things back to normal, we got a visit from a friend that had been in the youth group that we ran years earlier. She said she was starting college classes and wanted to know if she could stay with us through the week when she had classes or had to work. It was more convenient for her to get to and from work and school from where we lived than from where she lived. We didn't have any problem with it and she stayed with us for a while. She was a great kid and was trying to make something of herself. Her boyfriend was also in college and they had plans to marry and get a house together after they graduated. One winter morning I got a call on my cell phone while at work. It was December 9th 2011. I don't normally answer my phone right away while I'm at work but I was completely stopped in a traffic jam so I answered it. It was Marie and she was more upset than I had ever heard her before. She said our house was on fire. The girl staying with us had been asleep on the couch and smelled smoke. She jumped up and ran outside with her cell phone and called 911. Then she called Marie at work who then called me. I was stuck, unable to move and my family was in the middle of a crisis. I told her I would get there as soon as I could. I stayed as calm as possible and inched forward enough to get off on an exit and took off for the office to clock out and go home. When I turned onto our street, the flames were bursting out the side of the house and climbing into the air. I pulled into the neighbors drive and jumped out of my car to go find Marie. I ran past the blazing house with dark black smoke billowing out of every opening. It didn't feel real at first. I thought to myself "Is this really happening?" When I got to Marie she was holding back her hysteria the best she could. She couldn't take her eyes off the house. I put myself between her and the house to block her view and to keep my back toward it. I needed to be strong for her and if I turned around and looked at all our hard work going up in flames, I would have lost it for sure. I was barely keeping my cool when the next thing I know we were surrounded by friends. They were there almost as fast as the fire department. These ladies were right by Marie's side trying to console her. I stood there in complete shock. I didn't know what to say or do. I had no idea why this was happening. We had worked so hard to provide for our children and do the right things and be good people. We had gone back to church and I even quit smoking. I had given up everything that could be considered sinful. I was trying to be a good influence and a good example to those around me. Why was everything being taken away? I didn't understand.

A fireman came running out of the burning house with an armload of something covered in black soot. He had saved our children's photos from our living room wall! The fire was starting to get under control and when he saw the opportunity to save something that he knew would be important he did it. Another fireman saved one of our two dogs that were in the house. These were incredible acts and I'll never forget it. I am grateful for all the firemen who were there that day. They did a great job and kept the house from burning completely to the ground. Once the fire was out and they deemed it safe to enter we walked in and tried to take inventory of the loss. It was everything. The fire had been so hot that it torched, melted or damaged everything. If didn't burn or get wet it was so smoke damaged that it wasn't salvageable. We pulled the clothes that didn't burn out of the closets and a friend took them to the laundry mat right then and washed them for us so we would have something to wear. It was impossible to get the smell of smoke completely out but she was a huge help in getting us started. We saved as many pictures as we could but a lot were too damaged to do anything with. The Red Cross was there that day before we left. They offered help and it was exactly what we needed to get a few things to get us started and on with our next step.

The kids were at school during the chaos of the fire. We had to pick them up and take them to Marie's moms' to break the news to them. Our pastor had come to check on us and asked if he could be there when we told the kids. They had lost their home and their things and two pets, a dog and a rabbit. They cried so hard and for so long. There was nothing I could do but hold them. I felt completely powerless as I watched my children hurting and wondering what was going to happen to us. I found it a little ironic that our pastor came to talk to us the day of the fire and seemed concerned but then told the people of the church not to donate anything to us. He told them to wait and see if we got paid by the insurance company. I tried to understand his reasoning but at that moment we had lost nearly all of our possessions, our home and the only money we had was what the Red Cross had donated to us. The small community we lived in however took it upon themselves to raise a generous sum of money for us. Marie had lived here her entire life but I had only lived here for ten years. I was impressed at the compassion and willingness of this small town to help someone in need. There were so many that helped or donated and I don't want to leave a single person out so to anyone who helped or donated anything at all we sincerely thank you. We had a few people who came over to personally deliver clothes, goods, checks or cash. Someone who wanted to remain anonymous donated brand new shoes to every member of our family. I was astonished at how many people came to our aid at this time of need. I decided then that this is exactly the type of place I wanted to raise my kids.

Marie's parents offered to let us stay with them for a while. Now that their kids were grown, they had moved back into the house we had rented from them. They had rented out the larger house to another family who had a fire not long before we did. The six of us lived in the basement bedroom. Marie's parents stayed on the road most of the time to give us more room in the house, which was beyond anything I would have ever asked them to do. They wanted to help in any way they could and we needed all the help we could get. We stayed there while we waited on the insurance company to get things figured out. Once all the details were taken care of, they deemed it a total loss and paid us for the house and the value of our belongings. Now we had to decide what to do and where to start. We started by cleaning out the house.

The smell. I can't describe well enough the smell of all your hopes and dreams and memories covered in thick black soggy soot. Seeing the charred remains of what was once a happy home took a toll on us. We went through every single thing in that house, piece by piece trying to save anything we could. There wasn't much. Going through all of our belongings that were unsalvageable and having to throw it in a dumpster was not an easy task. We had just finished our Christmas shopping a week before the fire. Looking at the disgusting pile of wet ash that had once been our kids Christmas gifts was gut wrenching. We didn't let it stop us or slow us down. We were determined to rise from the ashes stronger than ever. So many people were in our corner that I felt like I could accomplish anything. I was willing to do whatever it took to get my family stable again. Our faith was strong and I had no doubts that God was going to lead us to something better. Our family bond grew stronger and we took this time to really cherish having each other to lean on. For years after the fire, I would be right back to that moment every time I would have to haul a dumpster for someone else who had a house fire. That smell can bring up so many strong emotions in a flash.

After a month of living in my in-laws basement I was ready to get a place of our own. I love them and appreciate everything they were doing for us but we needed to have our own house. While we were trying to put some kind of plan together Marie got a call from her grandmother. She said she would give us some acreage to build a house on if we wanted to live by her and help her with the farm. Marie was so excited she started crying. It was her dream to live on that farm. She had fond memories of spending time there when she was a child. She was so emotional she could barely tell me the news. She thanked her and we immediately started looking at homes. We spent the next few days trying to figure out what type of home we wanted that we could afford. We made up our mind and Marie called her grandma to tell her what we decided but her grandma said she changed her mind. She didn't want to give up any of her farmland. Marie was devastated! She was more hurt by this than anything I think her grandma could have ever done. I was angry that I had to watch my sweet wife get her feelings trampled on like this. We were both reeling from the blow and just couldn't imagine why she would lead us on like that and then pull it away. It was cruel, just plain cruel.

We were back to square one and we knew we would have to rent for a while. Marie had made friends with a woman she worked with who had recently gone through a divorce and her and Marie bonded. She had a house that she was willing to let us rent temporarily. We agreed to rent it for six months and Marie and I decided that we were going to start looking for our "forever home." It would be the place we would eventually retire to and live the rest of our lives. Our goal was to buy a house with some acreage at the end of the six months. We began to pray earnestly that God would lead us to the place that would be perfect for us, not just another house but the exact one that was for us. I refused to believe that God would allow this to happen without having a plan.

CHAPTER NINETEEN

God's Plan Is Revealed

We paid off the debt we owed for the house that burned and a vehicle loan and sold the remains of the house and the lot it sat on. We spoke with our friend who was a real estate agent and we had her show us every property in the area that came with land. We found a few that we liked but none that felt like they were the right fit for us. After how our community had come to our side at such a difficult time we wanted to stay in the school district. The only places we looked at that came close to what we wanted were out of the school district. The end of the six months was coming up fast. We were looking hard and had not found exactly what we were looking for. We came very close to settling on something that we knew wasn't perfect but then Marie got a call from her grandmother. They were not on great terms but she answered the call. She told Marie that someone she knew was considering selling a house just outside of town with land. We didn't take her seriously at first. We sort of blew it off as another dead end. A couple weeks later, the lady she was talking about happened to come into the bank where Marie worked. Marie figured it was worth asking about so she asked the lady if she was considering selling a house. The lady looked a little confused because it was not on the market yet. She said "yes, I'm thinking about it. How did you know?" Marie explained to her how she found out and the lady said "why don't you come see it and we'll talk it over." Marie told me about it and we decided to drive by and just look before we took it too seriously. We found the address and right away we just knew that this house would be way out of our price range. It was beautiful and it was huge. It had large barns and buildings behind it like it had been an operating farm recently. I told Marie we shouldn't waste this ladies' time because there is no way we can afford something like this. We talked it over and decided to follow through with the meeting and set up a time to get a better look at the property. Before we went, we sat down and hammered out the finances and decided exactly how much we could afford to spend on a house payment and how much we could borrow without getting ourselves into trouble.

We pulled up the drive and waited nervously for the woman Marie had spoken to. We had been looking at houses for months and tried to be open to what God had to say. We kept telling each other to keep our eyes and ears open for a sign. We had asked our friend to come along, unofficially, to get a professional opinion. When the woman arrived she explained that she didn't live here but it was inhabited. She and her husband were separated and he lived there. It had been his parents' house. She began telling us the story of why they wanted to sell it. It had been a huge hog farm and was known all over the area. His father passed away several years before and his mother was in a nursing home. The man wanted nothing to do with farming or hogs. They had already sold anything in the house that had been of any value and did not want to have to spend money for the upkeep of the place. She warned us before we walked in that her husband had a drinking problem and that he was eccentric. It became clear what she meant right away. He was obviously well educated and extremely intelligent. He spoke well but also made it a point to make comments that were out of the ordinary just to see the reaction of the people he was talking to. I believe he was sizing us up to see what kind of people we were.

Upon entering the 5000 square foot house we immediately saw a gorgeous fireplace that separated the living area from the huge dining room. Once you looked past the junk that was everywhere you could see the potential of this home. There was a rustic motif that I loved right away. The kitchen looked like something out of a magazine from a few decades ago. It was a big room with beautiful cabinetry and a large island in the middle. As we were making our way throughout the house I started to see more things that I liked. The master bedroom was enormous. It had its' own bathroom that was bigger than any bathroom I had ever been in. There are two bedrooms and two and a half bathrooms on the main floor alone. We went downstairs to the basement and it was like walking into another house. You could live out of the basement if you wanted to. It had a bedroom, living area, another fireplace, full bathroom, laundry room, a full kitchen and extra storage areas. It wasn't completely finished and needed some repairs but I was starting to get a little more nervous about what the price tag for this place was going to look like. We hadn't seen the acreage that was going to come with it and I had already seen enough to make the assumption that this house was worth a lot more than we could afford in two lifetimes. I worked up the nerve to ask how much she was going to ask for it as we walked back upstairs. She responded with the exact number Marie and I had decided we couldn't go over. It was too good to be true! It took everything I had to not look like I had just won the lottery. I almost started jumping up and down. If this was not a sign from God that we were about to receive the blessing of a lifetime I couldn't tell you what would be more clear. The place had some quirks and needed to be updated in several spots but I had not seen one thing that was not fixable. A few minutes later our friend asked me how much they were asking. When I told her, she had a look on her face that I hadn't seen before. I whispered to her "That's good right?" She said "yes, I've shown houses like this for twice that closer to the city." I was about to lose my mind I was so excited!

We went outside to take a walk around the property that they were selling with the house. She said it would be something close to ten acres but it had to be surveyed and separated from the farm land they were keeping that surrounded the house. We walked down a small path that curved around some very old hog buildings. Everywhere we went the weeds were at least as tall as I was. It was hard to tell what we were actually seeing that first time through. They had been paying someone to mow the front yard but the rest of the property hadn't been touched in something like 15 years. What it boiled down to was, if we agreed to buy the house we get the property that these old buildings sat on just so they could get rid of them. She was willing to keep the price affordable for us if we took all the junk they didn't want. We were young and healthy and had four healthy kids that could help us do the work so we didn't need long to decide that this was a project we were willing to take on.

We signed a contract and once the place was surveyed we started the process of buying the house and the 12.73 acres it sat on. When the word got out that it was for sale people came out of the woodwork offering to buy the house out from under us. By now I knew this house was meant for us and I really didn't have any doubts that we would be the ones who got it. There have been very few times in my life that I was this confident about something. As the closing date came close, the lady's husband made his intentions clear. He said he would take his clothes, his computer and whatever he could carry in his arms as he left but anything he left behind was our problem. He wanted nothing to do with this place anymore. I don't know what the whole story was and to be honest it was none of my business. When we walked in the house for the first time after the closing, we saw that he had done exactly what he said. There were still dishes in the cabinets, old furniture in the living room, an old bed in the bedroom, a soiled mattress left in the master bathroom, an entire bookshelf full of books, old family photos, clothes in some of the closets and junk everywhere. The youth pastor at our church brought the entire youth group over to help us get started. We had a 40 yard dumpster filled to the brim before we could start moving in.

We put as much of the insurance and donation money as we could spare toward the down payment so our monthly payment would stay affordable. We had the carpets replaced and did the cleaning ourselves. We had been given some furniture to get us started but there were still many things that needed replaced that had been lost in the fire. Right after we moved in, I took some vacation time to start working on the outside. Marie's cousin came down to help us out. He brought a large tractor and brush hogged the entire property for us. Even with his large equipment he had a hard time getting through all the obstacles on our property. We bought a very small used tractor with a small brush hog and I got into the smaller places with it. We found so many things that needed to be done. It was a monumental undertaking to get this place in shape. The kids and I spent my two week vacation getting a small area cleaned up enough to put the horses in. We found a mound of liquor bottles and mangled sections of fencing and cattle panels. It was the middle of summer and the kids hated it. I was very proud of how hard they worked and how little they complained for as young as they were. We kept at it every day and they worked right alongside me every step of the way. We kept working until a project was done and then I would decide what project to start next. Amber wanted a horse of her own and Marie found one that we thought was just right for her so we bought it. Marie's cousin had been keeping it for us, for the couple of weeks it took us to get the lot ready for the horses. The time had finally come that we had talked about for so long. We had found our dream home and were able to have our horses on our own property.

As soon as we were settled in we invited all our friends and family over for a barbeque to see the new house. I felt like anyone who wanted to see it should be allowed to see what we invested their donations on. I wanted to be as transparent as possible to everyone who helped us. Our home was an incredible blessing to us and we wanted to be a blessing to others. We had no idea at the time of the fire but God had already put this in motion before we even knew what happened. He had to take away what we had, to give us what we could have only dreamed of before now. This place had enormous potential and we had plenty of plans for the future.

We bought the supplies we needed to get a permanent fence up around the perimeter of the property. The youth pastor came over again with a few workers to help clear a path for the fence. It was hard hot work and it took time but we got the fence put up. I started looking around for the next project to work on when I noticed the roof was not in as good of shape as we originally thought. I climbed up to get a better look and it was way worse than it looked from the ground. There were places that had no shingles at all and bare wood was showing. We had spent all the money we had saved, so now we had to take out a loan to have a new roof put on. It was expensive but it's comforting to know that it is something we won't have to worry about for a very long time.

As I got stronger in the Lord we were asked to help more and more around the church and I was asked to be one of the deacons. I told the pastor that I didn't feel worthy of a position like this. We had a private meeting and I told him I had a lot of things in my past that were not things that I was proud of. He said I met the criteria and he could tell I was a good person. He said one test of a man's character is how his family is run. He said my family was exactly what he was looking for. My wife and I got along great, our kids were well behaved, we were involved in the community and he had not heard any negative reports about us. I was a little surprised that we were thought of this highly. I didn't think of myself this highly. I accepted the position and tried to do my best to not disrespect the church, the pastor or God.

Being a deacon was nothing like I expected. I was very surprised at how much of the meetings were about money. It felt much more like running a business than operating a church. I thought we should be concentrating on how to help and lead people, not where the money was coming from and where it should be spent. I know that's a big part of the burden of leading a church but I don't believe the money should be the main focus. It should be about God and his plan for the people. I seemed to be the only member of the board who felt this way and I felt very out of place. I made my opinions clear, that I thought the church I had started attending before the two were combined should be allowed to operate itself. I was shut down. I continued pushing my ideas and it became clear that I was not popular as a member of the board. I resigned as a deacon when it started to feel confrontational and didn't attend services for a short period of time. Then a member of the church asked me to attend a meeting about the two churches becoming their own separate churches again. It was a popular idea among the congregation. The board disagreed but finally gave the people what they wanted. I met with the person in charge of the district at the time and recommended the youth pastor to fill the new pastor opening of the church. I thought it would be a smooth transition and he had showed interest in becoming a pastor. He didn't think the youth pastor was ready for this kind of position but was willing to give him a chance. The youth pastor accepted and we started attending services again and tried to get things back to normal. Please understand that I don't want to sound like I'm trying to take credit for anything that took place. On the contrary, I think God used me and my stubbornness to put something in motion and he took it from there.

We spent all our spare time trying to clean our property up. It was exhausting but we continued to make progress and it kept looking a little better with each project we completed. We found a lot of things lying around that Marie would find buyers for rather than throwing everything away and we hauled all of the mangled metal out to the scrap yard. We saved any money we made and used it for upgrades later. Marie was continually looking for new or different animals to introduce to our little hobby farm. We started with the three horses, Marie's horse the Belgian, my horse was an Appaloosa, and Amber's horse was a Quarter Horse. Then we got a couple fainting goats. If you've never seen fainting goats, they are hilarious, look them up. We eventually got another goat and started breeding and selling them. We moved here with three dogs, a Chihuahua mix that I accidentally ran over while putting up the fence, a husky who passed of old age a couple years after we moved here and a mutt we adopted that is now 15 years old. Marie surprised me with a Pit Bull Terrier puppy who became a valued member of our family. Anytime Marie found an unwanted or mistreated animal she had to have it. She found a free horse for me that was younger and faster than mine. She found a miniature donkey someone wanted to get rid of. She named him after me because I can be... well you know. We call him Junior for short. She also found a miniature pony that had been neglected and mistreated who has been a headache since we brought him home. Marie has chickens that she sells the extra eggs from and rabbits that she breeds and sells. I decided to try a little riskier investment and bought some calves to raise.

We took the blessings God had given us and turned the tragedy of our house fire into a life for our family that we are extremely proud of. We had both been at our places of employment long enough to know we had stable incomes. I didn't dread going in to work every day because I found a position I enjoyed. I had been approached about moving into a supervisor position but decided to continue doing the job I had. Marie made friendships at work that I believe will last a lifetime. We were spending time together as a family. The kids were very involved in sports and other activities. We were steadily trying to make improvements on our property and continue the clean up process. We had our niece and nephews come for visits during the summers. We were happy and thriving. It was our own personal slice of Heaven and we were enjoying it.

CHAPTER TWENTY

Not Out Of The Woods Yet

My Sister Anna had gotten divorced and started partying very heavily. She was running around with men who weren't good for her and doing drugs. She became addicted and it ruined her life. Her daughter has been through a lot, being dragged along through my sisters' life. Anna has lost custody of her daughter and it doesn't look like they will ever be reunited. I talked to my sister Lucy about the idea of letting my niece come live with us. Lucy stepped up and took our niece in before I could actually make it happen and now has custody. I've offered more than once for our niece to come live here with us but Lucy stopped talking to me. She even went as far as to change her phone number so I couldn't contact her. I'm not sure why she became so defensive when I was only trying to help. I don't think I was ever mean or rude about it but Lucy made it clear that our niece was staying with her and she didn't want me around. At least she is with family that can care for her. I keep hearing my sister Anna's voice telling me that her life was ruined because I left her there with mom. I think back to the time I gave her marijuana for the first time. Is this on me? Did I do this? Maybe offering her pot one time is a bit of a stretch and I know she made a lot of bad decisions to get to where she is but I introduced her to her first drug. I'm her big brother, the only person she had to look up to. If her story was written, would I be the gateway to her future drug use? This weighs on me and bothers me to my core. I don't hear from her much at all anymore. I pray for her but it seems like anytime I hear about her it's not good news.

My mom and her husband spent years drinking and fighting before she finally decided she wanted out for good. Actually, I'm not sure if it was her or him that made the decision this time but I got a call from her asking to stay with us again. Marie and I talked it over and decided that since we were doing so well we would give it one more try to help someone live a better life. I set ground rules that I told her she would have to abide by. They were: 1. No alcohol at all 2. You must attend church with us 3. Once you have been sober for a while you have to get a job and support yourself 4. This is permanent; we are not taking you back to Missouri in a few weeks because you changed your mind. She agreed and we turned a storage room into a bedroom for her. It went better than I expected it to. She stopped drinking alcohol completely and didn't complain about going to church. We gave her a long time to dry out and made sure it would stick. Eventually there was some tension but we talked it out and everybody got along as well as possible. It was stressful at times but the overall feeling was that what we were doing for her was actually helping and was better than the alternative. She needed cataract surgery and Marie found a program for her to get both of her eyes fixed free of charge. Once we knew she was alcohol free, stable and in good health, we had a talk about what she wanted for the future. She decided she wanted to get a divorce and get her own place. We helped her get a job and start saving money to accomplish her goals. She offered to try and help out or pay for things and I refused. I wanted everything she did to be towards her goals. She really didn't have much of anything that had any monetary value. She was quite literally starting from scratch. When she was ready we took her to Missouri to get her divorce official. She continued making progress as time went on and everything was going as planned.

I got a phone call from Jimmy one evening. It had been a long time since we talked. He had a baby boy now and he called to ask me for parenting advice. He was having trouble staying sober and dealing with the stress of being a parent. I tried to give him the best advice I could. We talked for a while but it didn't seem like anything I said really helped that much. I wanted to help but felt like my hands were tied. What kind of dad did he want to be? This was something he needed to figure out. He said he wanted to have the type of relationship with his son that I had with my kids. I did the best I could to steer him the right direction but it seemed like there was a piece of the puzzle he wasn't telling me. We hung up on good terms and I started praying for him. I hoped and prayed that this child would give him the incentive to change his life and be responsible.

Just when I thought the really tragic parts of my life were over, I lost one of the people I loved most in this world. In early 2014 Jimmy died of a heroin overdose. I had told Marie of all the good times Jimmy and I had as kids but we hadn't been close in over 15 years. The only good conversation we had in several years was that last time we talked on the phone. I had always told him to be more responsible but there was a part of me that resented him for how carefree he lived while I worked non-stop most of my life. There was even a short time where I thought maybe he was right and I was wrong for working my life away. I thought hard all the way to Kentucky for the funeral. I had myself convinced that this had been an accident and he made a dumb mistake. When I finally got the whole story out of someone, I found out it wasn't an accident and it wasn't the first time he had tried. He committed suicide. His son had been born with severe birth defects and it was believed to have been caused from Jimmy's drug use. The guilt of the life he had condemned his own son to, was more than he could handle. He took the cowards' way out instead of manning up and taking care of his responsibility of helping his child through this life. He left that burden solidly at the mothers' feet.

I held it together very well the whole trip until I saw Jimmy in the casket. I tried to talk and just started crying uncontrollably. I couldn't believe he was gone. I remembered back to when we were kids and all the crazy things we did. I also remembered that day I gave him his first hit off a joint. I gave him his first drug and it turned into this. Is this on me? Is this my fault too? I know he looked up to me and wanted to be like me. Did I send him down this path? Are the struggles his son will face for the rest of his life caused by me? I can't answer these questions. I can't help but wonder and the guilt eats at me. Anytime I see his face I see the pain in his heart. I knew he was hurting and I had no idea how to help him.

Once again, I dealt with a heart breaking event and went right back to the grindstone. I went back home, back to work and back to normal, or so I tried to make everyone else believe. Marie could see through my hard outer shell most of the time. I know she cares about me and would have done anything she could to help me through it. As hard as she would have tried, I don't think she could really understand how truly deep this pain is. No matter how I felt, I couldn't sit around wasting time feeling sorry for myself. I couldn't afford to not go to work or to not be there for my family so I had to keep on. I shoved all the pain down inside and tried to rationalize what happened. I tried to not let my feelings interfere with how I interacted with my family but sometimes they could tell I wasn't myself. I started praying for Jimmy's son and asked God to help him and his mother through the struggles they would inevitably face. I tried reaching out to her but it was a little strange and I got the feeling she preferred to keep her distance from Jimmy's family. I continued praying for them and it helped me get through the toughest part of it.

As things were getting back to normal, I had a rough day at work. I was asked to haul a dumpster that someone else couldn't get. When I tried, I got stuck in the mud. I got pulled out and then got ready to haul the load. It started sprinkling on my way in and the wind picked up. The tarp covering the dumpster started flapping and my supervisor who was behind me radioed to tell me that I had some loose trash blowing out. I pulled over and got my straps out to tie it down and climbed up onto the truck. It had sprinkled just long enough to make the truck rails slippery and I fell off. On the way down I hit my rear end on the rail. I hit hard and it jerked me which sent pain all the way up my back and into my neck. I bounced off the rail and landed in a ditch. I got up and finished my job but I was furious because I knew right away something was wrong with my back. I went home that night and tried to rest it. When I came in the next day I asked to get it checked out. After a few doctor visits and some imaging, I found out I had two damaged disks in my lower back and one in my neck. This was definitely not what I needed right now. I opted to just let it rest and see how things went. After a few weeks of sitting at home resting, I went back to work. It felt better but I knew this was something that could come back to aggravate me again in the future.

We were still going to church as a family but the recent changes didn't go nearly as smoothly as I had hoped. I felt that the majority of the congregation shared similar views but I also felt like I had caused a lot of strife when I pushed for our church to have its' own pastor again. There was a lot of tension and it became clear that money was still going to be a big focus. I couldn't help but wonder if it was my fault. I couldn't be a part of it any longer because I felt like I was doing more harm than good. It started to feel like people were going for some other reason than to be close to God and we stopped attending. I'm not telling you that you should not go to church or that all pastors are money focused. I'm saying, I wasn't comfortable with the direction my church was going and I decided to make a change. I fully believe in God the Father, God the Son and God the Holy Spirit. There is nothing more important in my life than God and then my family. I know beyond the shadow of any doubt that God has led me to exactly where I am today.

After talking it over with Marie we decided to teach our kids about God and do our own Bible studies at home rather than search for a new church. This is a dangerous option for a person of faith because it would be easy to get lax or be led astray by ideas that do not come from God. There is strength and renewal in being around other Christians. I have walked this path for several years now and it is how I choose to lead my family. It has worked for me but I know I am absolutely solid in my faith. I know what I believe and I stand on it continually. The times that I feel like I'm wavering, my wife is always there to pull me back up. Together we have grounded our children in faith and belief. The road I have chosen is not for everyone but it works for us. This was a tough decision to have to make with my mom so new to being back in church. We continued having Bible reading on Sunday mornings and we taught the kids and my mom about what we read and made sure we all understood it. We were all learning new things at our own pace. Mom was doing well and kept growing stronger emotionally.

Mom's next goal was a car. She saved enough to get a cheap used car and we started looking for one. Marie's parents helped her by selling her and old car. It ran great and they sold it to her for what she could afford to pay. I took her to get the title and license and Marie showed her how to get insurance and pay her bill. My mother was in her fifties and this was the first time she had ever owned a vehicle of her own. I was proud that we helped her achieve this accomplishment. We told her the next step would be for her to get a place of her own. She started looking for places she could afford and we started finding cheap or free furniture for her to move in with. She found an apartment she liked that was close to where she was working and she was set to move in the next month. My mom had been living with us for two years. She had been sober the entire time. We had done everything we knew how to do for her and she was finally ready to move out on her own.

I was asked to be the assistant coach for Alex's soccer team a couple years before this and the coach and I got along well. We weren't the type of friends that hang out every day or meet up for lunch once a week, but we understood each other and when we did hang out it was always fun. There was never a dull moment and we had grown close over the last few years. His wife helped us with the purchase of our home and they were there for us at the time of our house fire. He and his wife made a decision to move down to the gulf coast. I was sad when I found out they were leaving but also happy that they were getting to make their dreams come true. I told them we would have to come visit them and hang out on the beach sometime. Her parents decided to move to the same area with them and they had a horse to sell before they moved. We were familiar with the horse since we had boarded our horses with them and her dad asked Matt if he would be interested in buying this Tennessee Walker. They had a lot to do to get ready for the move and were willing to exchange some manual labor for the horse. Matt agreed and was really excited to have his own horse.

CHAPTER TWENTY-ONE

Tragedy Strikes

The kids were doing great. They were making good grades. All the boys were playing football. Amber made the middle school cheer squad and played summer softball. I was volunteering as a coach for Alex's football team. Work was going really well for both me and Marie. I enjoyed my job and I was good at it. I made good money and had earned quite a bit of seniority over the years. I was making over twenty dollars an hour and had good benefits. The only thing I didn't like about it was how much time I had to spend away from home. It was starting to look like we had life figured out. I made comments to Marie from time to time that if we could afford for me to stay home and work on our little hobby farm full time, I could really clean this place up and do something with it. I could also spend all the time I wanted coaching the kids' ball teams. It was one of those "if I ever win the lottery" conversations. How many people can say that if they hit the lottery they would stay in the house they live in and be happy? Yes, I might make some upgrades but overall I was so happy with my life that the only thing hitting the lottery would have changed was not going to work so I could work at home and spend more time with my family... .... Be careful what you wish for, you don't know what type of package it will come in when you get it.

There was a going away dinner at a local restaurant for one of our friends. Neither of us felt like going anywhere that night but this was a long time friend and we wanted to be there for her. We thought it might make the night more fun if we rode my motorcycle into town. I loved riding the bike and having Marie with me made it even better. We left the restaurant after dinner and it was a beautiful August night. The temperature was perfect for a bike ride. As we headed toward home, I slowed down at our turn and then decided to go past it and ride a little longer and enjoy the nice weather. I turned off my turn signal and picked my speed back up to the speed limit. Marie gave me an approving tap on my leg that told me she was game for a ride too. It was about 9:30pm and the sun hadn't been down long. As we rode along, I saw three sets of headlights in the oncoming lane. One of the sets of headlights came into our lane and headed right at us. My eyes darted right and left looking for a way out as I thought "Oh God No!" I put my foot to the brake but they never had time to engage. By the time I finished the thought "oh God no," we had already been struck head on by the oncoming minivan. I saw a flash of light and heard a ringing in my head as I felt like I was floating for several seconds. I kept waiting to feel myself hit the ground but I never did. I woke up face down on the pavement.

At first I didn't feel anything so I tried to get up and look for

Marie. When I tried to get up I couldn't and it sent extreme pain all through my body. It was the worst torment I have ever felt, in every single part of my body, all at the same time. There have not been words invented that describe what this wretchedness felt like. I had hit face first into the windshield and I was not wearing a helmet. I couldn't see anything but shapes moving around because my eyes were so blurry. I'm not sure if it was from the damage or all the blood on my face. I could taste the blood and gravel in my mouth and I could hear the driver of the other vehicle saying frantically that he didn't see us. I started screaming for help. I cried out "God please help us!" I tried getting up again but my body wouldn't work right and I felt like every part of me was broken. After a couple minutes I heard a familiar voice. "Help is on the way." He was a police officer and our sons had played sports together. It calmed me down for a few seconds to know that someone we knew was there. I responded "How's Marie?" He said, "Marie's here too!?" I said "yes find her!" She had been catapulted over the vehicle onto the side of the road. As he walked away to find Marie I started to panic. I kept trying to get up and go to her. I had to know she was ok, no matter what it took to get there. When I couldn't, I screamed out in pain and kept asking if she was ok. Some of the people who were on the scene later told me that they had a hard time getting me to calm down and lay still. They said, they couldn't stop me from trying to go to Marie. Someone finally walked up and said "We found her... she's in better shape than you are." Considering I was awake and talking, I figured maybe she was ok. I had no idea how severely injured I actually was.

Having at least some comfort that Marie was going to be ok, I started noticing my pain more and then I heard another voice. I assumed it was a paramedic but it was actually someone who had been on his way to work and stopped to help. I asked him to lift my leg out of the position it was in to relieve some of the pain. He didn't think it was a good idea but I begged him to please lift my leg. I didn't know it at the time but I was a gruesome sight. I was told months later that nobody expected me to live because of how bloody and distorted my body looked laying on the pavement that night. He lifted my leg and I felt a little bit of relief when the muscle relaxed. I had very little control of any part of my body but all of it was in agony. This must have been when the ambulance arrived because I started hearing more voices. Someone was talking to the man who was holding my leg. I started feeling weak and dizzy. I could feel myself slipping into darkness. I tried to stay awake but when I knew I couldn't hold on any longer I had a short talk with God. I simply said "God if this is it, I'm ready." I knew my heart was as it should be and I had done all I could. I had turned my life into something positive and I had no fear in facing him because my heart was ready. At that moment all I saw was darkness and all I felt was peace. The most pure, soul releasing peace I have ever felt. I don't think there is anything on this earth that can compare to the peace I felt for those few moments. The only way I can even try to describe it would be to tell you to imagine all of your worries disappeared, I mean really disappeared without even a memory of a problem that ever existed and you were floating in space with your eyes closed. I felt no pain, no regret, nothing but a peace that enveloped me from inside out.

The next thing I remember was the sound of the helicopter as they were loading me in. I could feel blood running down the back of my throat so I tried to tell whoever was next to me about the blood and then I was out. I had a few crazy dreams about the helicopter crashing but that didn't really happen. When I woke up again, I was in a hospital bed and couldn't move. I had no idea where I was and I've never told anyone this but I didn't even know WHO I was. I could hear noises but I didn't see anyone in the room. I didn't know why I was there and I felt completely alone, more alone than I've ever felt before. I had a tube down my throat so I couldn't talk even if someone had been there. I was really out of it but eventually a nurse came in to change the bandage on my right leg.

The pain..... oh God, the pain. I literally felt like I was being tortured. Unable to move or speak and the only people I saw caused me unbelievable pain. This happened a few times before I saw anyone other than nurses. I finally realized what had happened and where I was. I had brief periods of consciousness where I would open my eyes and see a familiar face. I wanted to reach out to every one of them and talk to them but each one had looks of terror on their faces. I couldn't even ask about my wife. Her mom said she tried to tell me Marie was ok but that every time she said her name I would thrash wildly trying to get up out of bed.

I had a broken nose, broken eye socket, both bones in both wrists had broken and protruded through the skin. My pelvis was shattered and had also ripped through my skin at the crease where my leg attaches. It caused permanent nerve damage to my right leg which caused me to develop foot drop on my right foot and ankle. The ligaments and tendons in my right knee were shredded and I had a ruptured intestine. They gave me 22 pints of blood the first night and considering someone my size probably has around eight to ten pints in the entire body, I completely bled out more than twice. The trauma doctor in the ER saved my life that night. I was told he refused to give up on me and kept me alive. My kidneys started to shut down and they put me on dialysis. During the first two weeks the doctor had my kids come in to tell me good bye three different times because each time they thought I wouldn't make it. My leg had swollen to five times its' normal size. They said if I lived, there was a good chance I could lose my leg but they were able to save it. The doctors told my family that even if they save the leg, I may never walk again. These were devastating injuries that would take years to recover from, if at all. Marie told me that once she was awake and could talk she demanded to know how I was, as often as they would tell her. She said they kept telling her not to get her hopes up. Then one day the doctor came in and said "I don't know. Every time we think he won't last the day, he gets a little stronger. That man is fighting hard to stay alive."

Once I was able to start seeing people and actually remember it, there was a message stuck in my head. The message said "your job's not finished." As soon as I saw my kids, I knew exactly what that meant. I had worked hard and fought to change so that my kids could have a better life than I did. Those kids are my life. The day I found out I was going to be a father my life changed. I made a decision to be a better person and to be a father they could be proud of. I'm not a perfect parent but if I didn't make it through this my kids would have lived a very different life. Mike and Matt would have to live with their biological mother. With Marie's injuries she would have to rely heavily on her family to raise Alex and Amber. I had life insurance that would have helped but they would lose the life we had built together. Their lives would have been uprooted and changed forever. I fully believe that the only reason I'm still alive is to be here for my kids. I have a job to finish and nothing was going to stop me from doing it. My sole purpose in this life was to raise my kids to the best of my ability and make sure they turned out ok.

When I was conscious enough to know what was going on I remembered that it had been almost Marie's birthday when we got into the accident. I got the attention of the nurses in the room and tried to tell them but they couldn't understand me. I had external fixators on my wrists and pelvis so it was very difficult for me to move but I was able to scribble enough on the paper they gave me to get them to understand the word flowers. Then through a sort of game of charades they figured out that I wanted to send flowers to my wife for her birthday. I always sent her flowers on special occasions and sometimes just because. I wasn't about to stop now when she needed me the most. The doctors and nurses took excellent care of us. The nurses made sure the flowers got to Marie and anything we needed at all, they were right there. When Marie's Birthday came, they brought her bed from her ICU room into my ICU room. They didn't tell her where she was going and made it a complete surprise for her. Most of our family was in the room and it was the first time we got to see each other. This hospital stay was the longest we were apart for our entire marriage.

The people on the scene had not lied to me. Marie was in better shape than I was at the time but she had many injuries of her own. Her injuries weren't as life threatening but were very serious and some were permanent. She had broken her pelvis in two places. One of her legs was broken. Her left arm is completely paralyzed from the shoulder down. She had a bad cut on her head that went to the bone. Her bladder and spleen had ruptured and she had some road rash. She had lost memory of the accident and a couple of days leading up to it. She still doesn't remember anything about the accident or how she ended up in the hospital. She spent two weeks in ICU and was then moved to another floor. Part of her physical therapy was making it to see me in her wheel chair. It hurt me so bad to see her in pain. She would come into my room and sit by my bed but there was nothing to say and we couldn't even touch each other for a long time. She would stay in my room for as long as the nurses would let her and she would cry when it was time to go back to her room. There was one day that I saw that she was hurting pretty bad and I made the nurse take her to her room to rest. Marie didn't want to leave but I couldn't watch her sit there hurting just to be next to me when she could be resting and getting better.

The pain was far from over. There were many tests and surgeries to come. I had more than a dozen surgeries before I left ICU and that wasn't the last of them. Every time they moved me to take me for a test or another surgery it was excruciating. The pain was vivid and constant. They would lift me from my bed and move me to a bed that would be wheeled to another part of the hospital. Then I would be scooted onto a freezing cold table for whatever needed to be done. All the while, every movement intensified the pain to something I still have a hard time believing a human being can endure without passing out. It was what I can imagine hell being like. Constant torturing pain to the point you almost forget your own name.

I started getting phone calls from family and friends who couldn't make the trip to see us. I remember one call very clearly although I couldn't think very clearly at the time. My friend who had moved to the gulf coast called me and told me I had to make it through this. He said, you told me you would come see me at my new home and we would go to the beach. He told me I needed to pull through and I was too strong to let this get me. He made me promise that I would come see him on the beach. I made that promise not knowing if I could keep it but I was going to give it all I had.

I was getting regular visits from family and I tried to hide the pain but I could see the worry in their faces. I was on a lot of pain killers which made me a little sedated. They would talk to me and tell me jokes or stories about their week and I felt so bad for not being able to be a part of it or even be able to give good responses to their conversations. Marie's brother and his wife had moved into our house with their two kids to take care of our kids and home. There is no way I could thank them enough for putting their life on hold and making sure our kids were taken care of. They made sure the kids went to school and stayed busy to keep their minds off the turmoil as much as possible. They brought them to see us regularly and did all they could to make this easier for them. They spent a month at our home taking care of our family. When Marie was released they went back home. They continued to help with anything we needed at any time we asked. I couldn't have asked for more from them.

Marie was in no shape to take care of four kids and a home. It was recommended that she go to a nursing home where she could have constant care but she refused to even consider it. She wanted to go home and be with her family. Her mom and step-dad put their lives on hold and moved into our house. Her mom had been handling all our finances and insurance needs and was more than willing to continue doing anything we needed to get us home and safe. They moved our furniture and had a hospital bed set up in our living room so that Marie was able to be home and still get the care she needed to continue healing. Marie wanted to be at home but it was tearing her apart to leave me there alone. She was an emotional mess and cried all the way home from the hospital. The day she got to go home was Mike's birthday and it was also the day her grandmother passed away after a battle with cancer.

After a month I was taken out of ICU and I started physical therapy in the hospital. They were trying to help me learn to walk again but the damage was too severe for me to even hold my own weight. There were two therapists that worked with me. They alternated sessions with me and it worked perfect for me. The contrast of the way they approached my therapy made it clear to me what I needed to do. One therapist would have me stand up at a walker and tell me I needed to push past the pain and start walking. My right foot was still so messed up that it would not go flat for me to stand on. It was stiff as a board and stuck in a position that looked like I was on a 6" stiletto. My knee had not been repaired yet so it was not stable enough to hold my weight at all. I tried but it was like trying to climb a mountain barefoot with 200lb on my back. The other therapist wouldn't really push me at all. He let me go at my own pace and was very nice but I didn't accomplish as much. I knew then that if I was going to walk again it was up to me. God had saved me and given me another chance. I had to do something with it not sit on my butt and let life happen around me.

I wanted to do things myself but when I tried to get up from the mobile toilet they had placed in my room to get back into the hospital bed, I fell on the floor. That was when I realized just how weak and useless my legs had become. My mom was in the room and she tried to help me up but she wasn't strong enough and called for the nurses. The nurses came running in and helped me back into bed. One of them said "You shouldn't be trying anything on your own like that. You're going home soon and don't need to be hurting yourself." Home? Already? But I couldn't walk or get myself to the bathroom or get my own food or change my own bandages. I still had a drain coming out of my gut because of the hole in my intestine. I still couldn't use my hands enough to even write my name. How could they let me go home? I was afraid I would be a huge burden to my family. I didn't want them to despise me because they had to take care of me. It was my job to take care of them. The hospital had a therapist come in to talk with me about the emotional side of going home. I didn't feel any better about it but it helped me understand that it was time and the therapists started preparing me to go home. There were things I was going to need to know how to do, just to be able to get into a car or to the bathroom. I had to use a plastic board to slide from a wheelchair into a car or onto a toilet or onto a shower seat. Because of the damage to my wrists, I couldn't even push my own wheelchair. After learning some valuable tricks to get where I needed to be, the day came for me leave the Hospital. Just shy of two months, I was about to head home.

CHAPTER TWENTY-TWO

New Challenges

Marie called and said she heard they were preparing me to come home. She said there was something she needed to tell me but didn't want to. She said there was a lot of tension between my mom and pretty much everyone else. At the beginning of this ordeal my mom was not handling it very well. The doctors would come in and say I wasn't going to make it and Marie's mom would talk about things that needed to be taken care of like insurance, both health insurance and life insurance. I had a very large life insurance policy that would need to be managed if I died. My mom would flip out on everyone in the room and yell at not only Marie's mom but also my kids. It turned into a heated argument more than once so I'm told. She took offence at anyone for talking about things that needed to be done if I passed. What my mom didn't know was that there was no way I would have wanted her handling any of my finances or having any authority over my kids if something happened to me. I had spoken to Marie's mom and brother about taking care of things if anything like this ever happened. I don't blame anyone for how things went but it caused a huge problem. Marie and I were going to need constant care to be able to stay in our own home. Her mom and step-dad were willing to move in and do this full time. I trusted them to do the job more than I did my mom. Now that my mom wasn't getting along with anyone, I needed to have a talk with her.

Mom had been in the hospital room with me more than anyone else. It seemed like every time I woke up she was there. She didn't talk much and she would always leave the room when anyone else came in to visit, which I thought was weird, but I now understood why. I had asked her to not give up her job or the chance to get the apartment she wanted just to sit by my side. I had let her live with us for two years and put up with the stress of helping her get on her feet and she was almost self sufficient. It was passed the date she was supposed to move in and I knew she was giving up on it. I did not want all the work we had put in to be for nothing. I talked with her and told her that I didn't know for sure what happened in the beginning of this but that I knew things had been said. I told her whatever the problem was it had to stop. There were more important things going on than feelings getting hurt and we needed everyone to put their emotions aside and get along for this to work. I told her that Marie's parents were going to move in with us to help Marie and I get going again. I told her we needed their help and I didn't want her arguing with everyone. She didn't say anything but she decided to go to Missouri and stay with Lucy for two weeks.

When we got home and pulled into the drive I saw something

different. There was a spot next to the driveway that had been dug up and reburied. I was told that when Marie got home from the hospital, we had a water line break. Some friends of ours came over and fixed it for us at no charge. I thought, "How could our luck get any worse, but at least we have friends who are willing to lend a hand at times like this." When I was wheeled into the house, I saw a hospital bed in the living room. Marie was in it and happy as she could be to see me, I was finally home. Marie gave me her hospital bed even though I argued with her but she wouldn't take no for an answer. She slept in a recliner next to me that night. I felt despicable. My wife was in a chair, a very comfortable chair but still a chair, while I lay in her hospital bed. The next day a second bed was delivered and we slept side by side like that for over two months. Marie was able to get up and walk short distances but I was still bound to the bed or a wheelchair.

Marie started to fill me in on everything that had been going on while we were in the hospital. People had come out in droves to help us with anything that needed done. The animals had been taken care of, the kids had been taken care of, donations of all kinds were pouring in and people were dropping off food and supplies. My Facebook page was filled with people praying and asking about us. I had no idea I even knew this many people, much less that many that cared so much about us. I was moved at every turn. There was even a donor who paid our mortgage payment for a full year. Without all these people we would have had a very difficult time keeping our home. I can't say thank you enough to everyone who did anything at all because it added up to an amazing outpouring of love. The words, thank you, just don't seem like nearly enough for the blessings we received. God worked absolute miracles in our lives with our survival, our healing and the blessings poured out on us. It was incredible!

A couple days after my mother got back from Missouri, Marie had a doctor appointment. She asked my mom if she would stay with me and take care of me the few hours that they would be gone because I was still bed ridden. If I needed anything or even had to use the bathroom I couldn't do it by myself. Mom agreed but as soon as Marie was gone, she disappeared to her room. When she came back out mom said she was moving back to Missouri and asked if I would be ok if she left. I thought to myself, you want to leave? Marie just asked you to take care of me for a few hours and the second she's gone you want to leave? There were many things going through my mind but all I said was "I'll be fine." She said, "Are you sure?" I said "Just go." She loaded her stuff in the car that we helped her get as fast as she could, so fast she was almost running when she left. I was speechless. All we had done for her and all we helped her accomplish; stopping drinking, getting a job, getting her eye surgeries so she could see at no cost to her, helping her get established and getting her some furniture for her to get her own place, getting her divorce, so she could bail out the first time anyone asked her for anything in return. I hoped that maybe she would live with my sister and then get her own place but in a matter of days she was back living with the ex-husband who used to beat on her. That was all I could take from that woman and I really didn't care to ever hear from her again. I had reached deep into my past to pull up any member of my family willing to try to make a better life and this was the last straw. I can forgive the things that have been done to me but there is no more to give. I am always willing to lend a hand to someone but I have no desire to offer helping hands to anyone who doesn't show a desire to help themselves.

When Marie came home she was very angry that mom left me alone for hours after she said she would stay there with me. Her mom and step-dad stayed with us and waited on us hand and foot for over two months. Her mom handled all our bills, insurance, medications, doctor appointments, cooking, bathing, anything at all that we needed they took care of it. I could probably write a chapter just on how much of a daily grind it was to be with us and take care of all of our needs. I am eternally in their debt for what they have done for us. I hope that I can be a good enough person to make them feel like it was worth it.

I was taking so many medications that I wasn't even sure what most of them were. I had to give myself a shot in the stomach every day and there was a cupful of pills for me to swallow and I still felt miserable. The first procedure after I got home was to go back and have the drain removed from my abdomen. I was glad to have that gone! We had physical therapists coming to our home a couple times a week to get some of the simpler things worked out, like using my hands again. There's metal holding the bones in my wrists together and I still don't have full range of motion in either of them. I had no grip and had to relearn how to hold a pencil and write. After a while, I was able to start pushing myself along in the wheelchair.

I hadn't been home long at all when one of our horses passed away. She was the oldest of our horses but she had not shown any signs of bad health so it was unexpected. Marie and I were in no shape to handle it so there was nothing we could do. We had to call someone out to take care of her and Marie was very upset.

We were doing all we could to just survive and heal and one of our horses died in our pasture. I started getting upset at myself for not being able to get up and take care of things. Marie got the idea that she wanted a puppy of her own and found some puppies she really wanted to look at. I told her this was not the time to be bringing in another mouth to feed or a mess maker to clean up after. I had a very hard time telling her no and we ended up with a new puppy named Duke, after my favorite actor, John Wayne. It worked out because having to get up and take care of the puppy was great exercise for Marie and she started progressing a lot faster. She called him her therapy puppy.

In November, about a month after I got home there was going to be a benefit dinner for us. Our friend that worked with Marie at the bank, the same friend who rented us the house after the house fire, had organized a group of people to get this going. She teamed up with some others who were willing to help and put together a wonderful fundraising dinner. It was the first time we were out of the house for something other than a doctor appointment and had some fun. I was amazed at the turnout. It was a little overwhelming to have so many people there for us. I was very impressed at how our friends had worked together to make this happen. The pastor of the church we used to attend also organized a fundraiser with the youth groups in the area to sell t-shirts. It makes me smile every time I see one of these shirts being worn around town.

The next thing on the to-do list was to figure out how to get my foot in the right position. This meant I needed another surgery. In December I had surgery on my Achilles tendon to allow my foot to release from its stuck position. This meant more time in bed. When the boot was taken off, my foot flopped loose with hardly any control of it until it healed. When it healed, it locked back into place but in the proper position this time. I have some movement of it now but not much. The tendon going to my big toe was severed completely, meaning I have no use of it at all. I have no feeling in some places on my leg and foot but in other spots my foot is super sensitive to the touch because of the nerve damage. Still to this day, I have to sleep with my foot uncovered because even the weight of a blanket causes me pain. Any little bump would send waves of pain through my foot and up my leg. Sometimes it would happen out of the blue for no reason at all. I was in constant unwavering pain in every bone of my body, aching and writhing in mind numbing uncomfortableness. And as an added bonus, I would get what felt like an electric shock through my foot and leg that lasted for what seemed like minutes multiple times a day when the nerves would get aggravated. When this happened I would scream out in pain. Many times I've woken up in the middle of the night screaming in sudden pain. It felt like I would explode if I didn't let it out in a scream.

That year the kids did all the Christmas decorating. It became a tradition to let the kids decorate however they wanted after that. It wasn't always organized but it was way more fun this way. Marie's dad came to visit for Christmas and brought some really nice gifts for everyone. He seemed friendlier than he used to be, more genuine almost. He had come to the benefit dinner and since then he was making an effort to spend some time with Marie. I don't know if it was losing his mom or the accident that softened him up but at least it wasn't so uncomfortable when he was around. Marie started to talk to him more regularly than she had before.

We still had regular doctor visits and this meant multiple, hour long trips in the car every week. One of Marie's friends loaned us a motorized wheelchair for me to use for a while. Marie was walking and getting around pretty well by now but I still had a long way to go. This was a huge help for me to get around easier and be able to get out more. This chair made it easier to go see Amber cheer at the middle school basketball games. It felt good to be back out into the community and see people again. Most people were very friendly and genuinely concerned for us. We would get approached everywhere we went and we answered the same questions a lot but we didn't mind at all. It was nice to have people that cared about us. We didn't mind telling people about our story or how our lives were going. We even did interviews for three different newspapers and one radio interview. It was hard for me to believe that people were this interested in us.

It was difficult for us to make meals at home. Marie had one usable arm and I couldn't stand on my feet very long at all. The kids helped make meals often but we ate out at restaurants a lot. There were many times we would get to the register and our meal had already been paid for by someone. Occasionally a local church would bring us meals right to our house. It meant so much to know that people cared and noticed and wanted to help. I think a lot of this was because of Marie's amazing attitude. She was nice to absolutely everyone we met and always had a smile on her face. The outpouring of care and attention was more than I ever could have expected. I appreciate every single person who did anything at all with us in mind. After a while people started calling us an inspiration and it weighed on me. I was working hard to get better and stronger. Knowing that people were watching every move we made was both a blessing and a curse. I wanted to allow people to see our progress but it also made me feel like I couldn't make a single mistake without it being magnified. I felt like if I or my kids did anything people didn't approve of, they would turn on us. For instance, Marie spoke with someone about their teenagers' reckless driving close to where we live and the person took offense to what she had to say. The lady threw it in Marie's face that she had been to our benefit dinner by saying "I even came to your benefit" like that was supposed to somehow make it ok to treat us however you want? I believe that it's perfectly ok to consider it an investment in someone's future when you help them because you want to see them succeed and do well. It's bothersome when they go the other direction. I understand that all too well after the time and money I invested into members of my family. Believe me when I say we're not a wasted investment but that doesn't mean we have to agree with your opinion all the time either.

At first, I thought everyone who talked to us was being nice because they liked or respected us. This is true for the most part but there were other times that I wasn't so sure. There were some who just pitied us. Please understand, caring and pitying are two different things. Someone would ask how we were doing and if I tried to actually tell them how things were going they got very disinterested. I would feel like an idiot trying to talk to a wall. It seemed like they just expected me to say we were fine or give a one word answer. I had a hard time figuring out which ones were genuinely interested so I just started telling everyone who asked that we were doing great. This seemed to appease everyone and I didn't have to pick through the ones that didn't really want to know. Then there were others. Like the lady we saw in Wal-Mart. We were having a hard time sleeping and decided to get some new pillows. We bought two cheap pillows while we were picking up a few groceries. The pillows made our cart look like it was completely full. We finished our shopping and as we were about to leave I started hurting and we stopped at the benches by the entrance for me to rest for a minute. A woman who looked to be in her sixties was walking in the store and stopped to look at our shopping cart. She turned toward who I assume to be her husband and said very loud and angrily "See, a whole cart full!" She never spoke to me or Marie or acknowledged that we were even there. She turned and stomped on through the store like she was disgusted by us. I have no idea who this person was. I have never seen her before or after that so why she felt it was any of her business what was in our shopping cart I don't know. We weren't getting government assistance or borrowing money and we paid cash for everything we bought. We didn't buy new fancy things with money that was donated to us but we did have four teenage kids to feed. Even on a tight budget, it takes a lot of food to feed six people three meals a day. When we shop we buy things in bulk or we stock up for weeks at a time so we are not going to the store multiple times, wasting time and fuel. I started wondering how many people looked at us like that and just didn't have the outspokenness that this lady did.

Because of our story there are a lot more people who know who we are than we could have ever imagined. I know there were so many people who donated to us and I want to do right by every single one of them, from the smallest donation to the one who paid our mortgage. It weighs on my heart that I owe a debt that I can never repay. I started to worry that everywhere we went people were watching what we spent and what we bought. You might say I was over thinking it but I've seen the looks people give us. I know the conversations that take place about what others think we should or shouldn't be doing. I feared that I would let everyone down if we didn't meet a certain standard. What if my kids started acting up in the community or causing trouble? I made sure even the kids knew that eyes were on them now more than ever. This is a lot of pressure for someone who is just trying to recover from an accident. There were so many people who actually cared and I hate for them to not get the recognition. To those, I say thank you. I want to be the person you can be proud to say you helped at my lowest point. I promise to do the very best I can every day.

CHAPTER TWENTY-THREE

Moving Forward

A year before the accident we had invested in some cattle we were planning to breed. That winter one of our cows drowned in our pond. The pond was shallow enough to walk all the way across. It must have gotten stuck in the ice or something. I'm not sure what happened but I do know that we couldn't afford to keep taking losses like this. I had high hopes for the money we could make breeding cattle but now we were down to just two cows. I was still trying to understand why unexplainable things like this continued to happen. It was a slow moving avalanche of bad luck.

Now that my foot was in the right position, I started going to physical therapy to strengthen my leg. As I got more confident in my ability to stand, I started trying to walk and I noticed my knee would just go wherever it wanted. I really had no control of it. I had a knee surgery coming up in February but I had no idea just how bad I needed it until the doctor explained why my knee acted this way. I had several torn ligaments and tendons and my ACL was torn completely off the bone. My knee was reconstructed using cadaver parts and screws. I've been told by people who have had knee surgeries that it's very painful. To give you an idea of what I was going through, the knee surgery was painful but it was nothing compared to the pain in the rest of my body.

This was the new normal for a while. I would work my butt off in therapy and then it would be time for another surgery. We would go to doctor visits and therapy and then recover from surgery and start all over again. I asked Marie one morning for some coffee and she told me I needed to get up and take care of myself because she hurt just as bad as I did. I felt she had a point so I got up and started working harder to get better. It was a challenge just to walk at all. I continued to stretch and work my body the best I could and go to therapy three times a week. I went from being bed ridden, to being in the wheelchair, to using a walker and then using a cane. I was determined to get my strength back. I spent an hour every morning stretching and working on my leg and my core strength. I did every stretch and exercise that I thought would help. I knew if God would bring me this far he would help me keep going.

I had developed a blood clot and had and IVC filter put in while I was in ICU. When I went in to have it removed, I was surprised that they didn't put me to sleep for it. I got to watch them pull this large metal thing through my body and out of a vein in my neck. It got stuck half way through and I could feel the guy tugging on it. It was a very weird feeling to say the least. Now that all of my major surgeries were over I really hit the rehab hard. As soon as I could get down the stairs at our home I started trying to lift weights again with the boys. The first time I tried, I couldn't bench press the 45lb bar. Matt had to lift it off me. I had taken pride in my physical fitness in the past and now I was starting over from scratch. I was weaker now than I was the first time I ever touched a weight. I had no physical strength whatsoever and the limitations of my wrists kept me from holding anything properly. I kept trying until I could get the bar up and started using dumbbells for everything else. At physical therapy I went from working my wrists, to my ankle, to my knee, to strength and mobility training.

In April of 2015 there was a high school combine being held at the Rams practice facility in St Louis. The need for my teenage boys to decide what they wanted for their future was always on my mind so I signed them up. I knew that I couldn't help them get their future started but I could point them in the right direction. If there was any chance at all that one or both of them could attract enough attention for a scholarship I had to try. I wasn't able to drive yet so I had to guide a young driver through city traffic. It really wasn't that bad but I'm paranoid in vehicles now so it was very nerve racking. We had fun but at the end of the day it was obvious that they were not going to be college athletes. I started talking to them about other options and told them they needed to start making the hard decisions about their future. Mike wanted to go into law enforcement and Matt wanted to work with his hands. I had told them for a long time there were three options, college, military or a job but most important it all starts with a high school diploma. Mike made his mind up and went to talk to a Marine recruiter that summer. Matt had his mind made up for a long time to be a Marine but he kept his eyes open for trade schools that he might like.

In May 2015, Marie and I attended the court hearing for the man who hit us. I was angry and I wanted to be there to see him sentenced. I wanted him to see what he had done to us even though just seeing the physical damage doesn't tell the story of all we went through and are still struggling with. It doesn't tell of the pain, the surgeries, the emotional trauma, what our families went through or what this did to our kids. There is no way he could know the financial strain he put us under. He was drunk when he hit us. Actually he was more than drunk, he was three times the legal limit. He had only been out of prison for about a month when the accident happened and he didn't have a driver license. He was driving a borrowed vehicle and neither he nor the owner of the vehicle had insurance. He was charged with two counts of aggravated driving under the influence. He pled guilty and received a sentence of 4years and 3 months that would run concurrent with his previous sentence. This means his time in prison would count towards all of his crimes, not just the one he was sentenced to for hitting us. We were told he would be required to serve at least 85% of that time. It wasn't fair at all. We were sentenced to a lifetime of pain and suffering because of someone who couldn't stay out of prison for more than a month. I didn't understand God's plan but I knew there must be one. I had two choices. I could let the anger take over and it would most likely consume my every thought or I could find a way to forgive. Not for him, but so that I could move on with my life. There wasn't anything that could be done or said that would change the fact that Marie and I would deal with these injuries the rest of our lives but there was no reason to allow it to destroy the life we had left. Before we went to court that day I stopped and bought a nice new bible. After the sentencing he was escorted past us. Marie stopped them and said the words "I forgive you." I couldn't say the words but I gave him the bible. I thought if he used his time to read it maybe he could change his life. Maybe this wouldn't happen to someone else the next time he gets out. Whatever the result was going to be, I couldn't keep that hatred in my heart. It was way too powerful and it would have controlled me.

Later that month Marie had to have carpal tunnel surgery. Having only one good arm caused her to overuse it. The surgery went well and she recovered quickly. She wanted to do as much for herself as she could so she learned to do what she had to. In no time at all she was back to doing the things she enjoyed. She developed a passion for photography and started doing our family pictures herself. She had dabbled in it off and on for years but now she had time to really get good at it. She started taking pictures for others and was able to make a little money from time to time. She had a lot of crafts and artsy things that kept her busy and gave her a way to connect back into the community. She amazed me at how resilient she was. She always had a project going. This was a hassle for the rest of the household because she always needed an assistant. (Just being honest) Although I have to say that I'm extremely proud of her for all she was able to accomplish with one arm and fighting through pain.

Marie's grandma left her a few thousand dollars when she passed. She and I put our heads together and decided we needed one more really great family vacation before our kids started leaving the nest. We had been on cheap adventures in the past like float trips and camping trips but Marie and I were in no shape to sleep outside. We went over the finances and Marie decided she wanted to use the money her grandma left her to pay for a family vacation and wanted it to be awesome. We decided to go to Universal Studios in Florida. It was going to be cheaper to drive but there was no way I could handle sitting in a vehicle for that long of a trip so we had to plan wisely. We hadn't seen any relatives in a while so we thought we could stop and visit along the way and that would give us just the right amount of stops. So in June we traveled to see Marie's dad. That was about all I could take before it got too uncomfortably painful. We stayed one night and left the next day. We drove to Kentucky to visit my aunts and cousins that live in that area.

I couldn't drive at all yet and I was a basket case watching someone else drive. I had a melt down on the way to Kentucky and almost decided to go home. Once I calmed down, we got back on the road and had a nice visit. We stayed the night and left for Tennessee the next morning. We stopped at my Uncles' house in Tennessee and stayed the night. We drove from there to Pigeon Forge. We all had a great time there. By this time I was exhausted and we stayed an extra night to rest up. The kids didn't mind at all, they were having so much fun they didn't want to leave. We drove through the Smoky Mountains and we all enjoyed the scenery. Amber even said she might move there someday. We took our time and stopped often to get out and keep from getting too uncomfortable, which gave us a chance to see a lot of sights but also made the trip longer. We made it to Florida and got settled into a hotel. When we made it to Universal, I rented one of the motorized wheelchairs to ride around. I was so exhausted just getting to the gate that I thought I might have made a mistake for even trying. Once I was able to sit down, I kept up with the kids just fine and they were very patient and understanding. We all had fun but I felt weird sitting in a wheelchair again. Whe wearing pants and a nice shirt you can't see most of my scars and I would see people staring and I knew they were wondering why a guy my age who looked healthy was in a scooter. I tried not to let it bother me and went on with our day. We took another rest day and started heading to the gulf coast. It was a long drive but well worth it. Our friends welcomed us with open arms and invited us to stay with them for the weekend. We spent some time visiting and I was glad to keep the promise I made in the hospital and hang out on the beach with them. We headed home after that. I really wanted to make one more stop and see my fathers' side of the family but we promised the kids we would have them back home in time to get to church camp. We drove home and I think I slept for about a week.

Once I had recovered from the trip I went back to therapy. I had a long way to go and I needed to get back on track. The kids all continued to play sports. They had gotten a little behind after the accident, from the emotional standpoint along with just being able to make it to practices and things like that. They had to work even harder than normal to get back into the swing of things. I could tell Mike had a lot of anger built up towards the man who hit us and I couldn't let him go through life with that burden weighing him down. I explained that things happen for a reason and only God knows his plan. I told him that if it had not happened, Marie and I would not get to be home every day with him. We were going to continue getting better and we needed to enjoy this time together while we have it. He understood and he calmed down but I know this affected him deeply and I hope that he can let go of the past so he can have a positive future.

CHAPTER TWENTY-FOUR

Pure Determination

For the next few months I worked harder than ever to get stronger. My mind was healing faster than my body and I was getting very anxious sitting at home with nothing to do. I spent all the time I could handle exercising. It was a slow process but it was working. I was starting to see results so I pushed harder. It took everything I had to stay on track and not get discouraged. I was constantly tweaking my routine and adding stretches or new exercises. Many people told me to slow down or take it easy but I refused. I worked at it until I had nothing left every day. There were still parts of my body that didn't work or didn't work right and I wasn't quitting. I wanted to get back as much function as possible. Pain was still the norm. All day, every day I feel pain all through my body. There were times I became angry and blamed the man who hit us. Sometimes I thought this was the answer to my request to spend more time with my family but if it was, then why couldn't I enjoy it? Other times, I wondered if I did something to deserve this. Is this my punishment for my sins? I have lied, cheated, stole, done drugs, slept with married women, I've beaten men unconscious with my bare hands and I'm sure there's more. I know that Christ paid the price for my sins on the cross. I also know that things happen for a reason. Regardless of the answer, I prayed. I prayed hard and I prayed continually every single day. I prayed that God would give me wisdom to understand and the ability to get stronger and better. I prayed that God would take away my wife's pain. I've read that sometimes you pay for the sins of your father so I prayed, "Please God, let me bear the burden of their pain. Let me bear the burdens of my mistakes instead of my children. Whatever it takes, don't make them suffer because of me." I started to feel an uncontrollable guilt. I saw my children struggling and I saw the torment my wife was going through. I couldn't help but feel responsible. I was the one who had to have a motorcycle. I was the one who made the decision to ride it that night. I was the one who decided to go past our turn and take a scenic ride. I made these decisions and now my entire family has to suffer because of it. My wife was going through horrible pain, even months later. I felt responsible and there wasn't anything I could do about it.

I told myself that I had not made it this far in life to get knocked down and not get back up. I had overcome so much already. I have a wonderful family, we have our dream home and we had learned to work hard together to achieve our goals. I started hearing things like, just relax and enjoy being alive. To me that sounded like giving up and that's just not me. I believe there's always room for improvement. Even when I'm relaxing I'm usually thinking of the next step. God had saved us and provided for us in a miraculous way and I couldn't just sit back and let that slip through my hands. I spent a full year after the accident going through surgeries and physical therapy. By the time that year was up, I could walk and my surgeries were finished or so I thought at the time. I was told I had gotten all I could out of therapy but I was still exercising at home. I bought a couple pieces of gym equipment that would help me move forward. The knee surgeon was very impressed with the flexibility I had achieved when I saw him for my last check up. I was even walking without a cane. I had a very noticeable limp but I could walk.

I made steady progress and I got stronger and started looking healthier. I put some weight back on and got back to the weight I was before the accident. I started feeling stronger but I paid a hard price for every step forward. I was seeing an urologist to monitor the healing of some damage to my bladder. I was healing nicely but I was still having some issues. When my pelvis broke, it came out of the skin right next to my genitals. There's some scar tissue and a lot of numbness. I'm not sure if it's from the scarring or the nerve damage. The doctor did some blood tests and found that the damage had caused my body to stop producing testosterone like it should. Let me put this into perspective. Some of the side effects of low testosterone are; erectile dysfunction, lowered libido or desire, extreme fatigue, reduction of muscle mass, increase in body fat, back pain, reduced bone density, risk of heart attack, brain fog (difficulty concentrating), memory problems, insomnia, severe depression, lack of motivation, irritability, anger, and loss of patience. This meant that all the gains I had made so far were without a normal level of testosterone. I had driven myself past the emotions and physical limitations without the hormones that would normally fuel that kind of progress. It was pure determination and the will of God that had gotten me this far. The doctor prescribed an injection of testosterone for me to try and it worked, I felt better than I had before. It didn't do anything for the pain but I now had more motivation and energy. I looked for positive ways to burn off the extra energy I had now.

I started working on our hobby farm like we had talked about. There was always something that needed done. I pushed myself to do as much as my body would allow. In my mind I felt like I could tackle the world and maybe even go back to work. Reality on the other hand was not so positive. I would find a project to start and have the kids help me get it going. I couldn't do nearly as much as I thought I could. If I used a hammer it would fly out of my hand because I couldn't grip it and every hit sent sharp pain up my wrists. I had to stop often to catch my breath or work out a cramp. I would try to move something or lift something and just didn't have the strength I thought I did. My in-laws came over often to lend a hand. Marie's step dad was in his upper sixties now and had been a truck driver since he got home from Vietnam. He wasn't in that great of health himself but would work circles around me and I was in my thirties. I once considered myself a halfway decent athlete and a very good worker. To see everyone around me able to do more than I could made me want to work harder. The kids were patient with us and did everything we asked of them, even though I could see it was taking a toll on them. They had to pick up all the slack and they would get frustrated at times. After about an hour or two, I would be hurting so bad I could barely make it back to the house to sit down. Two hours of work would cost me three days of torturing pain to recover. What made it worse was that sitting for more than an hour was almost as painful as standing. My back would ache and my leg would start cramping. Standing for too long caused crippling pain and sitting too long caused miserable aching and cramping. I was always up and down without being able to do much.

I started doing some research on the medications the doctors had me on and I didn't like some of the side effects they came with so I stopped taking everything but the pain pills and testosterone. My body went into withdrawals. Some of the meds had mind altering qualities and this was an extremely difficult time for me and Marie to get along. I was irritable and angry and sad and would go off the handle over any little thing. It took me a while to realize what was causing the problem. Once I did I tried to explain it to Marie but she just told me I needed to get it figured out because she was tired of me yelling at her again.

About the time I thought I had it under control one of my doctors told me I needed to get off the pain killers. "By being on them so long your body has to be dependent on them. I hate to say it this way but by now you're technically a drug addict." I took offense to it. He said he was going to wean me off of them but I was stubborn and wanted to prove a point so I didn't take another pill after that. I came in the next month and showed him the full bottle of pain pills he had prescribed the month before. I said "I'm no addict." I didn't know it but I was going through withdrawals again. I thought I was acting normal but Marie and the kids said I had an attitude pretty much all the time. I tried to control it but at times I honestly didn't know what I was trying to control. It felt like everyone around me had the problem not me. I finally conceded that it was probably me that was wrong and did the best I could until the feelings passed. As much as I hate to admit it, the doctor was right. My body had become dependent on these drugs and now everyone around me was suffering for it. What made it worse was that the pain hadn't stopped. I wasn't taking anything for it any more but I still hurt constantly and now there was nothing I could do to relieve it.

I volunteered to help coach the eighth grade football team Alex was on. I needed to do something positive and constructive. I love football so this was perfect. I couldn't do much and they didn't really need me but it was fun. I felt like I bonded with a few of the players and the coaches treated me well. We had a great season and I enjoyed it but it took a toll on my body. After the games I would come home and collapse in a chair and try not to cry out in pain. All that pain just from being on my feet for a couple hours. I wasn't going to let it stop me from doing the things I enjoy. I kept going and pushing myself as far as I could. I got to a point that I had to make a decision. Keep doing what I was doing, knowing that the pain was only going to keep getting worse or quit and stay home. Quitting was simply not an option. I had to toughen up, that's all there was to it. I trained myself to ignore pain. I told myself "There's no such thing as pain, it's all in your head." I imagined those movies where a monk is able to withstand unbelievable pain without flinching because of his state of mind. Sometimes it would come on fast and take me by surprise but other times I could feel it coming and I was able to prepare myself and act like it wasn't there. It may sound silly but it worked. Sometimes I could just shut it off. I knew it was there but I was able to just ignore it. The problem would come later when I had pushed myself for hours and then get home and try to relax. The pain I had been holding back would come on like a tidal wave and last for what seemed like an eternity.

One year from the accident fell on a Sunday. The next morning Marie got a phone call from her employer asking her to come in for a meeting. When she got home she said they fired her. Before we finished the conversation I got a call from my employer. I was told that if I was not released to go back to work that I would be fired as well. I asked if I could get some time to get an appointment with my doctor and ask what he thought so they gave me one week. I went to see one of my surgeons and he said there was no way I could do the job I did before. I asked him to release me and he refused. I told him "I've never, not worked before, what do I do now?" He didn't have the answers I wanted to hear. He said maybe someday I would be able to work but it wouldn't be anytime soon. When I called to tell my employer, they said they were going to fire me. I asked if there were any other positions I could try. They told me if I couldn't come back to work at 100% and do the job I did before then they didn't want me back. I was in a bit of shock and anger. I had worked for that company for 14 years and spent 60 hours a week doing any nasty job I was asked to do and they just tossed me out as soon as they were legally allowed to. Upset just doesn't quite cover the emotion at the time. Our income had been the temporary disability from each of our employers which was less than we normally make. I had been told to apply for social security so I did. I went for an exam and they turned me down initially but approved it right away on the second try when they had all my medical records. We also applied for the state medical insurance. At least this way we would have insurance coverage and now we wouldn't have a co pay or if there was one it wouldn't be much. The medical bills for all of our combined care was somewhere around two million dollars. We had co pays on a lot of that and we had already used all of the donations we had been given to pay doctor bills and keep our regular bills caught up. The social security I started getting was even less than I was getting from the disability insurance through work. Marie was turned down twice for social security even with a paralyzed arm. She was still getting the temporary disability through her employer which helped. She applied for food assistance and we were turned down. They said our disability income was too high to get assistance.

There was a storm in Autumn that damaged the electric pole in our back yard. The pole was leaning so badly that the live wire was only about five foot off the ground. It was a serious hazard and had to be repaired. We called the power company to come out and look at it and they told us it wasn't their responsibility. How could it not be their responsibility? They said the pole had been put in so long ago that the rules had changed since then and when we bought the property we bought the pole with it. Any cost of this repair was going to fall on us. Why do these things keep happening? I believe that God gives you only what you can handle. I was starting to wonder if maybe he was testing me to see how much it would take before I break. We contacted a local electrician who was willing to do the job at a reasonable rate. We had to replace the pole and the entire setup needed redone. Even with the cheap rate it was still a huge expense for us but God will always provide when you need it if you have faith. We had just enough from the back pay from Social Security to pay for the repair. It was simply Gods' grace and mercy that provided at the exact time we needed it. It was just another step forward.

After eighteen years of working and teaching and parenting, happiness, stress, struggles, pride, fear, courage, faith and determination, Mike made it to his senior year of high school. I had the privilege of watching him play football and it really hit me hard on senior night. As Marie and I walked him down the track in front of most of the people we knew in town, all I could think about was how grateful I was to live to see this day. It had not been that long ago that I couldn't get out of a wheelchair. To be able to walk my son down that track at his last home football game was more of an accomplishment than anyone could know. It was nothing short of a miracle. I can't imagine how he would have felt if we had not made it and he had been alone on this day. As I limped down the track trying to keep up, I was choking back tears. This was Mike's night but a huge day for me.

CHAPTER TWENTY-FIVE

Trying To Find Normal

We went to Marie's brother's house for a visit and he mentioned something about wanting to hang out more like we used to. I said I have free time now so you tell me when and where and I'll be there. He asked me to start coming over once a week after he got home from work. I agreed and we made it a regular thing. We saw a couple movies but mostly just hung out in his basement and shot pool and talked. I probably did most of the talking getting things off my chest but it was nice to have a friend again. It only lasted a few weeks before he started cancelling our guy nights. He changed the day of the week to a day he thought would work better but it got harder to find a day that he wasn't busy or tired from work. He finally told me one night that he would call me when he had time to hang out again. I'm still waiting on that phone call.

I was still having some trouble dealing with my emotional outbursts so I decided to stop taking the testosterone shots to see if that made a difference. I thought that it would be better for my family if I was nicer and easier to get along with even if it meant I would suffer all the side effects of low testosterone. I had gone through withdrawals of other drugs; the ones they gave me in the hospital, the ones I got off by my own choice and the ones the doctor told me I needed to stop taking. It wasn't just that I didn't take the drug that bothered me. My hormones were all out of sync. The difference of how much better I had felt taking testosterone and what I was feeling now sent me into a very dark depression. I felt worthless and without purpose. I felt like I had become one of those people who live off the government and milk the system. I wanted to work and take care of my family. I wanted to feel like I was worth something to someone but I didn't. I know I had many people who cared about me but I didn't feel like myself anymore. I had worked since I was thirteen years old. The only period of my life I didn't work was also when I got into the most trouble. I was terrified of what would happen if I became too lazy. I had people telling me that I looked great considering what we went through. I may seem strong but even my closest confidant, Marie, didn't see all the pain I was suffering. She sees 99% of it but I'm afraid of what she would think of me if she saw how weak I really am on the inside. I hide as much of it as I can. I smile when all I really want to do is burst into tears. Sometimes I blow up in anger because the pain is so disturbing, both physically and emotionally. I refuse to look weak in my children's eyes. I would rather them think I'm a jerk than have them pity me.

The winter was awful. The cold caused my pain to intensify and I was in constant misery. I wasn't angry any more but the pain never ceased and sometimes it was all I could think about. I had no drive. I felt no desire to do anything. There were times the pain on the inside was more than the physical pain on the outside. This was the only time in my life that I gave serious thought to suicide. The physical pain was uncontrollable and if I took anything for it I was an addict. I couldn't take care of my family any more. In fact, they were taking care of me. My emotions were all over the place. I woke up in pain every single night. I was suffering from lack of good sleep. I was just suffering period and I wanted it to stop. After the peaceful feeling I felt when I slipped away on the pavement that night, I know the only time I will know true peace will be when I close my eyes for the final time. The only reason I'm still here to tell this story is because of my wife and kids. I knew all too well what it would do to them for me to end my life. I couldn't do that to them. They saved me without even knowing it. It took tremendous determination just to force myself out of bed every morning. I pushed my body to the limit and kept going. I can't quit! There is no room for failure! I will continue on, even during the times my own mind feels like a prison. I want to be an example of faith, strength and perseverance. For months I choked back feelings that were overwhelming me. I came up with a new motto. "Keep putting one foot in front of the other." You have to keep moving forward. It doesn't matter what happens or what obstacle is in front of you, if you can take one step forward you can keep going. If you can take one step, you can take another. I thank God every day for all he has done for me and my family. Even on the days I didn't think I could make it, I was still grateful for the life I was blessed with. As bad as it got at times, God always provided another step to take.

Marie and I had become dependent on our kids to handle

the work around our little farm. We had to ask them for a lot and we began to see that they were getting weighed down by it. I still believe it was building character for them. I don't regret having them do so much work but I do regret how I handled it at times. I tried to be fair but I'm not always an easy person to get along with. They did their part and more. They didn't give up and they stayed strong for us. I don't think they know just how strong they are yet but I'm sure some day they will. One day they will have a trial and look back and say I can do this because I've been through worse. I can do this because my parents went through worse. I know they will be great at whatever life they choose to lead because they know where their strength comes from and the examples were set. I'm incredibly proud of each of my kids and I pray that they find true happiness in their lives and are always there for each other.

Mike had enlisted in the United States Marine Corps delayed entry program. He was to leave for boot camp at the end of summer after high school graduation. I was in the same program my senior year, when I made so many bad decisions. I was terrified Mike would get into trouble before graduation like I did. I was so worried about it that we convinced him to move his ship date up to right after graduation instead of in the fall so he wouldn't have so much time to make mistakes. It was a hard decision to ask your child to leave even sooner than they planned but I believe idle hands are the devil's workshop. He came into our bedroom one night in January and said "Dad, I need your help." His recruiter told him he was overweight and if he didn't lose it he was getting cut from the program. At the end of football season he was 45lbs overweight by boot camp standards. He had lost some of it on his own and while working with the recruiter but had stalled out. I told him it was going to be hard, I wouldn't take it easy on him and he might hate me before it was over but I could get him there. He said he would do whatever it took to be at his goal by graduation. I put him on a very strict diet and put together a workout program designed just for him. He impressed me with how dedicated he was and he started gradually moving toward his goal.

Just before graduation I had a talk with him about dedication and perseverance. I told him "You come back a Marine or you don't come back at all." This was not meant to be cruel or said in a hateful way. It hurt me to say those words but I felt there was good reason for it. I didn't want him to get in a tough spot and think, oh well I can just quit and go home. I wanted him to make something of himself. I would always love him no matter what but I couldn't let him think that I would always be here to bail him out. I don't know how long I can keep things together and I don't want my kids to suffer if I fall apart. I've spent twenty years protecting my children from people like me. The time is quickly approaching that I need to protect them from ME. They cannot fail because I am not strong enough to continue taking care of them. It's time for them to become adults. It took me so long to figure out how to get my life together and I want my kids to have a huge head start towards that.

The big day came. We sat in the high school gym as the seniors walked in two by two. I had watched many of these young people grow up right before my eyes. I coached some of them. A few had been in our home and played in our back yard. A couple had been in our youth group years before. I felt connected in one way or another to this entire class of graduates. They all took their seats and the principal began her introduction. She recognized the graduates who were about to leave for the military and asked them to stand. As they did, the entire gym erupted into a standing ovation that was deafening. The pride I felt at that moment was unquestionably worth every second of time and effort I put into being a father. I had never felt that much accomplishment before that day. My heart swelled with emotion. I was overjoyed that my son had made it. We watched as the first of my family accepted a diploma. I had not graduated, neither had my parents or grandparents. I have cousins who have but no one in my direct lineage had a high school diploma. Right after the ceremony we took him to St Louis. The next morning he was leaving for San Diego California.

I had been holding in my emotions and tears for months. I didn't want Mike to see me break down before he left. He needed to see strength not weakness. Walking out of the building after seeing him for the last time for thirteen weeks, I couldn't hold it in any longer. I burst out into a hard cry and leaned on Marie. I could barely stand for the combination of sadness and pride from sending off my oldest son. The baby boy I held in my arms when he was only 4lbs 4oz and covered in wires was going away from home to become a man. There was no more I could do. There was no more I could say. It was up to him now. I did the very best I could. Was it enough?

We hired a lawyer to protect ourselves from the insurance company who threatened to sue us for all the medical bills which had gone up to around two million dollars. The guy who hit us had nothing and neither did the person who owned the vehicle. The one who owned the vehicle even filed bankruptcy to keep us from trying to sue them. We had insurance and our policy had uninsured motorist coverage. For the two of us we were covered for $100,000. My health insurance company was trying to take that before we got it. Our lawyer was able to get them to settle for less than half of it and after his fee we were given a check for $55,000. This was going to give us enough money to go to California to see Mike's graduation from boot camp. We decided to invest some of it into animals that had a high profit margin. We bought some Boer goats to raise and breed. Right after that our air conditioning unit went out. Marie's brother came to look at it and said if we could afford it, now would be the time to replace the system. The unit was over thirty years old and the furnace needed replaced as well because it was leaking carbon monoxide into our house. He did the work for us but it still cost us close to $8,000. Right after this job was finished, our septic backed up into our basement. This was the third time since we lived here that this had happened. We couldn't get a plumber out to fix it properly because it was an extremely old setup and it was out of code. Every plumber we talked to told us we had to have an entire new system put in. It cost us $23,000. Why it cost this much I don't know. It was explained to us and we were told there was no other way to get it up to code and we couldn't find anyone else willing to work on it so we went with it. While the septic repair was being done we had another water line break in our front yard. I rented some equipment and got some help from friends to repair it. So let's do the math. Septic-$23,000, Central air and furnace roughly -$8,000, Boer goats roughly-$2000, trip to California for five people to see Mike graduate-$5000, overdue vehicle repairs-$2,000, invested in a cd at the bank to save for Matt's boot camp graduation-$5,000 and the rest went toward our bills and upkeep. We were back to where we started financially but I can't even imagine where we would have been if that settlement had not come at that exact time. Should I have been upset that all those things happened and cost us the settlement? We chose to be grateful that it came at the right time to take care of the problems. Gods timing is always perfect.

For the next thirteen weeks I stayed busy. I couldn't just sit around and think about how Mike might be doing. The high school was looking for a football coach. I knew I wasn't qualified to be a head coach but I started asking questions about how to get involved. I spoke with the superintendant about volunteering. I told him that this community had been wonderful to my family. I said football is something I'm passionate about and if this was a way for me to give back, I'd be glad to do it. Once I had completed all the requirements I spoke with the now head coach. He had coached sports for fifty years and I thought it would be an honor to learn from someone with his experience. He asked what my intentions were and I told him that I hoped to gain enough experience to be a head coach someday. He agreed to allow me to volunteer and sort of took me under his wing. Another coach on the staff was an officer in the National Guard and a high school teacher. He stood out to me as someone who had a good rapport with the student athletes and was willing to teach me some of the things I would need to know and I grew to have a great respect for him. All together there were six coaches on staff and there were two of us who were volunteering our time.

Alex wanted to find a way to make money so he could buy a vehicle before his 16th birthday. I was happy to help him because I had made it a point to push my kids to work hard and make their own way. Mike earned the money for his first vehicle and Matt had an old pickup Marie's step-dad gave him but he spent an entire summer's wages fixing it up. All of our kids know what it's like to put in a hard day's work. This is one of the things I take the most pride in and hope they do as well. They all know how to work hard and not give up. I pushed each of them to go beyond the normal limits. They have all mowed lawns or shoveled snow or raked leaves. They know to help those in need and be respectful. Sometimes I may have been a little too hard on them but I believe it made them stronger. I knew I had done something right when my 13 and 14 year olds asked when it was going to be their turn to get a job because they wanted spending money. They knew things were earned and not just handed to them. Alex earned enough to afford a cheap vehicle and I agreed to pitch in to help him get something somewhat dependable. We found a truck he was satisfied with and he began to practice for driver education at school.

Amber surprised me by asking if she could play football going into eighth grade. She was strong and tough enough but I was against it at first. I'm not saying girls can't or shouldn't play football but it causes issues. I didn't want my daughter to be the kid causing issues or getting singled out by all the boys. She talked me into it and I decided to let her try it, as long as she was willing to give it her best. She wasn't a star athlete but she did ok and I was proud of how tough she proved she could be. She also surprised us by participating in the local beauty pageant. She didn't place but it was quite an experience. She had a great summer. How many little girls can say they were in a pageant, on a championship softball team, the cheer squad, the scholar team, rode horses and played football all in the same year? She's always had my heart but she really impressed me that summer. She did all that and still managed to keep her chores done and her grades were excellent during the school year. I attended as many of her practices as I could and we were at all of her games as well.

It's funny that just a year earlier I had told a friend of ours that my dream job would be to be a high school football coach and I would probably do it for free just to get the opportunity. Now, here I was coaching at the high school level and doing it just for the experience. God works in mysterious ways. I was right about one thing, this was definitely for me. I loved it but I had a lot more to learn than I thought. I approached it with an open mind and a desire to contribute any way I could. Matt was now going into his senior year and Alex was going to be a freshman. I felt like I bonded with several of the younger players but the seniors including Matt didn't respond as well. The head coach was now over 80 years old and had been involved in sports his entire life. He had a lifetime of sports knowledge and I tried to learn as much as I could. I did my best to be a part of every aspect of the team. There were times it was all I could do to just stand on my feet for the whole practice. Very early into it I realized I wasn't going to be able to last the season without the testosterone. I was completely drained and no matter how bad I wanted it, I was getting weaker instead of stronger. I talked it over with Marie and she agreed that I was in a much better place now that I had something I loved to do. She was ok with me starting back with the injections. It took a little while but I figured out the dosage that would give me what I needed without the huge ups and downs. This gave me the energy I needed to continue coaching but it didn't stop the pain. It was excruciating but I love the memories I have of that season. I have said many times that it was the most fun I've ever had and the most stressful job I've ever had all at the same time.

The worst part of coaching is that having my sons on the team wasn't the great bonding experience I thought it would be. I loved watching my kids play sports, especially football. Mike had been a very good middle linebacker. He had a way of knowing what the offense was going to do before the snap of the ball. Unfortunately after our accident he got emotional and out of shape and lost a lot of playing time. Matt was the star running back all through his time in the junior football league. I loved watching him run the ball. After getting into high school he hadn't played much. As a coach and a father I pushed them to try to be the best. I was harder on my kids than anyone else on the team and Matt started to resent me for it. He didn't understand that I wanted him to be the best. He had to earn that. It wasn't something I could give him, not that he would want me to. He was the hardest worker on the team and tried to be a leader but people gravitated toward the popular guys. This really bothered him but I kept trying to push him to be the best he could. He got angry with me as the season progressed and I decided it was better to let him do his own thing than to ruin his last year of football. He had a decent season but we didn't do as well as I had hoped. Alex worked very hard and moved up to a starting spot on the freshman and junior varsity offensive line and held it all year. I would pull him out of the game for the tiniest mistakes just to prove that I wasn't playing favorites with my kid. I am very proud of them and how hard they worked to earn their spots. It makes me sad to think that I will never get to see Matt run the ball again or see Mike make another great sack on a quarterback but man was it fun. Alex is still up and coming with a ton of potential. He's small but very strong and extremely dedicated. Who knows, maybe even Amber might make a decent ball player someday.

CHAPTER TWENTY-SIX

God Is Still Working

A friend of ours needed to see a specialist in St Louis and they asked if we could drive them there since they weren't comfortable driving in the city. We agreed and as we were killing time waiting for them to finish their appointment we walked around the hall. We saw an office and on the door it said they specialize in the type of injury that Marie had in her arm. Marie's brother told us about it months earlier but the doctors she had been seeing told her there was nothing that could be done for her. We passed it up and it took me a little while to convince her to walk in and ask about it. They gave her some information and Marie had her regular doctor refer her to this specialist. Marie explained that the nerves that control her arm had been pulled out of the spinal cord causing the paralysis. What was left behind was never ending pain because of the open nerves. They sent her to another specialist who was able to perform a DREZ procedure. This is where they open the spinal cord and cauterize the nerve endings to stop the pain signals. It was a dangerous procedure but it was successful and it was an amazing relief of pain for Marie. She felt renewed and happy again. She wasn't in constant pain anymore and she was able to feel more like herself again. The doctor we had originally went to see told us this was not all she was willing to do. She was going to do a set of procedures that in the end would give Marie some slight use of her arm. We were in shock! She just wanted to get the pain to stop and now this surgeon was telling us she could do what other surgeons said was impossible. This was yet another miracle God was about to perform in our lives! Marie had already started the six month preparation for a bariatric bypass so the arm was planned for the next year. It was like we were led to that office at just the right time. It still amazes me how this happened. We stumbled across a surgeon in a hospital that performs the exact procedures that Marie needed, that other surgeons said didn't exist. Not only that but we walked into one of three hospitals in the country where this surgery is performed. I'm here to tell you that with God anything is possible! The surgeon told us at one of the pre-surgery appointments that this injury was so unique that she wanted to take Maries' file with her to use it when she went to speak at conventions as far away as Italy.

Being back on the testosterone, came with a problem. I had figured out the best dosage and was learning to recognize when my emotions weren't right. The problem was that in my mind I was ready to take on the world but my body paid the price. I pushed past my limits and abused my body to be able to coach. Although, it did help fill the time as we were waiting to get the call we were waiting for. Thirteen weeks went by and it was time to fly to California to see Mike graduate boot camp and claim the title of United States Marine. It was a remarkable experience to see our son in uniform as a member of one of the most respected military branches in the world. This was a huge win! He proved his worth and was now going to start a whole new life of his own. He had already been promoted to Private First Class during boot camp. There is a fulfillment like no other to see your child do their very best and accomplish something few people would dare to try. The ceremony was something you would have to see to fully appreciate, especially when it's your son out there on the parade deck. There were hundreds of new Marines marching in formation waiting for the moment they were released to their families. We all wanted to hug him and talk to him but of course all he wanted to do was get off base for some well deserved rest. We stayed an extra day to hang out on the beach and have a little fun but we could tell Mike just wanted to go home. Once we got home it set in that he would only be here a short time before he had to leave again. It was emotional but it was ok because all the hard work and years of patience and dedication was paying off. He was a responsible adult, well …for the most part. He was still only 18 and had some growing up to do but I couldn't be more proud of him and what he had accomplished. Not only had we raised a child to graduate and leave home but he was a Marine! The next few months revolved around where he was and what he was doing.

Marie had her bariatric surgery and was miserable for a month or more. She was in pain, couldn't eat much and had very little energy. I wasn't sure she should have the surgery at all. I wanted to help her get in shape without it but she insisted on going through with the surgery. She decided to do this because of all the weight she had gained over the years that only got worse after the accident. She was physically unable to exercise because of her permanent injuries and the medications she was on that caused weight gain. The weight was causing more pain on her joints than what she already had from the injuries. Her blood pressure was high and she was starting to have other health problems related to her weight. The surgery was successful but took a while to recover from. Once she started losing weight it came off so fast she was running out of clothes to wear. When she was able to eat somewhat normally she started feeling a lot better and was able to start getting some exercise. She was feeling great and looking better than she had in years. She was very strict with her diet and her routine. I was very proud of her dedication to make this work. She did a great job, she looks amazing and more importantly she feels much better. For her this was a major life changing event. She struggled with her weight her entire life and now she had to actually make sure she ate enough. Before the surgery she was taking handfuls of medication daily and after the surgery she was not on any medication at all. As worried as I was for her to have this done, I have to admit it was definitely the right decision.

As soon as football season was over Matt enlisted in the Marines and began making plans for his future. He scored so well on the ASVAB (Armed Services Vocational Aptitude Battery) that he qualified for a great job and was very excited. He had struggled with his schoolwork for a very long time and I was ecstatic that he did such an outstanding job on this placement test. He had also taken my advice to get his difficult classes out of the way early in high school and was now eligible for early graduation. His recruiter said he had two options to get the job he wanted. He could wait until September or he could graduate early and leave in February. He chose to get a head start and applied for early graduation.

Mike was able to make it home for Christmas after his next phase of training was finished and he filled Matt in on what boot camp would be like. It was nice to have everyone together for one last Christmas before they were truly off on their own. After the holidays we took Mike to the airport to see him off to Japan for two years. He had been talking about going to big cities and seeing the world for years and when he got the chance, he requested to go there. I tried to fill him with good sound advice while he was here. I choked back the tears and even scolded Marie for crying in front of him. We wanted him to head into this new adventure with positive feelings, not the ones of missing home. The problem with that is the pain that builds up inside. The added weight to the mountain of emotions and memories that have yet to be processed that cripples me into not feeling like a normal person. I did a good job of seeing him off without showing the sadness. I couldn't help feeling like a failure as we walked away. I know this doesn't make sense but I'm not going to see my son for two years. I don't feel at all like I did enough to prepare him for this. I was on my own at an earlier age than him but I never spent two years in another country. I don't know if I did a good enough job as a father to make him strong enough for this. Can he make good decisions? Will he be in any danger? Does he have the skills and common sense to get out of a jam? Are these things he simply needs to learn on his own or did I send him out into the world unprepared? I guess every parent feels this way at one time or another.

A short time later we were at a party for a friend. As I watched people who had been through divorces and kids who had been raised in broken homes and even some people who have given up on happiness altogether, I realized just how truly blessed I am. I looked across the table and saw the most beautiful woman in the room, my wife. She is so loving and caring. She has such a warm heart and is the only person on earth who actually understands me. I have felt alone most of my life, even when surrounded by family and friends. With Marie, I never doubt that she loves me. She cares about how I feel, what's on my mind and she listens even when I don't make sense. Marie has been an absolute rock for me to lean on and an exceptional mother to our children. I know she would do anything in her power to see us happy. I am eternally grateful to my Lord God for blessing me and my children with this incredible woman. We may not be perfect parents but as I look at our children, they will always know they had parents who loved them. We didn't just have kids and let them raise themselves. I made it my life's work to raise good children. I don't know yet how they will turn out but I'm confident we have given them every opportunity we could. There are so many kids in this world that are not a priority to their parents and I feel for them. In our home our kids and the example we set for them are the top priority. I'm far from perfect but I have taken the knowledge and experiences of my life and used them to steer our kids to better futures. My hope is that someday they will have wonderful, happy, prosperous lives and look back and know, Marie and I did all we could. We have wonderful children who fill me with pride every single day. It's not easy but it's very rewarding to see the faces of my kids mature into happy, intelligent young adults.

Matt was approved for early graduation and was going to be

headed for San Diego on February 13th 2017. The previous year had been all about Mike. Now Matt is about to leave early to start a new chapter in his life. Did I fail Matt by spending so much time on Mike? Is Matt ready? Here I am again, trapped in my own mind with no escape. I think Matt is more ready for boot camp than Mike was, but am I right? We went to St Louis to see him off and it was a little different having done this less than a year ago when Mike left. It didn't hurt any less but I was able to control my emotions until I made it home. Amber made the comment that I must have spent all my emotion on Mike. We dropped Alex and Amber off at school and I made it to our drive with tears in my eyes. Once I shut the car off, I lost it. I didn't want the kids to see it again so I held it until I got home. It boiled over and I cried harder than I ever have in my life. I told Marie I didn't know how much strength I had left. I was feeling weaker every time we sent a child off to their future. Matt had turned into a heck of a young man and now he was about to start his path to becoming a Marine. I know he didn't understand some of my parenting choices but what he doesn't know is that every decision we made about him was intended to make him a stronger and better person. He fills me with pride every time I see him.

I had to fill my time to keep myself from going mad and I needed to get stronger for the next football season so I spent a lot of time in my weight room. I was doing all the same workouts but now with my testosterone level being back to normal, I started seeing results in my appearance as well as my ability. I felt a huge difference when I would work out and now that I had energy, I could do it more often. I had spent an hour every morning stretching my leg and working on core muscles ever since I was able to get out of the hospital bed at home. If I didn't do this every day I couldn't walk because my leg would give out or cramp up throughout the day. Before the testosterone I was in the weight room for another hour three times a week. Now I could go four times a week if I really pushed myself. I started catching people's eyes looking at me around town and people would tell me how great I looked. I admit I loved it. I didn't feel like they pitied me anymore. I was asked weekly if I was back to work now or when I was going back. That's when I would get a little uncomfortable. I know that seeing my progress and knowing that I'm coaching a sport makes people think I'm all better now but they don't see what I go through daily to be able to do normal things and I try not to show weakness to people if I can help it. I've had people offer me jobs, even driving jobs. They don't know I wake up hurting every morning and have to get out of bed because the pain is too bad to lay there. They don't know the hours I spend in the morning to get ready for my day. They don't know that for me to walk "normally" I have to constantly flex every muscle from my abs down to my toes, to make my walk look normal. It takes so much concentration to walk without a limp that sometimes I don't hear when people are talking to me because I'm concentrating so hard on my walk. I don't do it just to look better. It's less painful for me this way as well. They don't know how much pain I'm in after I've been on my feet for more than an hour or even sat for over an hour. They don't know that to drive my car I have to push my leg over to the brake with my hand because the muscle in my leg that performs that action doesn't work anymore. There's no way I would be considered safe to be a professional driver any more. They don't know that I have trouble seeing now, much worse than ever before. They don't know that I have panic attacks in vehicles when another vehicle gets too close or that I can barely drive at night at all because I have flashbacks of the headlights running into us. I've been pulled over multiple times for driving erratically because I was afraid someone was going to hit me head on again. I know they don't know any of these things so I try to be polite and answer their questions and be friendly. All the while, I know they probably think I'm just too lazy to go back to work.

This drove me to work out harder and see just how far I could push my body. I pushed it too hard and I started cramping all over my body. My bones started aching; especially in the places I have metal, like my wrists, pelvis and knee. I was working out five days a week to see if I could get strong enough to go back to work and my body started breaking down. I would hurt for days trying to recover. I had to take weeks off of working out to get to feeling better. I tried but I have decided that worrying about going back to work to please others is absurd. I don't normally worry about what people think but to have people think of me as lazy drives me insane. I'm still trying to come to terms with the fact that I have limitations now. One thing is for certain, I have a great life. Even with the injuries, my life is wonderful. I feel for those who will never figure out how to escape the misery they are stuck in.

I was helping with the offseason workouts for the football team three days a week. I had taught my kids how to push yourself and work hard and the proper exercises and techniques they need to get in shape or even excel in the weight room if that's what they chose. There are so many kids that I feel like I could help if I could talk to them one on one. I want to reach out and instill the drive they need to make a positive future for themselves. Most of them have no idea how much potential they have and so many kids are falling by the wayside. As coaches we see it but most of the time, I feel like my hands are tied. It's ultimately up to the parents and the kid if they want to participate or not. I have so much I could teach them, not just about sports but about life. They have to be willing to listen and I definitely don't want to overstep my boundaries and cause problems. I'm just a volunteer, right? How involved should I get? Would someone get offended if I had a serious conversation with their kid? I've tried tiptoeing that line and occasionally I get just a little over zealous but overall I think the kids understand what I'm saying when I get chances to speak to them.

Amber was determined to play high school football and she talked me into letting her try. She started lifting weights with the other eighth graders and was doing great. The new head football coach said Amber may be good at shot put for the track and field team because she was so strong. She tried it and really liked it. She was good at it too. She placed first in her first meet. She started becoming more competitive after that and I started seeing even more of myself in her. She ran the one hundred meter and the four hundred meter until she started having pain in her leg and hip. This was the same injury she had complained about the previous summer. It started when she was sliding into a base in the championship softball game. After resting it over the winter I thought she would heal up but it kept getting worse. We took her to a specialist who saw a few problems in her MRI. There was a strain or possibly a small tear in her thigh that had not healed all the way. She also had something on her knee but they weren't concerned with that. What they were concerned about was a tumor in her hip. My heart sank. I couldn't believe after all we had been through that something like this would even come up. I immediately turned to God in prayer and in faith and asked him to take care of this. I felt peace right away and just knew that this was not something I needed to worry about. At the next visit the doctor said it wasn't uncommon and did not think it was cancerous but that it would need to be monitored to make sure it didn't become a problem. She started physical therapy but could not participate in any sports. This included track, football, softball and even horseback riding. Amber was very upset. Mostly about not being able to ride her horse but everything else too. The only thing she could participate in was the pageant. She did well and she got second runner up this time. As time went on she made progress in therapy but it didn't quite get back to normal. When she was released from the doctor she jumped right back into lifting weights and playing football.

CHAPTER TWENTY-SEVEN

Past Present And Future

After thirteen weeks of staying as busy as I could, it was time to fly to California and see Matt graduate from boot camp. This was also when we found out that Marie's disability income was being cancelled. We weren't told a reason and her arm was still paralyzed. We could have taken the money we put back for the trip and used it for bills but there was no way I was going to miss seeing my son become a Marine. I was holding back tears of joy as soon as we got on base. Knowing I was going to see him very soon made it hard to stay calm. As soon as I laid eyes on him I had tears running down my face. I had kept myself busy enough to not think about it constantly but now there was no avoiding it. Every time I saw him, all I could think of was that sweet little boy who wanted picked up all the time so long ago, (yet almost like yesterday). Now he has completed one of the toughest boot camps in the world to become a United States Marine. I am bursting with pride to have two of my children become one of the few. For me to actually be there to see it is nothing short of miraculous. I couldn't even come up with words to tell him how extremely proud of him I am. I felt like I had finally made my life worth something because my children were making something of themselves. I was finally starting to feel something that resembled peace in my soul. I had to make sure I didn't relax too much so that Alex and Amber could get the same effort from me that I gave their brothers. I also know that they are learning quickly not only from me and Marie but from their brothers too.

We went straight home after the ceremony, partly because Matt requested it that way and also because we were now broke. Mike tried to make it to see Matt graduate. He couldn't but he did manage to get home to visit for a few days and he was there when we got home. It was nice to have everyone home at once. It felt normal again. I tried to enjoy every second with them I could and still let them have time to see friends and other family. It took some self control to not try and hog all their time. Mike seemed more mature now than ever and Matt had changed as well. He told us how much he appreciated how we raised him. He said seeing others in boot camp who did not have good parents and watching them struggle helped him to see that. We had a party for Matt, similar to the one we had for Mike, the Sunday after we got back. It was family, friends and food. Later that night the boys had some of their friends over for a bonfire. They cut loose and showed that they were in fact still kids. I figured they had earned a little childish behavior under the safeguards of being at home. The next day I explained to them that they are about to be out in the world with only themselves and the Lord to really depend on and they needed to realize this in a hurry. We spent some quality time together and had some fun, yet I am still their father and I'm always going to have advice for them. When Mike had to leave to get back to Japan, I wasn't nearly as worried this time. I know he still has a lot to learn but he is getting there faster than I did. I don't think there is anything serious to be concerned about and I am very proud of him. I know he misses home and I still pray for him daily but I also know that he will cherish this experience later in life.

After seeing Mike off, we started preparing for Matt's high school graduation. It worked out perfectly for him to be home on leave in time for him to walk with his class. It was great to see him get his diploma but the ceremony did pale in comparison to seeing him become a Marine. I'm very pleased that he got to do this though. I'd hate for him to look back and wonder what it would have been like. It was a wonderful visit but it was time for him to get ready for his flight the next morning and I was not ready to let him go. I had to watch another one of my kids walk away to get on a plane not knowing when I would see him again. It hurts so bad to be without them but I know it's for the best and I wouldn't have it any other way.

It's pretty much back to normal, weight lifting with the football team and lining up our summer plans. Alex is doing exceptionally well in the weight room. He is exceeding my expectations by far and I am truly impressed with his dedication at such a young age. He worked hard to get better and stronger and it's showing. He has made good grades and is well on his way to being an honorable man. School let out and he got offered a summer job that he ended up loving. He will be getting his driver's license in no time. I've watched him grow and follow his brothers and learn from them and from me. I can't wait to see what he decides to do with his future. The opportunities are endless for this kid. He still has a heart of gold and he never quits. We've continued to make progress on our property and I got a couple yards to mow for a little extra cash. Marie's brother was fixing up a house a few miles from us with plans to move into it so he can be closer but the house was a disaster. There was so much work to be done. We went to help as often as we could but between coaching, mowing and helping her brother I was pushing myself so hard my body started regressing. I started being in a lot of pain again and I wasn't ever in a good mood anymore. It started to get really bad and I had to take a break for a few weeks to recoup. I didn't want to give up any of the things I was doing but my body wouldn't allow me to keep up this pace. I had set a goal to get my body in the best shape I could by my fortieth birthday, which was in November 2017. I had been making incredible progress and now I could barely walk again. I had proven that I could ignore pain and go far beyond the limits set before me but it took so much out of me that I was mentally and spiritually exhausted. After talking with Marie, she convinced me to ease back enough to not hurt so bad without having to give anything up so that's what I decided to do. I'm still searching for that perfect combination. I just have to learn the definition of the word "moderation." I've lived most of my life in an all or nothing type mentality and that's going to have to be adjusted.

I was invited to my 20 year high school reunion in 2016, even though I didn't graduate. I wanted to go but the timing didn't work out for us to be able to make it. I saw the photos online of the people who went and it didn't really surprise me that the ones who showed up were all the people who didn't give me the time of day in school. I didn't see a single photo of anyone I had more than one or two conversations with from kindergarten to 12th grade. As bad as I wanted to go, I don't feel like I missed out on anything. About a year later, I got invited to a barbeque at an old friend's house that I hadn't talked to in over twenty years. There were a lot of people invited that I had actually hung out with. They were the crowd that was mostly dropouts and druggies. I didn't live that lifestyle anymore but I felt like this was something I couldn't miss. I needed to see for myself how my old friends who still lived in that area turned out. When we got there and started catching up, I found out a girl I had dated got into an abusive relationship and even after getting out of it didn't seem very happy. Another girl had gotten married but her husband was in prison for shooting and killing someone. Most of the guys that I actually got to talk with had been to prison and one of them was pretty much homeless. Another was still dealing drugs and two of the guys I had considered friends wouldn't even see me. They had started trying to turn their life around and didn't want to see anyone from their younger days and I respected that. There were a few people that moved away and no one had heard from them. There was only a couple who had actually gotten good jobs and had normal lives. This visit was the most eye opening thing I have seen yet. I know I made the right decision to get out. I would have been another bad statistic if I would have stayed. I know it's about the choices you make and not where you live but I also know what my mindset was like back then and I would have only gotten worse. My wife still tells me I need to loosen up but I could tell when I talked to one friend in particular that I don't have nearly as sharp of an edge to me as I used to. He was still one hundred percent in that mentality that if you cross me or get in my way there's going to be trouble.

I did a lot of thinking on the ride home. I have been blessed so greatly but sometimes it's hard to see that without stepping back and looking at what my life could have been like. I have achieved my goals. I have four responsible and trustworthy kids who work hard and have what it takes to make a nice life for themselves. I have an amazing and stunningly beautiful wife who would do almost anything to see us happy. We have the home of our dreams and an affordable lifestyle. I have time to spend with my family and on the things I enjoy like coaching. I gave my heart to God a long time ago and like I said, I didn't always hold up my end of the bargain but I put forth the effort and God has blessed us for it. He has protected me and my family and he has guided me to places I never thought possible. It took a lot of heartache and pain to get here but I think for the first time in my life I feel satisfied. That's something I never thought I would feel. I love my life, my family and my home. I still struggle with things but what I have overcome has made me strong. There are days the pain is unbearable. There are days the emotions take over and there are days I'm not someone you would want to be around. Then sometimes there are those perfect days where the pain is under control, the weather is nice, I'm able to feel normal and good, I'm able to have fun with my family and it makes all those terrible days worth it. Sometimes I get frustrated because I want to show people how to be strong but I think it's something you have to experience on your own. Take what God has given you, no matter how great or small, and make something out of it. There is a line in one of my all time favorite movies that says, "Change your stars." The meaning being, you can change your destiny if you want it bad enough. I changed mine. How about you?

With the start of the new football season I decided to contribute as much of myself as possible. I was more confident in my knowledge of the game and wanted to make sure I passed that along to the players. By the week before the first game I had given all I could and felt like we were ready. Just as I started wearing down and feeling like I needed to take a break from it, I got a message from a player who told me they appreciated what I was doing for them. A day later I got another message from a different player saying something very similar. I've had several players tell me they personally appreciate me being there and giving my time. This means more to me than any gift they could have given me. I felt they truly meant the words they were saying and it touched my heart in a way that I knew God was telling me I had made a difference. If I never coach another day in my life I will still be satisfied that what I'm doing matters to these kids.

The first week of the season Amber rolled her ankle and tore a ligament. I knew as soon as she came off the field she wasn't going back in. She was so upset with me that night because she wanted to play and I wouldn't let her back on the field. I was proud of her. Some players would have called it a day and been happy to sit out with an injury like that. She was ready to go and chomping at the bit to play. She spent most of the season going to physical therapy and only played in one more game by the time she came back. She didn't quit and was determined to prove she could play. Tough? I don't know if tough is a strong enough word for my daughter.

CHAPTER TWENTY-EIGHT

Looking For The End

The football season was in full swing and most of my time was spent at the field. Things were going along about as close to normal as it gets around here and then the craziest day I've had in a long time happened. I got up and got ready to take Alex and Amber to school, like any other day. As I was pulling down the driveway I saw a very noticeable wet spot where our water line runs. I applied the brakes and the car did not stop like I expected it to. It slowed down just enough for me to coast to a stop at the end of the drive. If I had not seen the water, I may have ended up in the ditch across the road. I got the car back up the drive and found that I had a rusted out brake line that had to be replaced. I got the kids in the truck Alex had bought. He was still waiting for his sixteenth birthday to get his license so I drove the kids to school. When I got home, Marie and I went out to investigate the water break. As we were walking out she noticed a large amount of antifreeze under the truck. It had sprung a large leak in the radiator. I looked up to the sky and with my hands in the air I said, "REALLY?!?", as if God was laughing at my misfortune or just continuing to test my resolve. We found the source of the water leak and I left to get supplies to make repairs while Marie called a friend to get some help with the digging. When I got home, Marie was frantic and asked me to look at her dog. Someone had run over our dog and left him for dead in the road in front of our house. Luckily our other dog was smart enough to come to the front door and get Marie's attention and bring her to him. He was alive but very badly wounded and needed stitches at the very least. She rushed him to the vet while I stayed home to start work on the water line. She came home just as we were finishing up the repairs and checked the mail. To put the cherry on top of a not so great day, she got a letter saying she was to report to jury duty. After the vet bill, the water line and the vehicle repairs we were now overextended financially. When is it going to be enough?

When Marie showed up to court for jury duty, she was told they were going to pick jurors for a case that involved a guy who was trying to get out of a drinking and driving arrest. Talk about irony. When she was asked if she could be unbiased in this case, she answered honestly and said no. She gave the very short version of our story that she and I had been hit by a drunk driver and after almost losing our lives and three years of constant surgeries (that were yet unfinished) she had a paralyzed left arm, not to mention the torture our family has gone through. They said thank you for your honesty and you can go. They didn't want her anywhere near this case.

Maybe two weeks later, we discovered another water line

break in our front yard. This was the fifth break in the three years since our accident. We have a big yard and a long water line with huge trees growing along where the line runs. The tree roots were tearing the line up all along the yard and driveway. We had no money left to even buy the supplies needed to fix it. Marie's step-dad offered to pay for the repairs and helped me every step of the way. We got enough line to replace it from the house all the way across the front yard to the driveway, in hopes this would prevent another break in the near future. This took some time and I had to miss a few days of football practice and a couple games that Thursday and Friday night. I was glad to get the job done right but this took a lot out of me and by the time it was over, it took all I had left just to finish the football season. I started to wonder if I should be spending my time coaching, when there were so many things at home that need my attention.

Matt finished his training and found out where he was going to be stationed. I was surprised to hear him say he was going to Japan, very close to where Mike was stationed. For him to enlist months after his brother and have a completely different MOS (job) and end up on the same island with him on the other side of the world is incredible. Mike was doing well but we could tell he had become a little homesick. When he found out his brother was coming to Okinawa he was more excited than I think I have ever seen him. He was beside himself waiting for Matt to get there. Matt got to come home on leave for a couple weeks before heading to Japan. The difference in him was amazing. In just a short time he had matured so much. He had been chosen as squad leader during boot camp and his leadership skills were starting to show. I felt a little lost as a father because I wanted to continue giving advice and helping him along but this time I really had nothing to say that he had not already figured out. He was glad to be home and tried to make the best of the short time he had. It was hard to let him go when we took him to the airport but I have no doubts that he is going to do great things.

We did everything we could to prepare for Marie's big surgery. We tried to get every detail taken care of before the big day so nothing would hinder her recovery. On a Friday in October, I woke up sore with a stiff neck so I made some coffee and tried to loosen up. When I finished my coffee, I got up out of my recliner and something happened. A terrible pain started in my neck and ran down into my shoulder. It lasted for what felt like an hour and then it lessened somewhat but didn't go away. I had recently had an injection to relieve pain in my lower back because there are several disks that are damaged but none serious enough to consider any type of surgery. There was some arthritis already building up around the metal that holds my pelvis together which was part of the problem. The pain I was feeling now was a pain that had come on much more suddenly. I had a CT, an MRI of my shoulder and finally an MRI of my neck. It was clear that I had a herniated disk in my neck that was pressing on a bundle of nerves. It took a month to get through all the tests and get back in to see the specialist who diagnosed the problem. All this time I had been dealing with constant pain and the doctor still treated me like I was addict and only gave me one week worth of pain meds. When I finally got the diagnosis the specialist told me he wanted to try another injection first but that I would probably need surgery. It was now November and Marie's surgery was in two days. There was no chance I was letting them do anything that would keep me from taking care of Marie. I told them I wouldn't do anything until I knew she was recovered enough to be ok while I was having it done. The injection could be done in one day but the earliest they could do it would have been the day of Marie's surgery. They tried to get me to go ahead and schedule something and I refused. I told them I would call them when I felt she would be ok without me for a day or two. I stopped going to physical therapy and stopped going to the doctor so I could devote all my attention to Marie and the kids. Luckily, I still had a month supply of pain meds from when I quit cold turkey after the doctor called me an addict two years earlier. I started taking those to help me keep the pain under control enough to take care of Marie, the kids, the house and everything else.

Thursday, November sixteenth 2017 we were at the hospital at 5am for Marie to have her miraculous surgery. The staff at the hospital was amazing! They kept me updated every two hours and couldn't have been nicer or more professional. After a long day of intense waiting, I got the call that the surgery was finished ahead of schedule and it was a complete success. The surgeon had been so positive and so confident all these months leading up to this day that I really had no doubt it would work. Even the way we found this surgeon was a chain of events that could only have been the design of God. When the doctor came out to tell me how it went, she came right up to me and gave me a hug and said it went perfectly. She must have seen in my face that I needed that. I told her I was never so happy to see a doctor in my life. When I was finally able to go see Marie, she wasn't quite awake but looked great. My wife is the only one I know who can wake up from a twelve hour surgery looking amazing! When they got her settled into her room, I instantly felt woozy. It felt like I had the flu. By the time her visitors left the room, I was in the bathroom puking. I tried to be strong for her but it was no use. I asked the nurse if there was somewhere I could go, just in case I had something contagious so Marie wouldn't get sick. Marie needed me to be there for her and here I was puking until 2am. I left the next morning to go home and rest up. I told Marie what was going on and she said she would rather me stay home than for her to get sick too. I felt like the biggest heel on the planet. I had put off having my pain taken care of to be there for Marie and then this happens and I can't be there anyway. I was frustrated beyond belief but I was able to get back to see her after some rest.

She had great care at the hospital for six days and then it was time to come home. She was asked if she would like to go to a facility that could give her the professional care she still needed. It would have been a lot like a nursing home and she was adamantly against this idea. I agreed with her at the time. After everything we had been through, I was confident I could handle anything she needed. We got home and I did all I knew how. She was extremely weak and in a lot of pain. She wasn't able to do anything for herself so I was at her beckon call 24-7. I started to realize that the facility they mentioned was probably as much for the family of the patient as it was the patient because this was stressful. My hat is off to all nurses and care givers and I was even more impressed at how well her mom and step-dad cared for us after the accident. I did the very best I could and it wore on me after a week and a half. Luckily, by that time she was feeling a lot better and was able to start doing some things for herself but emotionally I was hanging on by a thread. Marie asked what was wrong with me and I tried to pass it off like it was nothing but she saw right through me and pressed for an honest answer. I figured she deserved the truth but I didn't want to put her under any stress while she was trying to recover. I had not told her that I was in as much pain as I was. I had not told her that the doctor had told me I would need surgery for the disk in my neck. I was gritting my teeth and pushing past the pain to take of her. I told her that I love her and I didn't want to hinder her recovery but I was doing all I could. I'm not a nurse. I didn't go to school for this or choose this as a career but even nurses get to go home at the end of the shift. I had been taking care of her every need and I was in a lot of pain myself. I always got very stressed after Marie's surgeries anyway because I absolutely hate seeing her in pain. It all added up and I wasn't being myself. I was back to having an attitude and she didn't like it. I told her that I was doing my very best to take care of her but it was stressful. I said that I could do the job but for her to expect me to do all this and to be in a good mood all the time was asking too much. Needing me to take care of her is one thing but telling me I need to do it with a smile felt a little insulting. Of course, this hurt her feelings and now I felt completely worthless because I couldn't give her what she needed at her weakest time. I know part of my attitude was because I had been taking the pain pills again but I don't want to use that as an excuse. I stopped taking them as soon as the pain let up enough to stand it and my body had to adjust to it again.

While we were trying to talk things over we actually went as far as discussing whether or not we should stay together. Her version was that I was a complete jerk to her when she couldn't take care of herself and she needed me. My version was that I did the best I could and my best wasn't good enough. I'm sure the truth is somewhere in the middle. Looking back, it seems ridiculous that this would even come up after everything we had been through together but everyone has their weak points. Marie and I are very different people. We look at almost everything from different points of view. We can usually meet in the middle on most things but there are times our differences become a struggle.

It's been over three years since the accident and Marie and I are still going through surgeries to repair what damage can be repaired. I'm tired and in pain. PAIN, every single day, forever. That just doesn't sound appealing to me. I started to feel like I had once before. I had thoughts of ending the pain once and for all. I felt tired of being alive, tired of just breathing. It takes so much more energy now to accomplish anything. I have to put out three times the effort for half the work. I started to think about taking revenge on the man who caused all this. He would likely be out of prison before we were finished having surgeries to repair the damage. Would that still be a sin? Yes, because the Bible tells us that vengeance is Gods. These are actual thoughts that went through my mind. I am not better or stronger than any average person. I don't want you to think that these thoughts never entered my mind. They are there and I'm still working through them. I look myself in the mirror and sometimes I'm not sure what I'm seeing. Am I as broken as I feel inside at times? Am I as strong as I have heard people say that I am? I wonder if there is truly a purpose or plan, like I've believed all along. Is God preparing me for something great or am I hanging onto something that will never come true? I would love to someday hold my grandkids in my arms and give them life advice to avoid the landmines I've stumbled on. Can I really be strong enough or tough enough to fight through this pain for another twenty or thirty years? Can I go that long and stay me or will I become more bitter and hateful as time goes on? I know one thing for sure. I have fought hard to get where I am. I have accomplished most of my goals and while I'm here, I have a wealth of life experience that I love to share with people. I'm not too embarrassed to share my story, any part of it, with anyone I believe it will help.

I have had a lot of time to do some thinking and reflecting. I don't regret most of the choices I have made, with the exception of dropping out of high school. I don't envy those who have better or easier lives than me. I do wonder, if I had made better choices or if I was given an easier path to follow would I have had this same level of determination and if so, just how far could I have gone? Where would I be if I had graduated high school? What if I had joined the Marines? Would I have made a career of it, and if so, would I be retiring from it right now? Would I have been happy with that kind of life? Would I have still met Marie? Would I have still had my kids? I guess questions like these are not meant to be answered and will drive you insane if you think about them too long. I believe that the choices I made have led me to be a better father than I would have been because I can guide my children through the trials of life with some knowledge of what not to do. I was meant to be their father and I have done the absolute best I can. I'm excited to see what they decide to do in the future. I have high hopes but mostly … …. I want them to know true happiness, peace and satisfaction.

CHAPTER TWENTY-NINE

A Pain Worse Than My Own

No matter how bad you feel at any moment, there is usually someone who has it worse than you. This is something that was hard for me to understand until it hit me in the face. We got word that some friends of ours were headed to the hospital to see their 11 year old daughter who was in an ATV accident. Marie and I decided to go see how she was doing the next morning after we dropped the kids off at school. We were thinking we would visit and find out how she was doing and how long before she would be back home and back to her normal fun loving self. We had no idea what we were walking into. When we got to the hospital on that Monday morning, our friends had already had to make some very hard decisions. The little girl who had been to our house many times to ride horses with my wife and daughter was not going to make it. Her brain had been damaged and the hospital staff was doing everything they could to keep her alive long enough for her family to say their goodbyes. Her parents made the decision to donate her organs and preparations were being made. While all of this was happening, our friends who were doing all they could to keep it together spoke with the hospital clergyman who had stopped by to see if there was anything he could do to help. He asked if they would like him to pray over their daughter. They turned to me and asked if I would do it. I didn't know what to say. I'm not a pastor or a minister but they knew me as a man of faith and they wanted someone their daughter knew to be the one who said her final prayers. I was honored that they looked to me for this. I was speechless but I knew this was something I had to get right. I prayed quietly that God wouldn't allow me mess this up. I asked him to help me do right by this family who was giving me such an honor. I did the best I could to keep it together and be there for this family who was feeling the pain and emotions I have hoped and prayed that I would never have to feel. After seeing what they went through, I am positive that I would rather go through what I have been through my entire life than to feel the pain they must be going through. After praying, I walked down the hall of the pediatric intensive care unit. I was trying to grasp some kind of understanding that I could pass along to this family. Room after room was child after child that was in very grave situations. Some of these were infants struggling for their lives. How could this be? These children couldn't have done anything to deserve this kind of life. Why was this happening? Why are there so many children in so much pain? Why are there so many families struggling with tough decisions like the ones this family had to make? I told the nurses on duty that I appreciated what they do. It's not something I think I could handle. They must be doing Gods' work because my heart was heavy just seeing this. I can't imagine seeing this every day. All kinds of thoughts went through my mind about different ways I could try to help but none of them seemed right. It felt as if my hands were tied as I watched children drowning in misery. Why would the great almighty God that I serve allow these things to happen to innocent children? I just couldn't seem to come to terms with this.

I was asked to be with them in the final moments late into the night and early into the morning. By the time we were leaving the hospital we were informed of just a few of the peoples' lives that were going to be changed for the better by the organs donated. I couldn't believe it. This little girl who was always active, fun loving and determined lived her short life to the fullest and was now giving life to others. Maybe God had a plan all along? We all have a purpose in this life. Some of us spend a lifetime trying to figure out just what that purpose might be. This little girl spread happiness everywhere she went for eleven years and then she had life to give for others. She was destined to make miracles happen in other peoples' lives. I believe that every time the recipients of those gifts thank God for the miracle they received that God will turn and look at her with a warm smile for the sacrifice she made to make it happen.

I had the surgery to repair the disk in my neck in January 2018. It was a strange experience. I woke up with a stiff neck, some new pain and swelling but nothing terrible. People had told me that it would be excruciating and I would need round the clock care and wouldn't be able to do anything for myself but it really wasn't that bad. The nurses seemed to be surprised at how well I was handling it. Marie even said she was shocked at how little help I needed. I told her this wasn't as bad as the pain I feel on most winter mornings when I'm really hurting from all the other injuries. This told me that I wasn't just being dramatic when I felt like I was really hurting. The daily pain I feel is as bad as the pain from a disk replacement surgery. To me this was a revelation. Pain had never stopped me before and I wouldn't let physical or emotional pain keep me from moving forward now. It wouldn't make any sense to give up after all I had overcome. I do feel stronger and able to withstand any storm. I will be productive and move forward with my life. I will not let the actions of one irresponsible individual rule my world. I will make my own choices and move forward putting one foot in front of the other in a positive direction. I will not give up or quit when the pain or emotions take me to places I know I shouldn't be. I will be here for my wife and kids to lean on and learn from for as long as God allows.

CHAPTER THIRTY

What's The Point?

Why right this? Why would I want to let anyone read about the most intimate details of my life? I'm nervous to let ANYONE see this story much less strangers. My original intention was to write down things I wanted to tell my children one day. I've noticed some memory loss and it seemed to be getting worse because of head injuries and the battle of keeping my hormones in check. I wanted to be able to tell these stories to my kids as life lessons with a point to them someday when I felt they were ready. My worry was that I would forget the things that happened before I could relate them to the lesson attached or they would eventually come out as the ramblings of an old man nobody wanted to listen to. I began writing whatever I could remember that I felt was relevant in a notebook. The more I wrote, the more I remembered. The more I remembered, the more I wanted to write. The deeper I got into it, I started to realize that maybe this was the type of story that could help someone who is struggling with life. It's for someone who needs to know that someone understands and has been through it too or just that there is still hope. I felt as if God wanted to use what I have been through to help people and I don't have any problem with that. Hopefully there will be a few that get something they really need from this story.

All through the Bible there are stories of people who did astounding things. Moses took on all of Egypt when he lacked confidence in himself. David battled and waged war his entire life. He was one of the greatest men of the Bible and he never knew peace. Job was an upstanding man of faith yet he was tested over and over again. Solomon was the wisest man of the Bible and he had his weaknesses. No man is perfect and we will all face trials and temptations. Am I or you any better than these great men? Of course we're not. Why should we expect an easy peaceful life if men of God that were that great didn't have it? Whatever we face, we must know that God has a plan and giving up is simply not an option.

So, what have I learned? I learned early on that you have choices. Jimmy and I were close as kids. He knew the same stories about our family that I did and he saw a completely different path than I did. He saw the excitement of being bad. He romanticized the outlaw life. The thrill of getting away with something or pushing the envelope was what he lived for. He wanted to be respected for all the wrong things by all the wrong people. He told me when we were very young that he wanted to live that kind of life. He basically wanted to be a successful outlaw. He couldn't understand that our family members who had lived that life were not happy with the outcome in the end. He lived for the excitement now rather than the result later. He couldn't see the collateral damage it did to everyone around us. I have always been proud of who I am and I wanted to stand for something positive. I dreamed of having a nice home and being surrounded by family. I wanted to be loved and respected. I came to understand that love isn't found easily and respect takes a long time to earn. In my younger days, I thought that if people didn't love or respect me, having them fear me was a close second. My mom told me once that I had changed. She meant it to be an insult but I took it as a compliment. It felt as if she resented me for wanting a better life than she could provide but if I was still thinking like that 17 year old who couldn't stay out of trouble I would be in prison or dead right now. That's a fact I believe whole heartedly. That's not the life I wanted to provide for my family. I wanted more. I just had to learn how to get more.

I've learned that anything worth having is worth working for. No matter where you are starting from if you are willing to work hard and make good choices you can make your life better. You can change the things in your life that you don't like. You just have to keep moving forward one step at a time. It takes time and patience but it's worth it. Even if you don't see the results you want in your lifetime, you can change things for the better for future generations. I don't want my children to go through the things that I have but I want to pass on the knowledge I gained from those experiences. Once you are in a position that you can pass on that wisdom don't hold back. They won't always want to hear it and they will usually think they've got it all figured out. That doesn't mean that they don't still need to hear it. You never know when someone desperately wants a kind word or piece of advice. People are usually going through more than they let on. Don't be the person that thinks they've got it worse than everyone else and always complains about how terrible it is. Keep a positive attitude, remember that everyone is going through something and always be willing to help others. God will repay you in his own way.

One of the things that took the longest for me to understand is that not everyone wants to change their life. Not everyone sees what they are doing as wrong or destructive and you can't force someone to change. They have to want it for themselves or all the help in the world won't work. This doesn't give us the excuse to not want to see them do better but praying for them to see their own mistakes is a good start. When you find that special type of person who really wants to know how to lead a better life, be all you can be for them. Lead a good life in front of them and lend that helping hand in any way you can.

There are kids in broken homes all over the world. I don't have any plans of traveling the world but there are plenty of kids right here in this country, in your state, in your county and your town. You don't need a lot of money to be someone they can trust. You don't need a degree in psychology to listen to their problems or give helpful advice. Just be careful you're giving Godly advice. You don't need a mansion to take someone in who needs a chance to turn their life around or a step in the right direction. Most kids in these situations believe that no one truly cares for them. Prove them wrong.

Hardships and losses can break you if you allow it. It can also make you stronger than you ever thought possible if you are willing to keep marching forward. Find something positive and rewarding to invest your time in. For me it was football. I loved staying physically fit and the battle of facing an opponent on the field. You need to find that thing in your life you can be passionate about. There will most definitely be times that it doesn't make sense to those around you. They may question why you are so involved in something that doesn't appeal to them. It's for you, not them. Enjoy it.

There are times in everyone's life that things are simply out of your control. As a kid I wanted to live in one place but my mom and sisters wanted to live somewhere else. I resented that about my mom for a long time. There will be jobs or employers or situations in life that you simply have to get through to find the start of the next chapter. Keep your head up, keep smiling and don't let someone else's misery change your direction. Find your purpose and the path to get you there. Don't settle for less than you know you can achieve. There are so many programs and scholarships now that I didn't know existed when I was in school. Open your eyes and look around. Don't settle because you don't know how to move forward. Find out how to take advantage of every opportunity you can.

Please pay attention to this if nothing else. Love isn't something that you have to find by the time you get out of high school. It doesn't work that way for most people. It's ok to be alone for periods of time while you work on yourself. You don't always have to be attached to another person. We settle for people we know aren't right for us at times just so we won't be alone. Then when time passes you don't know how to escape or worse you bring children into a relationship that wasn't good from the start. Would you really be willing to punish your child with a lifetime of misery just because you were afraid to be alone? That may be a little harsh but think about it for a minute. The better you make yourself, the higher quality people you are going to attract. Wait until you have figured out what you want out of life and have a plan to get there. Then you can look for the person who has similar goals and plans that might be right for you to share a wonderful life together.

Don't get sidetracked. People will always be either a help to you or a hindrance. They may push you along toward your goals or they may push you to anger. When you get angry, stop and think. Is this worth my time? Is this something worth arguing over? Is it worth me getting into trouble over if it escalates? There may be times when the answer is yes, but most times if you are honest with yourself you will see that the trouble isn't worth the fight. You can accomplish more by staying within the confines of the law because it will always catch up to you sooner or later. As for dealing with people, kill them with kindness. You can't control another person or their opinion of you. Control is nothing more than an illusion, you never really control anything. Treating people with more kindness than they deserve makes you feel better about yourself and drives them crazy when they can't get under your skin.

Be the person your family can be proud of. If you come from a family that holds you back or treats you unfairly, don't allow them to take away your happiness. Take the initiative to make your own happiness and destiny. What do you want out of life? What kind of person do you want to be? What do you want your children to see when they look at you? Many of my decisions were made because I wanted to be a person my kids could not only look up to, but also look to for anything they need. I want them to know that I will always steer them the right direction, even when it's not what they want to hear. A family is a very intricate and fragile thing. It can be a source of great strength or horrible broken emotions. I have been blessed enough to know both sides of that coin. My kids asked me one time, if I had such a rough upbringing how did I become a good parent? I simply didn't want to make my kids feel the way I did at times. I avoided doing things that would put them in those positions. I also wanted to instill in them the things I learned from a hard life so I was not easy on them. I made them study, exercise and taught them to work hard. They have been shown how to avoid the really bad stuff and how to move forward positively, always putting one foot in front of the other. If they choose to stray from that path, it won't be because they were not taught. It would be because they chose to stray. That is for each person to decide for themselves. I hope and pray that they have a strong enough foundation to always be going in the right direction.

If you find yourself in a bad situation be smart enough to recognize it and strong enough to change it. Don't take for granted the people that care for you and are willing to lend a helping hand. Let people help you from time to time. Nobody can travel this life completely alone all the time. It takes a lot of different pieces to put a puzzle together. You are one of those pieces. Take the time to carefully pick the other pieces you want in your puzzle. Always look for the silver lining. No matter how bad a situation is at the moment, keep looking up and waiting on God to show you the positive that can come from it. Most importantly, be grateful. God didn't give you a hard time to be mean to you. He wants us to be strong and sometimes great strength can come from great tragedy. Be a warrior not a victim or a statistic. Take the world by the horns and make it yours.

I write this out of love and compassion for anyone who has

taken the time to read this. I hope that if you or someone you love is going through something terrible this will be a source of renewal and strength. Pray, read the bible and learn from your mistakes. What doesn't kill you makes you stronger and hopefully smarter. Every great journey begins with one step forward.

This has been an incredible journey and I know beyond the shadow of any doubt that God came into my heart and has been by my side every step of the way. If you are struggling or even if you have it all figured out, give God the opportunity to do something great in your life. It may not be an easy road but it's worth it.